# THE GOVERNANCE OF INTERCOLLEGIATE ATHLETICS

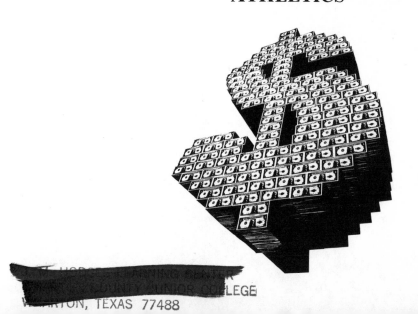

# THE GOVERNANCE OF INTERCOLLEGIATE ATHLETICS

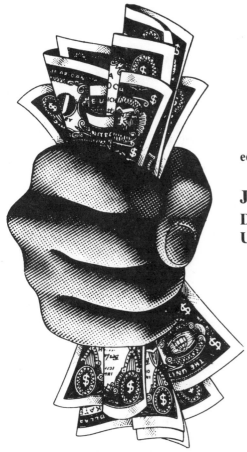

69451

edited by

## James H. Frey
**Department of Sociology**
**University of Nevada, Las Vegas**

**Leisure Press**
**P.O. Box 3**
**West Point, N.Y. 10996**

A publication of Leisure Press.
P.O. Box 3, West Point, N.Y. 10996
Copyright © 1982 by Leisure Press
All rights reserved. Printed in the U.S.A.

ISBN 0-88011-004-4
Library of Congress Number: 81-83014

# CONTENTS

# PREFACE

Once again intercollegiate athletics is a subject of controversy. Recent revelations of illegal recruiting practices, bogus transcripts from obscure two-year schools, questionable alumni/booster involvement in athletic administration, cash payments for extra rebounds or points scored, grade fixing and the pathetic graduation rates of athletes as compared to non-athletes have raised two questions: one is very practical; the other is more idealogical or philosophical.

The glaring exposé of college athletic excesses has stimulated the first question: "Who is in control?" The public, the press and even the federal government are asking how could these violations of institutional, conference and regulatory agency (e.g. NCAA, AIAW) rules take place if there was even a modicum of supervision at the level of the athletic department and the slightest demands for accountability from upper-level college and university administration. How could an athletic director, an institution President or even the Board of Trustees permit practices which could only put the athletic program and the institution in some disrepute if these nefarious practices were revealed? As we shall see, the answer to this question is not a simple one.

Institutional control of intercollegiate athletics is a subject which has attracted controversy since the first intercollegiate event in 1852. Yet, despite the continuous revelations of impropriety and the associated debate over their impact, college athletics thrived. It became the object of interest for external constituencies and soon came under their control in many ways. Some college and university representatives are fighting to regain, or perhaps to capture for the first time, ultimate institutional authority over intercollegiate athletics. Institutional administrators recognize that while athletics is of considerable benefit to community and populace, it is the institution, not the public or booster club, that is responsible for governance and for fiscal accountability. The latter is of particular significance in an age when the sources of athletic dollars are not so lucrative as they once were.

The second facet of the recent controversy is also one which has been raised before. This is the more fundamental, yet perhaps more ideological query: "What is the relation of an athletic program to the educational function of an institution of higher learning?" The commercialization and professionalization of intercollegiate athletics have resulted in a classic case of goal displacement, where the original purposes of enhancing the mind via physical exertion has been replaced by a guiding maxim which holds that the dollar-producing entertainment and public relations purposes are now the desired outcome of athletic endeavors, not the stimulation of knowledge-seeking capabilities. The mark of a "good" athletic program is one with a favorable winning percentage, not a high graduation rate.

Until recently, few cared who controlled athletics or how these programs related to academic purposes. The controversy takes on greater meaning today because colleges and universities are fighting for their political and financial lives. These institutions cannot afford adverse political relations or financial irresponsibility. Thus, the issue of governance, and ultimately control, rises to a level of prominence and attention which it has not achieved in the long history of intercollegiate athletics.

The contributions, both original and pre-published, were solicited with the two questions of control and academic justification in mind. Authors were also asked to address their comments to a particular constituency of intercollegiate athletics such as boosters, student-athletes, faculty, administration, etc. Thus, this anthology is not designed as a handbook or technical manual on how to govern an athletic program, although some very innovative and significant operational suggestions can be found in several of the chapters. Rather, this text was designed to delineate all facets of the governance issue and to provide some insights into the complexity of this phenomenon as it relates to intercollegiate athletics.

Special thanks must go to the contributors of the original chapters, since they had to endure with my constrictions of theme and time. The patience of Leisure Press editor, Dr. James Peterson, was also appreciated particularly when I missed what was an original, but overly ambitious, deadline. Lillian Havis, Judy Robinson and Alyce Wasden provided invaluable clerical services, and Ms. Joyce Standish lent her editorial wizardry to each chapter to enhance consistency and readability. The support of the Sociology Department and the University of Nevada, Las Vegas was also crucial to the completion of this project.

James H. Frey, Ph.D.
University of Nevada, Las Vegas

# CONTRIBUTORS

JACK W. BERRYMAN is an Assistant Professor in the Sport Studies Program, Department of Kinesiology, at the University of Washington, Seattle, where he is responsible for teaching courses in sport history. He also assists with the graduate programs in Sport Studies and Sport Administration. He did his graduate work at the University of Massachusetts and the University of Maryland where he concentrated in sport history and American social history. He has published numerous articles and book chapters on sport history and is currently the Editor of the **Journal of Sport History.**

ROBERT CARTER is affiliated with the Department of Political Science of Texas Tech University in Lubbock, Texas.

JAMES H. FREY is an Associate Professor of Sociology at the University of Nevada, Las Vegas. He has authored several articles on sport, survey research and deviance as well as **An Organizational Analysis of University Environment Relations (1977).** Dr. Frey is the editor of the **Journal of Sport and Social Issues** and is working on research in the areas of youth sports, gambling and the role of sport in international diplomacy.

ALLEN GUTTMANN is a Professor of American Studies at Amherst College. He published several books and numerous articles in the fields of American history and literature before turning to the history and sociology of sports. His **From Ritual to Record: The Nature of Modern Sports** (1978) has appeared in German and will soon be translated into Japanese as well. He is the translator of Bero Rigauer's modern classics **Sport and Work** (1981) and is presently engaged in a study of Avery Brundage and the Olympic movement and a sociological history of sports spectators from antiquity to the present.

*Contributors*

GEORGE H. HANFORD is president of the College Board and a member of the American Council on Education's Commission on Collegiate Athletics. He was director of the 1974 American Council on Education Study **The Need For and the Feasibility of a National Study of Intercollegiate Athletics.**

STEPHEN HARDY is currently an Assistant Professor of Sport Studies in the Kinesiology Department at the University of Washington, Seattle. His duties include teaching courses in sport history and sport administration and coordinating the masters program in Sport Administration. After graduating from Bowdoin College, he received his doctoral training at the University of Massachusetts/Amherst, where he concentrated in Sport Studies and American social history. From 1976-1979, he was an Assistant to Commissioner Scotty Whitelaw of Eastern College Athletic Conference.

HOWARD HOHMAN is a consultant on sports administration with the United States Sports Academy in Mobile, Alabama. He was formerly Director of Athletics at the University of Louisville and Dade County Florida Community College.

RICK HORROW is a member of the law firm of Garber and Buoniconti of Miami, Florida. He is author of **Sports Violence: The Interaction Between Private Lawmaking and the Criminal Law** (Carrollton Press, 1980) and the principal advisor on legislation relating to sport violence which has just recently been introduced into the United States House of Representatives.

ERIK KJELDSEN is an Assistant Professor in the Department of Sport Studies at the University of Massachusetts/Amherst. He holds degrees in physical education from Springfield College and a Ph.D. in sociology from the University of Massachusetts. He has taught physical education and coached seven different sports at the high school level. He served as gymnastic coach at the University of Massachusetts for ten years in addition to teaching a variety of academic and activity courses. His research interests focus on the process of management/leadership in sport organizations and on contemporary social issues in sport.

JAMES V. KOCH was formerly a Professor of Economics at Illinois State University. He is now Provost and Vice President for Academic Affairs at Ball State University. He has authored several articles on the economic aspect of intercollegiate athletics.

CYM H. LOWELL is a member of the bar of Indianapolis, Indiana. He is the co-author (with John C. Weistart) of **The Law of Sports** (Bobbs-Merrill, 1979) which deals with the variety of legal problems facing amateur athletics. He has also published articles on this topic in **Educational Record** and the **Journal of College University Law.**

GREGORY F. LUCEY, S.J. is Vice President for Educational Development and Planning at Seattle University. He earned a doctorate in Educational Administration at the University of Wisconsin in 1978. In 1964, he was ordained as a Jesuit Priest. In his position he supervises institution-wide planning for the University and assists the University administration in addressing numerous key issues: personnel development, productivity in academic units, assessment of intercollegiate athletics. In late 1980 Father Lucey assumed responsibility for University Relations while continuing his role in planning.

FRED L. MILLER is a Professor of Health and Physical Education at Arizona State University. He was formerly Director of Athletics at California State University, Long Beach (1967-1971) and Arizona State (1971-1980). After playing three years of professional football he earned a Masters Degree in 1958 from the University of Southern California and a Doctorate from Indiana University in 1963. In 1978-1979 Dr. Miller was president of the National Association of Collegiate Athletic Directors.

DAVID M. NELSON is Dean of the College of Physical Education, Athletics and Recreation at the University of Delaware. He coached football for 19 years and is credited with devising the now-famous "Delaware Wing-T Offense." He has served on a dozen NCAA committees, authored six books, and has served as a broadcast analyst for ABC Television.

DONNIE D. PEERY is Director of Athletics at Pensacola Florida Junior College. He earned a Masters Degree in 1962 from Florida State University in Physical Education and a doctorate in Administration of Higher Education in 1976 from the University of Miami.

ROGER R. RAEPPLE is Executive Director of the Florida Community College Activities Association. In this position he is responsible for supervising the promotion, coordination and regulation of intercollegiate activities among the state's community/junior colleges. He earned a masters in Business Administration from the University of Miami in 1972 and a doctorate in Public Administration from Nova University in 1977.

ALLAN L. SACK was a monogram winner on Notre Dame's 1966 National Championship Football team. He was also one of the 10 players from his class to be drafted by a professional club. Upon graduation from Notre Dame, Professor Sack attended graduate school at Penn State where he received a Ph.D. in Sociology. He is presently an Associate Professor in Sociology at the University of New Haven. Professor Sack has published numerous articles on college sport in both the popular media and in scholarly journals. Professor Sack's most recent project is the creation of a Center for Athletes Rights in Education.

11

GEORGE H. SAGE holds a Bachelors Degree and Masters Degree from the University of Northern Colorado and a doctorate from UCLA. He has recently received Honor Awards from the Colorado Association for Health, Physical Education and Recreation and the Central District American Alliance for Health, Physical Education and Recreation. He is President of the National Association for Physical Education in Higher Education, 1980-82. Professor Sage is editor of **Sport and American Society**, now in its third edition; co-author (with D. Stanley Eitzen) of **Sociology of American Sport**, and co-editor (with Gunther Luschen) of **Handbook of Social Science of Sport**. His current research interests are in socialization and sport, sociology of sport occupations, and sport in education.

H. A. SCOTT was formerly head of the Department of Physical Education at the University of Oregon, Rice Institute and Brooklyn College. He is the author of **Competitive Sports in Schools and Colleges** (1951) and **Professional Preparation in Health, Physical Education and Recreation** (1954).

LEE SIGELMAN is an Associate Professor of Political Science at the University of Kentucky.

DR. BONNIE SLATTON is an Associate Professor of Physical Education at the University of Iowa and is the President-elect for the National Association for Girls and Women in Sport. Having been involved in athletics as a competitor, coach, official and administrator, she has practical experience as well as academic and professional expertise on which to draw. Slatton's degree emphasis was on philosophy and sociology of sport, earning a Ph.D. from the University of Iowa in 1970, MA from University of North Carolina at Greensboro and BS from Middle Tennessee State. She served as Acting-Executive Director for AIAW in 1978-79.

TED C. TOW joined the NCAA staff in 1972 as director of publishing and was named assistant executive director in 1973. His responsibilities include supervision of the Association's legislative process, long-range planning and other general administrative assignments, in addition to all of the NCAA's publishing activities. A 1957 graduate of Wayne (Nebraska) State College, with graduate work at the Universities of Iowa and Wyoming, he taught journalism for 10 years at the high school, junior college and college levels. He has also been a sports information director, director of college information services, owner-editor of a weekly newspaper and owner-operator of a public relations counseling firm.

# PART I
# A LOOK AT THE PAST

# INTRODUCTION

The questions of institutional control and academic relevance have been raised a number of times in the history of collegiate athletics whenever discussions of the role of these programs on campuses took place. The first article in this section by Hardy and Berryman presents a historical survey of major events in the life of intercollegiate athletes which have occurred because of some controversy over the educational value of athletics. They describe how from even the first intercollegiate event—a crew race between Harvard and Yale in 1852—external, noneducational interests were prominent in the promotion and conduct of that competition. From that time the history of intercollegiate athletics has been one of balancing the demands of external interests (e.g., alumni/booster, entertainment and promotion) with those of the internal, educational constituency who asked questions about institutional control.

The selection by H.A. Scott, a prominent physical educator, is representative of a number of statements which appeared over the lifetime of intercollegiate athletics. The arguments seem to be the same, whether they were heard in 1910 or 1956 or 1981. The theme of these treatises is essentially based on the call to evaluate the educational role of athletics, particularly in a context of the commerical enterprise they have become. Scott Laments the apparent divestiture of institutional control from the hands of educators into the hands of external interests. This article is as applicable today as it was twenty-five years ago.

# A HISTORICAL VIEW OF THE GOVERNANCE ISSUE

by
Stephen H. Hardy
Jack W. Berryman

The athletic scandals that rocked a number of college campuses during 1979-1980—altered transcripts, "shadow" courses requiring no attendance by athletes, "slush" funds for athletic personnel—have raised serious questions about the effectiveness of current governance structures and methods. Yet, even a brief historical survey of college sport reveals that similar complaints have appeared with some regularity. For the last century, critics have continually worried that college competition was running "out of bounds," and have suggested that tighter controls and new structures of administration were necessary to make athletics "educational." Thus, the questions of athletic governance and athletic philosophy have been closely intertwined.

Intercollegiate sport was still in its infancy on American campuses when it felt the first cold sting of public criticism. The following poem exemplified the notes of discord raised by those who wondered whether athletics did not tend to taint the good name of higher education:

> Grammar, Algebra, and History glimmered in a hazy mystery, school terms softly sped away, while he practiced day by day — week by week, and through vacation. This his friends in desperation, vowed the boy was not for knowledge; so they sent him off to college. (Stacy, 1889: 532)

> 'Learning? Where's the use of learning,' Johnny cried, his lesson spurning. 'As for me, I'd rather run!' So from morn to set of sun, Johnny's legs were never still; he could distance Bob and Bill, Jim and Tom, and Dick and Peter. Not a youth in town was fleeter.

Several years later, Francis Amasa Walker, future President of the Massachusetts Institute of Technology (1893: 1), wondered if "it will soon be fairly a question whether the letters B.A. in a college degree stand more for Bachelor of Arts or for Bachelor of Athletics."

The concerns have continued in this century. Educational organizations have conducted three major investigations into college athletics. All have examined the match (or mismatch) of athletics and education. In 1929 (Savage, 1929:vi) the Carnegie Foundation for the Advancement of Teaching suggested that any foreign visitor to an American campus during football season would immediately ask what relation such an "astonishing athletic display [had] to the work of an intellectual agency like a university?" The American Council on Education asked similar questions in studies during the early 1950's and late 1970's (Hanford, 1979: 354; Marmion, 1979). Indeed, from the first intercollegiate sporting event, a "jolly lark" in 1852 on Lake Winnepesaukee, between crews from Harvard and Yale (Lewis, 1967, 1970b; Whiton, 1901), the historian may trace an ever-accelerating recognition on the part of students, faculty, college administrators, alumni, and the public-at-large that athletic competition played an important role in campus life. But this acknowledgement was coupled with a growing concern that athletics, at least at the intercollegiate level, might be incompatible with the general mission of the college or university.

Reactions to the early growth of campus sports ranged from laudatory justification (Adams, 1890; Davis, 1883; Richards, 1884) to severe condemnation and abolitionism (Deming, 1905; Godkin, 1892, 1894; Woodward, 1910). By the turn of the century, however, both supporters and detractors had adopted the posture that proper governance and regulation were necessary to (depending on one's position) improve, reform, or salvage the athletic pastimes which, like a weed, could neither be left alone nor completely eradicated (Hart, 1890: 69). An example of this posture may be found in the attitude of the presidents of the state universities of the North Central States, who met in Madison, Wisconsin in 1897 to consider the problems in college sports. These executive officers wanted to insure that intercollegiate athletics "be made to subserve the interests of higher education in a large sense" (Powell, 1964: 22). They further suggested three specific means of reform:

- More careful and systematic organization of the boards, councils or committees having control of athletics.
- Greater care and uniformity in the adoption of rules determining the eligibility of players.
- Some modification of the rules under which certain of the games are played.

These sentiments, offered so many times before and since 1897, go to the very heart of the historic problem of collegiate athletic governance - namely, the need to match goals with organizational structures.

Finding a workable marriage between goals and structures has proved elusive, possibly because both elements have been protean in nature. The university presents mentioned earlier desired only to make athletics "subserve the interests of higher education in a large sense." But what exactly were these "interests?" Students, coaches, faculty, presidents, alumni and boosters all had differing notions as to the athletic interests of their individual institutions. Clearly-defined goals might have limited the need to carefully govern the "who, what, where, when, and how" of college sport. This was not to be, however, and the historical attempts to regulate this burgeoning campus enterprise experienced recurrent frustration precisely because administrative structures were ill-designed either to represent or to control the divergent interest groups at work in the athletic arena.

The control of college sport has changed hands a number of times during the last one hundred thirty years, as students, alumni, presidents, faculty, and professional administrators (athletic directors) have enjoyed periods of absolute or shared domination. The gradual evolution witnessed overlaps of control, and, to be sure, variations existed between colleges. But the transfer of athletic governance from students to alumni to college faculty and administrators has been clearly outlined (Lewis, 1965, 1969b, 1970a, 1970b 1972; Lucas and Smith, 1978; Powell, 1964; Stagg, 1946). By further examining the efforts of these groups to determine and then match organizational goals with mechanisms of management, one may gain a greater appreciation of the historically-rooted obstacles confronting athletic reform today.

Collegiate athletics began as unorganized student pastimes; and while sports existed on colonial campuses, they were intramural in nature. As Lewis notes (1970a: 209), "at no time did participation ever become a meaningful part of campus life." By the 1820's, however, certain contests had assumed some importance in the establishment of class honor. At Harvard, the freshman and sophomores competed in an annual mass game of "kick-ball," or from the descriptions, "kick-shins!" The 1827 version of this "Battle of the Delta" enjoyed coverage by a youthful bard writing for a new college magazine, the **Harvard Register.** As this would-be Homer described it: "The college clock struck twelve—that awful hour when Sophs met Fresh, power met opposing power" (Prince, 1923: 312). The bloodiest versions of these class struggles drew the ire of college authorities, but little existed in the way of structured governance by students or faculty (**Forum,** 1894: 630).

This all changed with the development of intercollegiate competition. The goals of the Harvard and Yale crews in 1852 combined pleasurable recreation with honorable competition. Harvard was answering a challenge from Yale to "test the superiority of the oarsmen of the two colleges" (Mumford, 1923: 24). But despite the Harvard victory, the contestants enjoyed a week of "much good feeling." Institutional prestige, however, had assumed greater importance by the time of the rematch in 1855. At that time Yale questioned the eligibility of the Harvard cox, who had already graduated. Unfortunately, Yale had neither an arbiter nor a regulation to which it could appeal. Clearly some form of collective governance was in order (Lucas and Smith, 1978: 198).

Stern (1979: 247) has suggested that two major questions of competition have historically urged the formation of athletic "control networks." The first involved the rules of play; the second concerned eligibility of players. These students, however, perceived a third and prior consideration—namely group recognition of a champion. As Smith (1976: 157-158) has argued, pursuit of the **prize** has always lain at the heart of intercollegiate competition. It was only logical that the student athletes from separate colleges would federate in order to elevate the significance of the prize itself. This, then, was the **raison d'etre** for the earliest "league" forms (Young, 1886: 145). Further regulation was **then** necessary to insure that the chance for victory was equitably available to all competitors.

It was in this spirit that the first intercollegiate governing body emerged. In May of 1858, an editorial in the **Harvard Magazine** called for the creation of a rowing association: "What say ye, Yale, Dartmouth, Brown, Columbia, Harvard," it exhorted, "shall we introduce a new institution into America?" Harvard, Brown, Trinity, and Yale responded by sending student representatives to a meeting in New Haven at which the College Union Regatta was formed. The members agreed to conduct an annual championship whose winner would receive a "set of colors" paid for by the boats entering the regatta. Further, the members agreed both to a set of rules governing the race and to a stipulation that "the race be between boats manned by undergraduates, including the graduating class" (Mumford, 1923: 32).

Although the College Union Regatta soon faded into oblivion, the interest in regulated crew championships remained and led to the formation of the Rowing Association of American Colleges in 1870. Students quickly recognized the prestige which victory entailed. The Massachusetts Agricultural College, only four years old, enjoyed such a surge in 1871 when it defeated Harvard and Brown for the crown. The press emphasized the significance of the "Aggies" rural lifestyle in the victory over urban "Brahmins." But more important, the race brought the college "immediate state and national recognition . . . . no demonstration of the college work could have been as spectacular as this crew victory" (Fidler, 1977: 78). Students at other colleges formed clubs or "navies," and by 1875 thirteen crews competed for the championship at Lake Saratoga. Winning, not carefree participation, was clearly the major goal. Indeed, as early as 1864 a student maintained in the **Yale Literary Magazine** that championships were "sacredly connected with the glory of Alma Mater herself." (Lewis, 1970b: 228).

Students organized clubs in other sports during the 1860's, 1870's and 1880's. Baseball entered the scene at Harvard in 1865, followed by football (1872), track and field (1876), lacrosse (1882) and tennis (1882). Yale was similar, with baseball organized in 1865, followed by football (1873), track and field (1874), lacrosse (1878), and tennis (1880). Parallel developments occurred on other campuses during these years, with the east showing the way to the rest of the country (Hartwell, 1886: 107-111). In most cases, organization was geared toward molding championship teams. Typically, the arrangement involved feeder groups (often class teams) for the varsity contingents which were tightly controlled by the individual captains. Moral and financial support came from student athletic associations, sometimes formed around one sport but generally encompassing all sports (Davis, 1883: 667; DeMartini, 1976: 530; Gates, 1961: 100; Hart, 1890: 65; Lucas and Smith, 1978: 201-03; Richards, 1884: 449-51).

As with rowing earlier, the clubs from different campuses quickly formed intercollegiate associations to govern their competition. For instance, track and field had emerged as a sidelight to the crew regattas at Saratoga. In 1975, students from Harvard, Yale, Amherst, Columbia, Cornell, Princeton, Trinity, Union, Wesleyan, and Williams met in Springfield to organize what would become, in 1876, the Intercollegiate Association of Amateur Athletes of America (Clark, 1923: 464; Lucas and Smith, 1978: 201). The ICAAAA, still controlled by undergraduates as late as 1929 (Savage, 1929: 212), has conducted its championship annually since 1876. America's Centennial year also witnessed the formation of the Inter-collegiate Football Association, by students from Columbia, Harvard, and Princeton. Three years later, Amherst, Brown, Dartmouth, Harvard, Princeton, and Yale organized the Intercollegiate Baseball Association. Lacrosse and Lawn Tennis followed in 1882 and 1883, and by the early 1900's, leagues existed in basketball, swimming, wrestling, and soccer (Fleischer, 1958: 7-9; Reid, 1923: 192; Stagg, 1946: 15-16). While most of the earliest associations arose in the northeast, students in other sections of the country quickly established their own groups.

The earliest intercollegiate governing bodies, then, were student-initiated and student-run. Their missions were generally three-fold: to sponsor and conduct championship competition, to outline playing rules, and to deter-mine eligibility criteria. Their control was **vertical,** involving one sport only. In other words, the membership and regulations for one sport might differ from those for another sport. This, of course, was quite distinct from later umbrella organizations, such as the NCAA, whose membership and eligibility codes were consistent across a number of different sports.

The pioneer student associations were commonly short-lived (only the ICAAAA has survived). But their failure may be attributed more to their fragile voluntary structure than to their inability to measure accurately the desires of athletic clubs on campus.

If anything, student governance of college athletics was victimized by its own success. Student-athletes had molded organization to college sports in an effort to make them more meaningful and prestigious. Their product met with an admiring public. So, partly by circumstance and partly by design, these collegians found themselves in control of an enterprise whose heart had the rhythm of business and not the flutter of fun and games. But why not? Athletics received no regular institutional subsidy, and the public was willing to pay. By 1889, the Yale-Princeton football games garnered more than $25,000 in gate receipts (Hart, 1890: 67). Moreover, presidents, alumni, and the popular press joined the students in recognizing the prestige value of athletic victories (Lewis, 1967). Even a sometime critic (Walker,

1896: 711) had to admit that "the college athletics of today do wonderfully light up the life of our people." While some (Richards, 1884; Shaler, 1889) considered the negative as well as the positive aspects of the campus sports boom, there was little suggestion for a radical change in the structure of governance.

A gradual evolution began, however, during the late 1800's—one which led to the diminution and defacto elimination of student control. During this period, alumni and faculty sought increased participation in the management of college athletics. Both groups agreed that the job had become too big for students to handle. But whereas the alumni desired to bring greater competence to the chase after gate receipts and championships, some faculty began to suggest that college students ought to be restrained from pursuing goals which appeared increasingly inappropriate to higher education. Ironically, within the context of their own goals, the students were accused of being—at once—both inefficient and overly successful.

The alumni felt that their presence would compensate for undergraduate inexperience at both the campus and league levels. They skillfully traded financial support (or the threat of boycott) in return for a voice in the conduct of athletic affairs (Lewis, 1965: 35, 38). Eventually, many athletic associations appointed "graduate managers," the forerunners of today's athletic director, to oversee scheduling, coaching, and finances. At the same time, the graduate lobby gained more power within the intercollegiate associations. The Intercollegiate Football Association was a case in point. In 1881, Walter Camp of Yale returned to the annual meeting despite his graduation the year before. His subsequent attendance, followed by the appearance of a Harvard "grad" in 1886 (distrust of Yale, you say!) led to Camp's suggesting the formation of an "advisory" graduate committee for "rules and appeals" (Davis, 1911: 461-478). By the 1890's, Camp's rules committee had become the dominant force in collegiate football.

A further threat to student governance came from faculty groups who expressed growing alarm at the "evil" tendencies and overemphasis displayed by the athletes and their supporters. As Lucas and Smith (1978: 214-216) have outlined, faculty were generally concerned about five areas of abuses: (1) professionalism, including the tendency to hire coaches and recruit athletes, (2) increasing size and mismanagement of finances, (3) lack of sportsmanship, (4) glorification of athletics over academics, (5) derivative evils such as drunkenness and gambling.

Like the alumni, faculty sought involvement at both campus and "league" levels. As early as 1882, Harvard's President Eliot appointed a three-man faculty committee which dismissed the "hired" baseball coach and drew up five rules regulating competition (Sargent, 1910: 252-253). Similar faculty committees arose at other colleges during the 1880's and 1890's, such as the one begun at Wisconsin in 1889 with an eye on putting athletics "under systematic control." (Curti and Carstensen, 1949: 1, 705; DeMartini, 1976: 535; Lewis, 1965: 175 ff). Students complained (Gates, 1961: 100; Mumford, 1923: 85) about these intrusions into their domain, but to no avail. By 1910 they had lost most of their authority to corporations, faculty, and alumni. Students did continue to be represented on the various joint athletic boards (Meylan, 1921: 375) which emerged on different campuses. Indeed the Carnegie Foundation determined in 1929 that "the most popular single type of board embodies a balanced representation of various groups, for example, the faculty, alumni, and undergraduates." (Savage, 1929: 82). But the students clearly were no longer masters of their own product.

At the center of these changes in governance structures stood the college or university president; and presidents were in a squeeze. On the other hand, they were pressured by students, alumni, and boards of trustees to promote institutional visibility and prestige through athletics. Indeed, many presidents needed little prodding before becoming prominent boosters (Lewis, 1972: 54-56). On the other hand, however, presidents could not avoid the serious issues, noted above, which critics from the faculty and elsewhere voiced with increasing volume. Some presidents, like Woodrow Wilson of Princeton, (1909: 576) were forced to worry that the "sideshows" had started to swallow up the "circus," leaving the performers in the "main tent" to "whistle for their audiences, discouraged and humiliated."

The expanded campus athletic boards, described above, were an attempt to achieve some kind of balance in athletic policy. As Lewis (1965, 1972) has noted, however, governing boards and alumni interest continued to dominate on athletic committees. Concerned presidents and faculty had to look elsewhere for mechanisms of restraint. One answer appeared to emerge in a new form of association or conference of several institutions bonded by concession to a particular code of athletic regulations.

As early as 1883 faculty representatives from eight separate colleges had met in New York City to discuss mutual resolutions to the athletic problem. This group drafted proposals that included confining all games to college grounds, prohibiting any professional coaching, and limiting all athletes to four years of competition. The regulations would have governed teams in baseball, football, lacrosse, cricket, and crew, but the plan died aborning, as campus colleagues balked at such a sweeping **coup de main** on student affairs (Sargent, 1910; Young, 1886: 148). This early diffidence quickly yielded, however, to the growing assault, during the 1890's, on collegiate athletic "abuses." (Forum, 1894; Hart, 1890; Pepper, 1894).

By the mid-1890's the interest in faculty-run athletic associations finally reached fruition, possibly because of the success of recent academic federations like the New England Association of Colleges and Preparatory Schools and the North Central Association of Colleges and Secondary Schools. These and similar groups in the Northeast, the South, and the Middle States had enjoyed some progress in achieving common standards for admissions and degree requirements (Savage, 1929: 26-27). Their athletic counterparts began in the 1890's. The first of lasting prominence was the Southern Intercollegiate Athletic Conference, founded in 1894. The following year, presidents from Chicago, Illinois, Michigan, Minnesota, Northwestern, Purdue, and Wisconsin met to discuss a similar venture.

From this meeting came the Intercollegiate Conference of Faculty Representatives (The "Big-Ten"). In 1898, delegates from the future Ivy League (minus Yale) met in Providence to outline a set of eligibility regulations which the group subsequently adopted. In the early 1900's, a number of other regional conferences developed, including the Northwest Conference (1904), the Intercollegiate Athletic Association of the Southwest (1907), the Missouri Valley Conference (1908; later the "Big-Eight"), the Rocky Mountain Faculty Athletic Conference (1914), and the Pacific Coast Conference (1915; now the "Pac-Ten"). Numerous state conferences also emerged during these years (Fisher, 1916; Needham, 1905; Powell, 1964; Savage, 1929; Stagg, 1946).

The new groups differed from the old student associations in several ways. Their format and control was generally **horizontal** in nature. In other words, their members agreed to certain regulations which governed athletes in a number of sports, not just one (although most groups were particularly concerned with football). This was clearly related to the fact that their business was conducted by faculty or staff representatives who were concerned with problems common to all sports, as opposed to students and alumni whose interests centered on one activity. Finally, their chief concerns (at least initially) were not providing championships or promulgating playing rules, but rather, limiting competition and controlling eligibility.

Many of the early conferences have survived to the present; many have faded into oblivion. But their general insistence on faculty control and their consideration of eligibility in terms of "educational" standards rather than notions of competitive fairness clearly mark them as a significant development in the evolution of athletic governance. Indeed it appears that their proponents believed that the new associations, removed from the pressure to "win at all costs" which thrived on campus, would insure that athletics served education, rather than the reverse.

The culmination of this early search for collective solutions was the formation, during the 1905-06 football controversy (Lewis, 1965, 1969), of the Intercollegiate Athletic Association of the United States, which changed its name in 1910 to the National Collegiate Athletic Association. From its inception, the NCAA stood for **faculty** control and educational principles. It's initial Constitution (IAAUS **Proceedings,** 1906: 29) stated its chief objective:

> The regulation and supervision of college athletics throughout the United States, in order that the athletic activities in the colleges and universities may be maintained on an ethical plane in keeping with the dignity and high purposes of education.

Some administrators were elated at the prospects opened by the new regional and national groups. The University of Oregon's President (Campbell, 1911: 688) claimed that:

> The rules adopted by these conferences, pretty generally much the same both in spirit and in letter, have happily resulted in freeing college athletics from at least the grosser abuses to which

they were subject in the old days of undisciplined rivalry and go-as-you-please methods of securing invincible teams.

Pittsburgh's Chancellor (McCormick, 1912: 141) agreed. Athletic evils, he said, would surely "eliminate themselves."

Faculty control was **more** fully realized in the area of womens' athletics, mainly because the students had never established their own control networks. (Gerber, 1975; Smith, 1970; Spears and Swanson, 1978). Even the early campus women's athletic associations were usually "carefully advised and directed by a woman faculty member." (Spears and Swanson, 1978: 185). The first intercollegiate governing body, the women's basketball rules committee of the American Association for the Advancement of Physical Education, was formed in 1899 under the leadership of Sendar Berenson, an instuctor at Smith College. The rules were designed to avoid the roughness of men's play. From this point, the advocates of strict control (generally faculty in physical education departments) chartered a course which guaranteed avoiding the abuses of the men's side. This included restrictions on travel, championships, and gate receipts. The apogee came with the creation in 1923 of the Women's Division of the National Amateur Athletic Federation. This group was so successful in promoting restraint and control in collegiate programs that one 1930 study concluded that "intercollegiate athletic competition for women does not exist in the colleges of the United States except in a very limited number and percentage." (Lee, 1931: 122). Play days substituted instead, and the womens' programs suffered no publicized abuses, only unpublicized neglect.

The men's programs, on the other hand, were not so successful, largely because of confusion over the difference between the **forms** of control and the **substance** of educational goals. Many athletic reformers of the early twentieth century sincerely believed that if the athletic department were treated as an "academic" unit (usually in combination with physical education), and if athletic directors and coaches were hired by governing boards as regular faculty, competition would become "more educational." In fact, the NCAA lobbied for this policy early and often (NCAA **Proceedings,** 1910: 35). By 1921, 187 institutions answering a survey from the American Physical Education Association, pointed out that their chairmen of athletics and physical education did, indeed, enjoy a seat on the faculty (Meylan, 1921: 374).

Faculty status for athletic directors and coaches, however, did not reorient athletic departments toward educational principles. In the first place, by 1930 it was clear that most chairmen held their position by virtue of their success as football coaches, not because of their academic degrees (Lewis, 1969b:39). More important, faculty status did not insulate athletic directors or coaches from the pressure to field winning teams and fill the department coffers.

In truth, the new conferences and associations were not able to solve the problems of governance. The 1920's witnessed continued agitation over college athletics. In 1929 the Carnegie Foundation for the Advancement of Teaching warned (Savage, 1929: 207-208) that it was "absurd" to assume that the evils would "automatically disappear if a conference is formed and passes rules of a nature sufficiently lofty and stringent." The foundation's report stressed that the "fundamental problem" involved not **enforcement** by conference administrators but "**honorable observance**" (or lack of it) of the rules "on the part of all whom they affect—alumni, graduate managers, coaches, faculty members, college presidents, and undergraduates."

But this was, in fact, only the symptom of a deeper problem. The rules of the faculty-directed governing bodies reflected a goal of bringing athletics into conformity with certain nebulous "principles" of higher education. Unfortunately, many of those affected by the new rules directed their actions toward a different set of goals which had emerged long before, when athletics existed in the student-run extracurriculum. Part of this involved what Smith (1976: 160; Lucas & Smith, 1978: 226) has referred to as "the ritual surrounding athletics," including the "mass meetings, bonfires, spirited orations, organized cheers and college songs . . . . the college colors, marching bands, homecoming, and the 'big game.' " The students, alumni, and administrators who shared this "esprit de corp" quickly linked it to the ebullience of victory. As Amherst's president observed in 1922 (Meiklejohn, 666) many of this constituency commonly believed that "victories indicated better than anything else the quality of the undergraduate life, and even of the college instruction and administration." A number of circumstances perpetuated this vexing situation. The new governing bodies had no way of inculcating in all constituents the precedence of "educational" goals over the goals of victory and prestige. To make matters worse, rules enforcement remained limited or nonexistent. The NCAA's mission was hampered by this deficiency until after World War II (Stagg, 1946; Stern, 1979). Finally, and ironically, the new organizations themselves lent inadvertent support to the alternative goals by establishing league, conference, or association championships. The pursuit of regional or national honors again fueled the competitive fires which, in turn, elicited the pejorative behavior which the new federations had been designed to minimize or eliminate!

Only women's athletics, under the tight control exerted by its leaders in the Women's Division of the NAAF and in the Committee on Womens Athletics of the American Physical Education Association, experienced widespread support of common educational goals and philosophies. Consequently, they had little need for complex enforcement structures. But their success came at the expense of intercollegiate sport itself (and possibly, as Gerber [1975: 25] suggests, contrary to student desires). As Lucas and Smith (1978: 351) put it, they were "sailing away from the mainstream of American athletics." This early course has complicated the contemporary quest for equal opportunity in meaningful competition. The new interest in intercollegiate sport, as symbolized by the creation of the Association of Intercollegiate Athletics For Women (1972), which now conducts 39 national championships in 17 sports (Lopiano, 1980: 62), has had to overcome entrenched "educational" philosophies which discouraged travel, publicity, championships, gate receipts, and glory. Women have now elected to open the doors for all of these elements. The NCAA has expanded its organization to include both championships for women athletes and representation for women administrators. Increased and intricate problems in governance and control will obviously follow.

This has been but a brief glimpse at some of the historical developments in the governance of American collegiate athletics. Such a summary cannot hope to convey the variety of experiences on different campuses, large or small, public or private, male or female. One general conclusion can be made, however. The past century of development in collegiate athletics reveals that ambiguous and often conflicting goals and philosophies among students, coaches, faculty, administrators, alumni, and the general public have made it difficult if not impossible for governing structures that represent but one or two parties to control the actions of all. At the same time, however, even a cursory look at this history suggests that there have been, are, and will be, no simple solutions to the problem.

# REFERENCES

Adams, Charles K.
    1890        "Moral Aspects of College Life." *Forum*, 8: 665-675.
Campbell, P.L.
    1911        "The Future of Intercollegiate Athletics in the Western States." National Educational Association. *Proceedings*, 688-693.
Clark, Ellery H.
    1923        "Track Athletics." In *The H Book of Harvard Athletics*. ed. John A. Blanchard. Cambridge: Harvard Varsity Club, 463-486.
Curti, Merle and Vernon Carstensen.
    1943        *The University of Wisconsin: 1848-1925*. 2 v. Madison: University of Wisconsin Press.
Davis, Andrew M.F.
    1883        "College Athletics." *Atlantic Monthly*, 51: 677-684.
Davis, Park H.
    1911        *Football*. New York: Charles Scribner's Sons.
DeMartini, Joseph
    1976        "Student Culture as a Change Agent in American Higher Education: An Illustration From the Nineteenth Century." *Journal of Social History*, 9: 526-541.
Deming, Clarence
    1905        "Money Power in College Athletics." *Outlook*, 80: 569-572.
Fidler, Doug
    1977        "The First Big Upset: American Culture and the Regatta of 1871." *New England Quarterly*, 50: 68-82.
Fisher, George
    1916        "A Study of Athletic Administrative Bodies: Their Points of Resemblance and Difference." *American Physical Education Review*, 21: 281-96.
Fleischer, Michael M.
    1958        "A History of the Eastern College Athletic Conference." Unpublished D.Ed Project, Teachers College, Columbia University.

*Forum*
1894        "Are Foot-ball Games Educative or Brutalizing?" 16: 634-654.
Gates, Charles M.
1961        "Early Athletics at the University of Washington." *Pacific Northwest Quarterly,* 52: 99-107.
Gerber, Ellen
1975        "The Controlled Development of Collegiate Sport for Women, 1923-1936." *Journal of Sport History,* 2: 1-28.
Godkin, E.L.
1892        "Glorification in Athletics." *Nation,* 55: 406-407.
1894        "Football and Manners." *Nation,* 59: 476.
Hanford, George
1979        "Controversies on College Sports." *Educational Record,* 60: 351-366.
Hart, A.B.
1890        "The Status of Athletics in American Colleges." *Atlantic Monthly,* 66:63-71.
Hartwell, Edward M.
1186        "Physical Training in American Colleges and Universities." U.S. Bureau of Education, *Circulars of Information,* No. 5, 1995, Washington: Government Printing Office.
Lee, Mabel
1931        "The Case For and Against Intercollegiate Athletics For Women and the Situation Since 1923." *Research Quarterly.* 2: 93-127.
Lewis, Guy M.
1965        "The American Intercollegiate Football Spectacle." Ph.D. dissertation, University of Maryland.
1967        "America's First Intercollegiate Sport: The Regattas from 1852-1875." *Research Quarterly,* 38: 637-648.
1969        "Theodore Roosevelt's Role in the 1905 Football Controversy." *Research Quarterly,* 40: 717-724. (a)
1969        "Adoption of the Sports Program, 1906-39: The Role of Accommodation in the Transfomation of Physical Education." *Quest,* 12: 34-46. (b)
1970        "Sport and the Making of American Higher Education: The Early Years, 1783-1875." National College Physical Education Association For Men. *Proceedings,* 208-214. (a)
1970        "The Beginning of Organized Collegiate Sport." *American Quarterly,* 32: 222-229.
1972        "Enterprise on the Campus: Developments in Intercollegiate Sport and Higher Education, 1875-1939." In *The History of Physical Education and Sport.* ed. Bruce Bennett. Chicago: Athletic Institute, 53-66.
Lopiano, Donna A.
1980        "The NCAA, NAIA and Women's Sports: The Price of Control." *Athletic Purchasing and Facilities,* 4: 62-74.
Lucas, John A. and Ronald A. Smith
1978        *Saga of American Sport.* Philadelphia: Lea and Febiger.
McCormick, Samuel B.
1912        "College Athletics from the Viewpoint of the President of a University." *American Physical Education Review,* 17: 137-145.

Marmion, Harry A.
1979      "On Collegiate Athletics." *Educational Record,* 1979, 60: Entire issue.

Meiklejohn, Alexander
1922      "What Are College Games For?" *Atlantic Monthly,* 130: 663-671.

Meylan, George L.
1921      "Report of Committee on the Status of Physical Education, Hygiene and Athletics in American Colleges." *American Physical Education Review,* 26: 374-5.

Mumford, George S.
1923      "Rowing at Harvard." In *The H Book of Harvard Athletics,* ed. John A. Blanchard. Cambridge: Harvard Varsity Club, 16-124.

Needham, Henry Beach
1905      "The College Athlete: How Commercialism is Making Him a Professional." *McClures Magazine,* 25: 115-128, 260-273.

Pepper, George W.
1894      "Faculty and Alumni Control of College Athletics." National Education Association. *Proceedings,* 808-815.

Powell, John T.
1964      "The Development and Influence of Faculty Representation in the Control of Intercollegiate Sport Within the Intercollegiate Conference of Faculty Representatives From Its Inception in January, 1895 to July, 1963." Ph.D. dissertation, University of Illinois.

Prince, Morton H.
1923      "History of Football at Harvard, 1800-1875." In *The H Book of Harvard Athletics.* ed. John A. Blanchard. Cambridge: Harvard Varsity Club, 311-371.

Reid, William T.
1923      "Baseball at Harvard." In *The H Book of Harvard Athletics.* ed. John A. Blanchard. Cambridge: Harvard Varsity Club, 149-250.

Richards, Eugene
1884      "College Athletics." *The Popular Science Monthly,* 24: 446-453, 587-597.

Sargent, Dudley
1910      "History of the Administration of Intercollegiate Athletics in the United States." *American Physical Education Review,* 15: 252-61.

Savage, Howard J., et.al.
1929      *American College Athletics.* Bulletin No. 23. New York: Carnegie Foundation For the Advancement of Teaching.

Shaler, Nathaniel S.
1889      "The Athletic Problem in Education." *Atlantic Monthly,* 63: 79-88.

Smith, Ronald A.
1970      "The Rise of Basketball For Women in Colleges." *Canadian Journal of History of Sport and Physical Education,* 1: 18-36.
1971      "Athletics in the Wisconsin State University System, 1867-1913." *Wisconsin Magazine of History,* 55: 2-23.
1976      "Reaction to Historical Roots of the Collegiate Dilemma." National College Physical Education Association For Men. *Proceedings,* 154-162.

Spears, Betty and Richard A. Swanson
1978      *History of Sport and Physical Activity in the United States.* Dubuque, Iowa: Wm. C. Brown.

Stacy, Joel
1889 "The Sprint Runner." *St. Nicholas, An Illustrated Magazine for Young Folks,* 16: 532.
Stagg, Paul
1946 "The Development of the National Collegiate Athletic Association in Relationship to Intercollegiate Athletics in the United States." Ph.D. dissertation, New York University.
Stern, Robert N.
1979 "The Development of an Interorganizational Control Network: The Case of Intercollegiate Athletics." *Administrative Science Quarterly,* 24: 242-266.
Walker, Francis, A.
1893 "College Athletics." *The Harvard Graduates' Magazine,* 2: 1-18.
1896- "College Athletics." *Report of the United States Commissioner of* 
1897 *Education,* 705-715
Whiton, James
1901 "The First Harvard-Yale Regatta (1852)." *Outlook,* 68: 286-289.
Wilson, Woodrow
1909 "What is a College For?" *Scribners,* 46: 570-577.
Woodward, Calvin, comp.
1910 Opinions of Educators on the Value and Total Influence of Inter-collegiate and Interscholastic American Football As Played in 1903-1909. St. Louis.
Young, C.A.
1886 "College Athletic Sports." *Forum,* 2: 142-152.

# NEW DIRECTIONS IN INTERCOLLEGIATE ATHLETICS*

by
Harry A. Scott

In seeking to understand intercollegiate athletics, it is necessary to consider one of the essential characteristics of American institutions of higher learning. College and universities are chartered by the several states primarily to provide for the education of young people and to promote the general welfare of society. It seems apparent, then, that everything that takes place in an institution of higher learning must in some way—through instruction, research, or services—contribute to the educational welfare of the students and of society. It is because colleges and universities promote the general welfare that they, along with religious institutions and charitable organizations, are exempt from public taxation. Colleges are not (nor were they ever intended to be) commercial institutions. Obviously, then, athletics must exist in institutions of higher learning in order to contribute to the goals of education and to the improvement of the social order. If the program cannot be justified as an integral phase of the educational curriculum, then it is exceedingly difficult, if not impossible, to explain why it belongs in the college at all.

*Reprinted with permission from *Teachers College Record,* 58(1956):29-37.

# FALLACIOUS NOTIONS

Certainly athletics cannot be justified merely because it provides amusement to the public. Nor can it be defended on the grounds that money derived from athletic contests is essential to the financial structure of the college. In this connection it is true that a few of the more powerful, favorably located colleges and universities, athletically speaking, earn large sums of money through gate receipts, guarantees, sales of television and radio broadcasting rights, participation in bowl games, and similar lucrative commercial enterprises. However, most institutions of higher learning that attempt to bolster their finances through athletics learn by bitter experience that it is easier to force the proverbial camel through the eye of the needle than it is to make money from athletics. Where financial profits from athletics are concerned, the question must also be resolved as to the extent an educational institution, exempt from public taxation, is justified in expecting to profit financially through the toil of non-paid amateurs, who are supposedly participating in the game because they love it.

Moreover, athletics cannot be justified for its propaganda values to the college, since the proof of a worthwhile institution of higher learning lies not in the championship quality of its athletic teams but in the contributions it makes to the world of scholarship and research and in the qualitative achievements of its faculty members and students. Obviously, then, if athletics cannot be defended because of its entertainment, money-making, or propaganda values, it must be justified on the basis of its contributions to the educational goals of the college.

# A PHASE OF GENERAL EDUCATION

Fortunately, as a component of the program of physical education, athletics, if properly conceived, organized, and taught, can be justified as an integral phase of the general education of all students. General education may be defined as "that part of the educational program which seeks to develop in the student the common understandings, skills, and attitudes needed to function effectively as a person, as a member of a family, and as a citizen in a democratic society," (Snyder and Scott, 1954:52). By and large it is agreed that general education seeks to develop skills, understanding, knowledge, attitudes, and appreciations which will help the individual live more effectively in a complex society such as ours. To accomplish this, the college is obligated to provide experiences which will aid the student in developing a deep and abiding concern for others, a high plane of moral-ethical values, and the means to live effectively and happily with his fellow man.

General education seeks to widen the student's perspective in terms of past and present, affording him an understanding of his role in the world at large. This background for the individual is not an end in itself; it is a means for a fuller life and for a stronger and freer democracy. In these trying days of international tensions, citizens are needed who are responsible, mature, resourceful, capable of making sound decisions on critical issues, and, if necessary, bearing arms in defense of these decisions. Thus, it may be seen that the goals of general education demand more than the mere mastery of a body of knowledge; they must be understood and interpreted in terms of improved behavior.

If athletics is to be made worthy of a place in the educational curriculum, then those responsible for the program must delineate clearly and concisely the possible outcomes of participation in competitive sports and the manner in which the activities of the program can best be organized and conducted to provide maximal education experiences for college youth. These programs must in fact, as well as in theory, contribute to the general education of **all** students. This means that athletics, working cooperatively with the traditional academic displines, will so conduct its program as to enrich the lives of students by helping them to engage in experiences designed to produce the maximum development of their total personalities; improve their abilities to live harmoniously and cooperatively with others; attain competences leading to economic efficiency and independence; and enjoy the privileges and discharge the obligations of enlightened democratic citizenship.

# FACULTY CONTROL

One of the troubles with athletics is that personnel in this area of education have never really been expected to solve the problems in the field. From the very beginning, in 1852, those involved in athletics as players or teachers were considered interlopers in the academic domain. To control this encroachment, special faculty committees were established to prevent the athletic tail from wagging the educational dog. Because of this unhappy assignment, perhaps, academicians tended to exhibit a superiority over, and a healthy distrust of, anyone connected with intercollegiate athletics. As the inevitable problems arose in athletics they were, therefore, resolved **for** not **by** personnel responsible for the program of competitive sports. When, in the course of events, faculty members were forced to control athletics through committee action, much of their attention was directed toward the formulation of prohibitions designed to **curb** the program and everyone who was concerned with it. The thou-shall-not philosophy of control, instituted in the early days of athletics, is very much in evidence today. The philosophy still seems to be "when in doubt, add a prohibition."

# OUTSIDE CONTROL

The early development of such athletic conferences as the Pacific Coast

Conference, the Western Conference (Big Ten), and the National Collegiate Athletic Association (NCAA), was merely an extension beyond the campus of the principle of faculty control. At present it must be clear even to the most casual observers that faculty committees on athletics, athletic conferences of faculty representatives, the faculty-dominated NCAA, and the faculty-operated regional and voluntary accrediting associations have not been eminently successful in curbing malpractices in the program of intercollegiate athletics. Had they been successful we would not at this very moment be plagued with the same unresolved problems that have faced organized intercollegiate athletics from its beginning, more than a hundred years ago. Conversely, while it is true that these organizations have been unsuccessful in solving many of the problems of athletics, it must not be assumed that they failed to add anything of value to the program. On the contrary, these groups stepped into the breach when little was known about intercollegiate sports and brought some semblance of order out of chaos. The NCAA particularly, through its rule-making functions and in many other ways, has fostered and strengthened understanding and gained the acceptance of athletics in the colleges and universities throughout the United States.

# IF YOU CAN'T LICK 'EM, JOIN 'EM

Not only has control by faculty members failed to curb traditional abuses in athletics, it sometimes appears that the academicians have joined forces with the athletic barbarians to create new abuses. If current practice is a criterion, it seems that in some institutions of higher learning there exists a giant conspiracy to bypass established rules and disregard principles of ethical conduct in order to achieve status in athletics. Otherwise it is difficult to explain why students of low academic qualifications are admitted to the college; or how athletes acquire lucrative "scholarships" which have little or nothing to do with scholarly performance; or why special dormitory and dining facilities not available to other students are open to the chosen few in athletics; or why special privleges regarding class attendance are accorded athletes but not other students; and how it is that special curricula are tailor-made for athletes, especially designed to keep them eligible. It is difficult to understand how these things happen when academic faculty members and administrative officers representing a cross section of the entire college are directly responsible for policy and practice in many of the areas involved.

# CRUCIAL ISSUES

Since the very beginning of intercollegiate athletics, faculty committees, conferences, and other groups have developed regulations covering the minutiae and superficialities of the program of competitive sports. Today, policy-making and policy-regulating bodies continue in the traditional pattern. In their eagerness to curb current abuses of one kind or another, these well-meaning groups consistently fail to resolve basic issues underlying intercollegiate athletics. The report of the College Presidents Committee of the American Council on Education was an attempt in this direction, but it was pretty generally ignored by athletic governing bodies (ACE, 1951).

These crucial issues in intercollegiate athletics do not lie alone in such matters as the recruitment and subsidization of athletics, or in the scholastic averages to be maintained by the participants, or even in the problem of whether or not to permit spring football practice. Although it is highly important to draw a sharp line between what is amateur and what is professional in athletics, the crucial issues do not center alone on attempts to enforce to the letter our outmoded amateur code, which was handed down to us with few alterations from ancient Greece, by way of eighteenth and nineteenth century England. These troublesome and sometimes reprehensible practices represent only the symptoms of more important and deep-seated malignancies which lie elsewhere in the field. Once these malignancies are discovered and removed, perhaps the annoying symptoms will wither and die.

If the problems mentioned above are not the most important in the field of athletics, then what are the basic issues? Among them are the following:

• Should athletics contribute to the general education of all college students, or should its primary function be to entertain and amuse the public by using only a few highly selected, narrow specialists in the field of sports?

• Should athletics be an integral phase of the educational curriculum financed out of appropriated funds and controlled by the institution in exactly the same manner as chemistry or biology; or should it be conducted as an **extra**-curricular activity that uses for its selfish purposes the good name of the college, its facilities, and a few highly selected students, but operates more or less independently outside the structure of the college under a different philosophy and set of goals, and different policies relating to finances, personnel, and other aspects of the program?

• Should the philosophy, policies, and practices adhered to in other areas of the college govern all action in the program of intercollegiate athletics; or should the principles and practices of business and commerce guide the action?

# REFORM: A PROFESSIONAL PROBLEM

If the crucial issues of athletics have not been resolved by faculty committees on athletics, athletic conferences, the NCAA, the regional and voluntary accrediting agencies, or by others, then who can be relied on to bring about this long overdue and much-needed reform? The answer is that reform in intercollegiate athletics is as surely a **professional** problem as are departmental problems in chemistry, biology, engineering, or mathematics, and must rest squarely on the shoulders of professional personnel in these fields. The colleges must rely for reform upon the teachers of competitive sports (many people call them coaches, but they are teachers) and those in the department of physical education who administer and supervise the program of intercollegiate athletics. Indeed, because of an amazing lack of foresight in the past and the pursuit of goals that are primarily uneducational, to say the least, these persons must now accept major responsibility for the sorry state of present-day intercollegiate athletics. These are the persons who have intimate knowledge of the malpractices in the field. These are the ones who initiate and nourish the abuses. For these reasons they should be held responsible for bringing them to an end. This is the way it is done in other departments of the college, and there is no valid reason why it should not be done in athletics.

This grass-roots approach to the solution of problems in athletics involves some of the basic issues relating to human conduct. One of these issues involves the delineation of responsibilities. The time has come in American education when the program of intercollegiate athletics should be accorded full curricular status. Those in charge should have responsibility for making the program conform to the educational goals of the college and should be held strictly accountable for their actions. The traditional distrust by academicians of anyone connected with athletics has served to deny status to those entrusted with this program. This fact is evidenced in many colleges by the faculty committee of academicians appointed to give surveillance to the program of athletics—primarily, it must be assumed, to keep it honest. Equally justifiable would be a committee of physical educators assigned the task of "advising" the department of chemistry on how to conduct its affairs. The practice would not and should not be tolerated by the chemistry department. The paternal system of faculty control through the committee on athletics serves as a buffer between the program of competitive sports and the academic and general publics. It also provides a billowing skirt behind which the bad boys of athletics hide to avoid accountability for their acts.

In encouraging people to exert their best efforts, it is essential not only that responsibilities be delineated clearly but also that a climate of confidence and trust be established in the college. If enlightened action is to be expected, then it should proceed on the thesis that personnel in athletics are intelligent, professionally trustworthy and honest, and fully capable of solving educational as well as athletic problems. Moreover, it rejects the notion that professional people in this field must be legislated into practicing honesty and integrity. While it is probably true that people can be forced to conform to a code imposed from above, honesty and integrity are most effective as guides to conduct when the individual draws upon his own inner resources to govern his actions. He does right, not because it is forced upon him but because it is the thing to do. Since persons operate programs, willing adherence by individuals to ethical principles seems to be the key to the solution of problems of conduct in many areas of human endeavor, including intercollegiate athletics. If the program of athletics does not adhere to ethical practices in a given college or university, it is probably because the wrong people are in charge.

# ROLE OF PRESIDENT

Before the professional practitioner can cope successfully with the crucial issue of athletics, however, he will need much help from many sources—particularly from the college president and the board of trustees, who are responsible for the over-all policy-making functions of the college. Because of the external pressures engendered by athletics, those in charge of this program find it extremely difficult to count on everyone concerned to hold the line once it has been cooperatively established. It is in strengthening the head of the professional personnel in charge of athletics that the college president can wield his greatest influence.

From the very beginning of intercollegiate athletics, the college president has been tremendously concerned about his part in the program. In the early days he issued proclamations and posted rules prohibiting the playing of games on the campus, but these were of no avail. When he relied upon the faculty to throttle the athletic giant he met with only limited success. Neither has the athletic conference nor membership in such organizations as the NCAA entirely solved his problems. The college president presently finds himself harassed and sometimes severely castigated for his inability to solve the problems of intercollegiate athletics. Indeed, as most presidents will admit, they are subjected to the same pressures as the football coach. They can be, and sometimes are, summarily discharged for the same reasons the football coach is fired.

At mid-twentieth century, however, the college president cannot ignore intercollegiate athletics, even if he did inherit rather than create the problems in this field. Neither can he abolish the program by killing the patient in order to cure his ills. Indeed, if reform is to come in athletics at all, the college president must come to grips with the problems in the field and assume a role of leadership in their solution. To bolster his efforts in this crusade he will need the steadfast support of everyone connected with the college, including the board of trustees. After girding his loins for battle the president can then involve himself in the following matters:

He can be instrumental in crystallizing the philosophy and objectives of his own institution and in delineating the part intercollegiate athletics is to play in achieving these goals.

He can acquaint himself with the crucial issues in athletics and familiarize himself with the recommended principles and practices in the field. He can then set about to discover what is taking place in athletics in his own institution.

35

Once he has knowledge of what the situation is, he can then set the machinery in motion to make certain that athletics in his institution is controlled through the same channels as all other curricular areas of the college.

As the opportunities arise, he can recommend to the trustees for appointment only professionally qualified educators who are specialists in physical education, including athletics, and who meet the same standards of competence as other members of his faculty. The source of such personnel is likely to be other educational institutions rather than the field of professional sports or business.

Moreover, since they are qualified educators, he can insist that these teachers (coaches) and administrators be accorded faculty rank consistent with their age, education, and experience, receive the same salaries, enjoy all the rights and privileges, and assume the same responsibilities as other members of the faculty. In addition, he can make the strict adherence to established educational principles a condition of employment, promotion, or retention in his institution.

He can insist that intercollegiate athletics be made an integral phase of the educational curriculum and its benefits be extended to all students.

As a phase of the curriculum, he can then seek ways of financing the program of athletics in exactly the same manner that other aspects of the curriculum are financed—generally from appropriated funds, tuition, student fees, gifts, and endowments.

He can insist that the teachers (coaches) and other personnel connected with intercollegiate athletics be evaluated in terms of educational goals rather than on such commercial objectives as wins and losses, money taken in at the gate, or the amount of publicity accorded the teams and individuals representing his institution on the field of play.

He can give continuous surveillance to the program of athletics in his institution.

He can make certain that entrance requirements for all students are equal and see to it that athletes are neither favored nor dicriminated against in meeting admission and retention requirements.

He can be instrumental in setting the qualifications and conditions pertaining to financial grants-in-aid and see that these are allocated to athletes, as well as to other students, through regular college channels.

He can make certain that athletes, along with other students, are enrolled in bona fide, educationally justifiable curricula, and in all other respects are treated the same as other students.

He can familiarize himself with the activities of personnel

connected with the program of athletics in his institution and dissuade, by force if necessary, those ambitious individuals who believe that, given the opportunity—and the athletes—they can beat "State University" every Saturday afternoon in the year.

And finally, the president can make certain that a competent, full-fledged educator is appointed to administer the program of athletics in his institution. In making this appointment he can assure this person of the same academic status, confidence, trust, and cooperation accorded heads of departments in other areas of the curriculum. He can then hold him accountable for qualitative adherence to established principles and practices in the field of competitive sports and in education.

In all these matters, the president will find his burdens considerably lightened if his college is a participating member of a conference of institutions attacking these problems cooperatively. Preferably, these conference members should be traditional rivals in the field of sports, hold to similar philosophies and practices, and be somewhat equal in such matters as size, financial worth, and scholarly accomplishments.

# SIZE AS A FACTOR

The size of an institution, enrollment-wise, has little to do with the size of its athletic program. Some small colleges with inflated levels of aspiration conduct programs of athletics far larger than warranted by the number of students on the campus. Conversely, numerous institutions with enrollments numbering in the thousands conduct modest programs of intercollegiate athletics. It is distressing, but true, that the smaller colleges, athletically speaking, form the last frontier in the quest for a program of athletics that is consistent with and contributes to the goals of higher education. The larger institutions, athletics-wise, that traditionally have formed the spear-head of intercollegiate athletics in this country, have long since passed the point where they can turn toward an educationally justifiable program of competitive sports. Even if they wished to do otherwise, they are now compelled to seek more rather than less power in athletics. Tremendous monetary commitments in facilities, equipment, and manpower are involved, to say nothing of conference-sanctioned commitments to bowl games and tie-ups with commercial television and radio interests.

The wooing of off-campus support of athletics has developed into a large measure of control by vested outside interests that have little or no concern for the goals of higher education, for those who administer the educational programs, or for the young people who play the games. Although a press agent type of justification may be made by spokesmen for the big athletic powers, little genuine concern is evidenced as to where all this fits into higher education, or what happens to the youth who are caught up in this maze of contradictions. Unfortunately, these practices have tended to set the pattern which is diligently aped—at the starvation level in most cases—by many small colleges of the country.

There is no earthly reason why colleges with modest athletic ambitions should not conduct programs of intercollegiate athletics that are educationally sound and justifiable. Most smaller colleges are relatively free from the aforementioned pressures; not by choice, perhaps, but simply because few people seem to be interested in televising their contests, inviting them to participate in bowl or other post-season games, or in paying large sums at the gate to see their teams perform. These colleges, therefore, are in a better position to engage in serious soul-searching and programs of self-improvement than their more powerful brethren, athletically speaking, who, under faculty control and guidance it should be noted, have been caught up in the vicious cycle of so-called "big-time" athletics.

# RESOURCES OUTSIDE THE COLLEGE

It is not too late for the smaller colleges to band together and determine to bring athletics into its own as a justifiable educational experience for college youth. These colleges can be anything they wish to be in athletics. As noted above, responsibility for the quality of the athletic program in any given college should be assumed by the professional practitioners in the field, the college president, and members of the board of trustees. There are, however, numerous avenues of assistance which may be relied upon to help the institution to help itself. One such source of aid is the National Association of Intercollegiate Athletics (NAIA). This organization concerns itself with the programs of more than 400 smaller and less prominent colleges in the field of competitive sports.

The NAIA can strike a blow for educational athletics if, through working conferences, it can formulate a philosophy consistent with that of higher education, develop principles, and formulate a set of objectives that are appropriate for and attainable by the colleges holding membership in the organization. Once these principles and goals are delineated and accepted by member institutions, then the NAIA might launch a program designed to help these colleges to achieve these goals at the local level. Since financial problems are at the base of all issues in intercollegiate athletics, the Association might engage in research designed to show how a satisfactory program of athletics can be conducted out of appropriated funds, thus relieving the program of the necessity of earning its way. If this could be accomplished, then it would be of no great moment who televised what game on any Saturday afternoon.

The NAIA might help personnel connected with athletics in its member institutions to place greater value on a type of professional education designed to equip them to be full-fledged college educators rather than sports technicians. If this were accomplished, then the Association might be instrumental in throwing the white light of unfavorable publicity on colleges that summarily dismiss their teachers (coaches) for other than good educational reasons. Indeed in situations where the persons so involved have been accorded full faculty status and the program of athletics is sound from the standpoint of education and of physical education, the American Association of University Professors might find sufficient cause to exert its influence on the colleges in behalf of the aggrieved parties. Conversely, the NAIA might draw favorable attention to the educational values of participation in college sports, and bring to the attention of the publics those colleges that organize and conduct their programs as an integral phase of the total educational curriculum.

Due to widespread publicity down through the years, almost everyone in this country is familiar with the problems traditionally associated with intercollegiate athletics. Up to now no organization has been eminently successful in singling out the crucial issue in the field and doing something about them. This could be the role of the NAIA in the years to come. Instead of attempting to walk alone, however, the NAIA should join hands with such ongoing organizations as the athletic conferences with which member institutions are affiliated, the NCAA, the College Physical Education Association, the American Association for Health, Physical Education, and Recreation, and the appropriate regional and voluntary accrediting agencies. Thus, working together, these organizations can aid the colleges in their attempts to make athletics an indispensable factor in creating a fuller and richer life for students and a stronger and freer democracy for everyone.

# REFERENCES

American Council on Education (ACE). 1951. *Special Committee on Athletic Policy*
1951    *of the American Council on Education. Washington D.C.*
Snyder, Raymond A. and Harry A. Scott
1954    *Professional Preparation in Health, Physical Education and Recreation.* New York: McGraw-Hill.

# PART II
# ATHLETICS AND THE CAMPUS COMMUNITY

# INTRODUCTION

Over the years representatives of the academic community, (i.e., administration, faculty and students) have seemingly absolved themselves of responsibility for intercollegiate athletics, particularly as it related to the educational mission of the institution. Students, who originally operated these programs, turned over control to administration and alumni when intercollegiate competition became complicated by commerical and political interests. Administrators were content to permit alumni control as long as athletics appeared to provide for visibility in the community, political clout with the legislature and financial support for the academic programs. Faculties have never had much of a voice in the governance of intercollegiate athletics except to call for investigations, personnel changes or program changes at various times.

This section contains selections which describe the role of the academic constituencies in the governance of intercollegiate athletics. It has been only recently that college presidents, perhaps the most significant figures in efforts to establish institutional control, have moved to demand greater accountability from their athletic departments. George Hanford, a leading authority on the nature of college sports, describes this effort and the difficulties presidents face in solving the complex problem of control. That presidents and other administrators have been inconsistent and unsure of their role in governance is the theme of David M. Nelson's contribution. Despite all of the verbal assaults on athletics, little has been done by presidents to institute change.

Making changes, however, in athletic programming may not be as formidable as once thought. There are reasonable procedures for making adjustments without alienating several constituencies. Gregory Lucy describes the procedure utilized at Seattle University to evaluate its athletic programs. Ultimately, a recommendation for de-emphasis was accepted, and reduced commitments to athletics were instituted without apparent serious effects on student life or community support.

The rather ambivalent attitude of faculty to athletic programs, and the abuses contained therein, is described by Allan Guttmann. The elimination of a literary magazine in favor of supporting the football mascot at a southern school is viewed as symbolic of the priority athletics has over academics on most campuses. Perhaps the most pathetic facet of this episode was the passive acceptance of this action by that university's faculty.

The final two selections describe the experiences of the student athlete and the athletic director in the governance of intercollegiate athletics. Allan Sack, himself a former varsity collegiate football participant, uses the organizational concept of "Who Benefits?" to outline how college programs exploit the athlete for his/her labor rather than promote academic achievement. Sack recommends that campus chapters of an organizational equivalent to professional labor unions be formed to protect the rights of the athlete. One of the most prominent athletic directors in the country, Dr. Fred Miller, asserts that the athletic director is perhaps the most difficult job within the governance structure because of the severe cross pressures he/she faces from the variety of formal and informal constituent groups with interests in the athletic program. The mark of a good athletic director is his/her ability to "balance" these pressures and meet program goals in a financially responsible and ethically creditable fashion. While a member of the campus community, the athletic director is more often seen as solving the dilemma of conflicting pressures in favor of external constituents, not campus groups.

Academic constituents have not done a good job when it comes to institutional control of their athletic programs. Either they have not wanted to exert much influence or they have not been able to wrest control from the extra-academic groups which have significantly greater political and economic power.

# INTERCOLLEGIATE ATHLETICS TODAY AND TOMORROW: THE PRESIDENT'S CHALLENGE

By
George H. Hanford

The challenge posed by intercollegiate athletics for the college or university president is complicated first by the complexities of the administrative, educational, moral, legal, and economic problems besetting college sports and second by an intricate and still evolving set of external circumstances. I summarized the problems this way in a report to the American Council on Education in 1974.

Big-time college sports find themselves competing with professional sports and television for the entertainment dollar and with each other for the talent that will produce a winner. In the process, the escalation of the potential for, and of the likelihood of, ethical excesses in the recruiting, subsidy, and care and feeding of athletes continues. As it does, the adequacy of existing enforcement policies and procedures is being more and more called into question. These circumstances represent the current and more volatile manifestations of a problem that was identified in the 1929 Carnegie report, looked at in the early 1950's, and has in the meantime remained unresolved—a problem of morality that is given new dimensions by the demands of women and blacks.

*Reprinted with permission from *Education Record*, 57 (1976): 232-25. © 1977 by American Council on Education

It was, however, not the old familiar problem of unethical practices but the new problem of dollars that prompted the call for this inquiry. It is a problem posed by uncontrollable operating costs, the costs of keeping up with competition, and the price-elastic nature of gate receipts. And it is a problem that exacerbates not only the ethical dilemma of intercollegiate sports by creating still more pressure for victory at any moral cost, but also the educational dilemma regarding the role of intercollegiate athletics within higher education by mixing dollar motives with educational ones.

The **Wall Street Journal** put it more succinctly on 3 November 1976 when it spoke of sports as being "increasingly regarded as the fat man in the crowded educational lifeboat."

One serious complication is that the problems posed by intercollegiate athletics do not constitute the only challenge facing college and university presidents today. In fact, getting presidents and other top administrators to pay attention instead of lip service to college sports has in itself been a challenge.

The inquiry I undertook in 1973 echoed the finding of the 1929 Carnegie report that intercollegiate sports were suffering from presidential inattention. Steve Horn, Richard Lyman, Maurice Mitchell, and others, at the price of being termed gad-flies or Robin Hoods or being called angry or unrealistic, have in the last three years been trying to turn things around. But my own experience tells me how hard the task is going to be.

# PRESIDENTIAL INATTENTION

I want to cite three examples of presidential inattention. First, the chancellor at Berkeley, when the violations that put the institution in the NCAA's doghouse surfaced, readily admitted he had no idea what was going on. His counterpart at another prestigious university explained that his football coach's success was all the more remarkable because he achieved it with so few players wanting to play pro ball. That season more players were drafted by the pros from his squad than from any other in the country.

My third example is a collective indictment. Although interested foundation staff members encouraged me during my initial inquiry three years ago to think about next steps in ambitious dollar terms, the American Council on Education received modest preliminary signals from foundation trustees to support a commission on collegiate sports. Within a few months, a $750,000 proposed goal had been progressively scaled down to $400,000. Two years ago ACE was within $50,000 of this last figure, but with one large chunk contingent on finding foundation support outside the effete East, which is presumably less athletics-minded than other parts of the country. For more than two years the trustees of ACE kept reaffirming their interest in the project and kept looking for that $50,000 (without success). Finally, two and a half years after we finished our inquiry, a much more modest effort is being mounted—at a level I personally consider minimal.

I draw one inference from this chain of circumstances: higher education establishment, of which foundation officials, college presidents, and ACE are integral parts, simply does not take intercollegiate athletics as seriously as it should.

Two other complicating elements of the challenge of intercollegiate athletics are all too familiar to chief executives in their more general forms—the influences of government and of economics. Women are slowly achieving parity in sports not because it is morally and educationally right but because it is required by law and regulation. The scrutiny of the costs of college sports in general—or of the issue of aid-based-on-need to athletes in particular—has been generated not by educational but by economic considerations. The nature of the challenge is therefore determined in large part by—and the freedom of response to it limited by—familiar circumstances of legislation and economics quite beyond the president's control.

A set of complications with historical roots is also present. Reconciling the differences between men's and women's sports is made difficult in part by the existence of three national associations for men and one for women. The leading agency for men was conceived full-blown, at Theodore Roosevelt's insistence in 1906, as a free-standing, institutionally based enterprise with a primary concern for intercollegiate competition, while the Association for Intercollegiate Athletics for Women has evolved only in recent years as a third-level subsidiary of a parent, individually based professional association of physical educators.

# "NEW ATHLETICS" FOR WOMEN

Three years ago, given the problems facing men's athletics, I concurred in the hopes of others that the women might possibly show the men the way out of the athletic jungle. At the time, I identified three not necessarily opposing forces impinging on women's intercollegiate athletics (the advocates of the movement; the physical educators from the American Association for Health, Physical Education, and Recreation; and the athletes) and based my hope for leadership from the women on the second group—the educators. But time and the federal government have intervened with the result that Title IX and the athletes are driving women's intercollegiate athletics into, not leading the men's out of, the jungle. But they are not yet fully in the jungle. There are still ties to the ideals of AAPHER. Opportunities still exist, and part of the challenge, therefore, is to use the "new athletics" for women as a mechanism for getting a handle on some problems still besetting the "old athletics" for men.

One complication really characterizes and defines the challenge: many colleges and universities are simultaneously supporting quite contradictory policies—one set in the NCAA and quite a different one in AIAW. Certainly a major aspect of the challenge is the reconciliation of those differences.

# POSSIBLE SOLUTIONS

The challenge, as I see it, is to dare to use the opportunity that Title IX has unwittingly provided—the opportunity to rationalize the role of intercollegiate athletics within higher education. The challenge is also to care enough to try to rationalize the connection between sport and academe in ways that are morally and legally fair to both men and women athletes, from the majority and minorities alike, in ways that are morally and fiscally fair to other students and other departments and in ways that make education and ethical (not just athletic and fiscal) sense. And let me emphasize here that I am not talking about the opportunity that Title IX intentionally and explicitly provides to get more money for women's athletics. I'm talking about the opportunity it implicitly and unintentionally provides to reassess the educational role of intercollegiate athletics for women and men.

I have thought about possible solutions to the problems and have discovered some possible points of leverage that might be used. For one thing, there is the proposal before the NCAA that one-half of its governing bodies be college or university presidents. Frankly, I'm not sure the way for chief executives to influence intercollegiate athletics is to try to run them. Except for occasional special events, I'm not convinced that going to AIAW and NCAA meetings is the most fruitful way for presidents to spend their limited time. Perhaps extraordinary measures are called for. Perhaps there is no other way to get control of the situation now but to get a few presidents to dive in. But I'm personally not convinced that the job should in the long run be left to a willing few, when it really needs the attention of all.

Now at this point let me acknowledge that I have never been and have never aspired to be a college president—and let me further acknowledge that it's far easier to criticize than to be one. But at the same time, I would note that I was once a dean and before that the son of a dean—so I know something of how colleges and universities work. Presidents don't often accompany their academic and professional school deans to their meetings and seldom act as voting representatives at them. Yet deans work for college presidents—and so do athletic directors.

Because athletic directors presumably do work for their presidents, they could follow broad policy instructions worked out in advance. I see, therefore, as part of both the solution and the challenge of college sports today, the need for all college and university presidents, each in his or her own way, to take the lead in developing institutional policies for intercollegiate athletics, to reconcile the programs for men and women within both the letter and the spirit of those policies and the law, and to expect their representatives to uphold the policies that have been established.

# POINT OF LEVERAGE

I think presidents might insist on a bit of crime prevention—or to put it more positively, might seek to legitimize collegiate sports as part of the academic enterprise—by inviting the regional accrediting associations to visit their athletic departments. (Crime detection after the fact by the NCAA has its limits.) Or the presidents might insist on putting the admission of the financial aid to student athletes back in the admissions and financial aid office where many think they belong. I suggest that presidents of big-time football powers might think of separating their gridiron programs from the rest of their intercollegiate athletic enterprise, treating football as an auxiliary money-making enterprise contributing to the general fund and the remainder of the collegiate sports program as a legitimate part of the educational enterprise supported from the general fund. Weaning other athletic activities—first physical education, then intramurals, now minor sports—from football has been going on for at least 50 years. Why not complete the process in an orderly fashion now?

Some might even think of putting training for professional sports on a par with training for business or nursing. They might even get professional sports to loosen their purse strings in support of such a venture.

Because the challenge is complicated, no simple response will meet it; nor can there be impractical responses. Too much momentum and too many vested interests exist to permit a quick and easy panacea. What is needed, as I have already suggested, are some practical points of leverage. I trust that the new ACE Commission on Collegiate Sports will be able to find a few.

# ADMINISTRATOR'S VIEWS OF ATHLETIC GOVERNANCE

by
David M. Nelson

University and college administrators' views on the governance of inter-collegiate athletics have never been without concern and even trepidation. Athletic governance was an adopted responsibility that came relatively late in the life of academia as an obligation never really wanted. It is still the view of many administrators that college athletics remain the stepchild of the academic community. Yet, these same administrators see benefits coming to the campus from the athletic programs. This is the problem: College and university administrators can't seem to make up their minds on the most desirable relation of athletic to academic life. The lack of consensus is true today, as it was historically.

## HISTORICAL VIEW

The games played by college students are as old as the colleges themselves and originally developed on campus without encouragement or direction from faculty or administrators. In the beginning, the administrators and faculty viewed intercollegiate athletics as an illegitimate offspring, and it was not until the end of the nineteenth and the beginning of the twentieth century that competitive sports were reluctantly accepted into university and college families. It was not a happy adoption, and like the family member locked in a room and fed under the door, intercollegiate athletics was tolerated because they had to be some place since the demand from students was high. Not promoting athletic programs could have a deleterious effect on campus life.

49

In the early days, the students supported and administered the programs in every detail. This arrangement was satisfactory with administrators until the operation on many campuses became so large that it got out of control. Concerning this period, Edward J. Shea and Elton E. Wieman wrote:

The scope of the operation had so increased that the details of administration were far beyond the time and ability of students to handle and the program frequently lost control. Students, being a transient group, failed to provide continuity from year to year. Such matters as financial management, scheduling of contests, employment of personnel, maintenance and care of facilities and equipment, hiring of officials, among others, often lacked proper direction or were neglected completely. The administration and control of the programs were at best haphazard in nature. Athletic injuries inadequately cared for, personality clashes resulting in bickering over disproportionate amounts of attention between sports, and mishandling of funds with subsequent suspicion of their use were not uncommon. On of the most crucial areas of concern over the student-operated program was the lack of uniform rules regarding eligibility both within the same institution and among associated institutions. This failure led to the most serious of abuses both to the participants and to the institutions being represented. (1967: 7).

Administrators, once they decided the students could no longer reasonably operate the athletic program, had to decide who would run it and how. The first decision was to use volunteers and then salaried graduate managers, with alumni providing revenue. Volunteers and graduate managers have disappeared, but alumni participation in governance directly and indirectly is an administration conundrum, as is alumni funding.

During the early years, Harvard administrators were coping when they did a fast switch or double take concerning athletics on their campus. In 1882, the **University Magazine** claimed competitive athletics to be almost a panacea for many of the colleges' problems:

Before the introduction of athletic games in colleges, the hours of recreation were wasted by students in lounging around campus or town or in smoking or card playing in their rooms. Sprees were of almost nightly occurrence, property was wantonly destroyed, faculties and townsfolk alike were continually annoyed by the dissipated and riotous behavior of the students. Now this is entirely changed; the hours of recreation are devoted to the practice of athletics or to exercise in the gym, and the nights are passed resting from the healthful fatigue produced by muscular exercise. (Harvard, 1885: no page).

A decade later, Charles William Eliot, the president of Harvard College, expressed a much different viewpoint:

Athletics present the colleges to the public, educated and uneducated, as places of mere physical sport, and not of intellectual training. They make familiar to the student a coarse publicity which destroys his rightful privacy while in training for intellectual service and subject him to insolent and vulgar remarks on his personal qualities. They induce masses of spectators at interesting games to hysterical excitement (Nelson, 1962: 24).

Just prior to the 1905 blowup that shook football for generations, administrators were influenced by Professor Edwin G. Dexter of the University of Illinois "who for several years had **quietly** been keeping a precise and accurate record of the injuries of the game and its kindred sports, and who also had compiled a table of statistics covering the scholarship of the country's football men. The deductions from these figures were so strongly in favor of the game and its players that the agitation subsided as quickly as it had arisen" (Davis, 1911: 109).

By 1905, the year of college football's Pearl Harbor, every college administrator had an axe to grind with the game. President Angell of Michigan itemized his concern as follows:

1. The absorbing interest and excitement of the students—not to speak of the public—in the preparation for the intercollegiate games make a damaging invasion into the proper work of the university for the first ten or twelve weeks of the academic year.

2. The present conditions constantly hold before the students and before the world false ideals of college life. Not only in the college journals, but in the newspaper press of the whole country, the students who by daily descriptions and by portraits are held up as the great men of the university are the men of brawn rather than the men of brains.

3. The university is necessarily viewed in a wrong perspective. It is looked on as training men for a public spectacle, to which people come by thousands, instead of quietly training men for useful intellectual and moral service while securing ample opportunity for reasonable athletic sports.

4. The expenditure of money in the preparation for the game is out of all proportion to what a rational provision for exercise and games for students ought to call for. I need not go into detail. I will only add that where so much money is handled for such purpose, the temptations to misuse are not wanting (Wilson & Brondfield, 1967: 74).

President Angell then proceeded to solve the problem and was one of the first non-copers. He proposed the following for the Big Ten:

1. Students must have a year of residence before competing in athletics,

2. They must maintain proper grades,

3. Participation is limited to three years,

4. Training tables are abolished,

5. Universities may play a maximum of five games,

6. Coaches must be regular members of the instructional staff at their universities,

7. There must be absolute faculty control (1967:74).

Despite voices of criticism, the advocates and devotees of college football worked diligently to convince administrators that intercollegiate athletics (especially football) were a valuable and necessary part of campus life. Administrators supported athletic programs because they believed in them as educational vehicles, a source of additional funds, and self-supporting enterprises. A campus-controlled program would pose fewer administrative problems than the alternative of a program operated by off-campus groups including alumni and politically oriented interests. However, efforts at self-control proved fruitless; it was not long before administrative control of athletic programs had been wrested from the hands of college and university officials. The problem of self-control is exacerbated by the modern emphasis on winning, post-season bowl and tournament participation, and the competition for television dollars.

The decision to bring intercollegiate athletics into the academic family under university administration control has been second-guessed by administrators ever since, but there was no other choice. Coping with problems, as opposed to solving them, was an early decision faced by intercollegiate athletic administrators. Nearly 100 years later, coping and not solving the problems facing college sports is still the **"modus operandi."**

# CONTEMPORARY VIEW

Administrators, as they were in the past, are well aware that competitive athletics in our educational institutions are, at best a paradox. Aldous Huxley expressed this view:

> Like every other instrument that man has invented, sport can be used either for good or for evil purposes. Used well, it can teach endurance and courage, a sense of fair play and a respect for rules, coordinated effort and the subordination of personal interests to those of the group. Used badly, it can encourage personal vanity and group vanity, greedy desire for victory and hatred for rivals, an intolerant esprit de corps and contempt for people (Nelson, 1977:1).

Huxley's thoughts perfectly exemplify the old sporting cliche, "You are never as good as they say and never as bad," which is something every athletic administrator has known since the first ball was blown up.

For a variety of reasons, university and college administrators, especially presidents, have been subject to pressures against college sports internally from congenitally prejudiced faculty and externally from disenchanted persons. For example during the 1930s, the late Paul Gallico, a sportswriter who wrote **The Poseidon Adventure,** represented the disenchanted by publishing a sizzling criticism of college football before leaving sportswriting to become a sentimental story-teller in England. Gallico voiced his concern about sports in the 1930s by attacking college football in his **Farewell to Sports:**

> College football today is one of the last great strong-holds of genuine old-fashioned American hypocrisy. During Prohibition,

naturally, it ran second, but with the coming of repeal and the legalization of betting on the horses in most of the states of the Union, it easily took the lead. Its nearest competitor is the Amateur Athletic Union, and that isn't even close. It is highly discouraging that, one by one, all of our fine and worshipped institutions based upon the American precept of saying one thing and doing another, writing laws and then breaking them, have been crumbling. But football has stepped into the breach nobly and seems only to be beginning to come into its own as the leader in the field of double-dealing, deception, sham, cant, humbug and organized hypocrisy. There are occasionally abortive attempts to turn football into an honest woman, but, to date, the fine old game that interests and entertains literally millions of people has managed to withstand these insidious attacks. Like the chronic drunk, it has it moments of remorse, but equally like the inveterate souse, the benders following the periods of repentance are that much bigger and better. The future looks rosy. (Quoted in **Sage**, 1970:111).

College presidents, closely associated with intercollegiate athletics, have not been averse to using sports to promote their university. Dr. John A. Hannah, president of Michigan State College, had a goal to make Michigan State College a great university nationally. He came to the conclusion that one way to gain recognition was to have a nationally recognized football team and Hannah was quoted as saying: "If it meant the betterment of Michigan State, our football team would play any eleven gorillas from Barnum and Bailey on Saturday" (Hyman and White, 1977:130). President H. C. "Curly" Byrd at the University of Maryland was similarly motivated and did his best to promote the university with a successful football team. President Byrd was different from President Hannah in that he had on-the-job training as a football coach from 1912 to 1934.

One-hundred and eighty degrees from Presidents Hannah and Byrd was President Robert Maynard Hutchins of the Chicago school of thought that pictured football as a pernicious barnacle in the American University. President Hutchins, for all the criticism laid on him by the devotees of college football, had the courage, clout, and resolution to eliminate football from a notable university where the Patron Saint of the game, Amos Alonzo Stagg, had conducted the most sanitary program in the history of the game. Chicago became the flagship for those administrators who campaigned for the elimination of football from the campuses of America's colleges and universities. Chicago abandoned football in 1939, and the demise of its big-time intercollegiate athletics came in 1946 when this famous academic institution resigned from the Big Ten.

Almost two decades after Chicago dropped football, it is interesting to note how the viewpoint of an administrator in the same university viewed the death of the game:

Alumni of the University of Chicago—among them some who are still loyal to the academic concepts of Bob Hutchins—sometimes fret that Hutchins' doctrines attracted too many undergraduate eggheads. (Sample short: 'The greatest collection of neurotics since the Children's Crusade.') Last week Dean of Students Robert Strozier, speaking to 200 alumni lettermen from Chicago's years as an athletic power, charged that the 'best students' are no longer 'fighting for the opportunity to attend the University of Chicago' as strenuously as 'to attend many institutions of less academic stature.' He also proposed a remedy: a return to intercollegiate football, which Chicago proudly abandoned 18 years ago (Nelson: 1962:17).

Strozier rejected popular canards about Chicago's students but added that "the unpleasant fact remains that a myth was created on a national scale and myths die slowly" (1962: 17). The school, he said,

"constantly meets a kind of blank lack of interest even from those who recognize its greatness and its importance. Too many young people do not even consider Chicago . . . There is still something lacking in our situation. It is a subtle, indefinable something, but it needs to be remedied dramatically and forcefully . . . I wish to state without equivocation that I favor the return of football . . . as soon as possible . . .

Had I been a member of the administration when we withdrew from intercollegiate football, I feel sure that I should have voted to approve the action . . . (My present) deep personal conviction (was) arrived at with difficulty. I believe that the resolution to return to football competition would say something which could not be said in any other fashion to the public, and something needs to be said. I believe that there are many institutions of real quality whose quality has never been affected by football. I also believe that Chicago was a great institution when it participated fully in all intercollegiate sports (and) I intend to bend efforts toward the return of football to Chicago" (Nelson, 1962: 17).

The perspectives of two well-known college presidents, John Hannah and Robert Hutchins, were light years apart, but it came to pass that President Hannah's Michigan State Spartans eventually replaced President Hutchins' Chicago Maroons as the tenth team in the Big Ten in May 1949. The Spartans did not compete in the football league until the fall of 1953, but in February 1953 the administrators in the league got a preview of the first of several transgressions that would put the Spartans on NCAA probation three times.

Administrators have had over a hundred years to develop their views on intercollegiate athletics and some have dropped football and others have promoted it to a multi-million dollar business. In 1960, Dr. Glen Olds, president of Springfield College and later president of Kent State, took notice of the attacks by extremists on college athletics by saying:

One of the favorite post-sputnik sports of college presidents has become the debunking of sport as an enemy of education and people. No one would seriously quarrel with their criticism of the perversion of sport into professionalism, exploited for the sake of spectators, motivated to win at any cost and threatening the integrity of the player and the game. Still, there is a danger of throwing out the baby with the bath through disparaging and destroying the real role of sport in the creation and recreation of men and culture.

It is not sheer coincidence that in a world divided by cold war and iron and bamboo curtains slowly parting, sport remains one of the few bridges between men as men. In sport the accident of birth, race, creed, or station is transcended by performance alone. Sport speaks a universal language of movement and morality recognized in every culture and tongue. In its arena kings may be brought low, beggars crowned, phonies found out and simple excellence celebrated for what it is.

Sport teaches self-discovery, self-acceptance, self-control and self-giving. Taken seriously, such principles could reform our culture, our education and ourselves. They would put the players, not the coaches, in charge of the game on examination day. They would put equalization of opposition, not power to win, as the aim of a good game, and real sport. They would make development of the total powers of the person, not skill in a few, the mark of sport as education at its best. They would affirm the proper mission of education as the molding of men who find themselves in action, accept themselves for the sake of others.

When this happens, sports will not be confused or abused but will become the school room of competence and character. Fail in this, and we lose not only sport—but ourselves as well (Nelson, 1962:25).

Administrators with a variety of philosophies at schools of all sizes and persuasions have not missed the hard cold facts that the NCAA, from 1952 to 1977, considered 993 cases for possible infractions of NCAA rules; and disciplinary actions were taken in 548 cases. Governance practices have been directly and indirectly affected by what happened during this 25-year period.

The reactions of administrators vary, but President William E. Davis of the University of New Mexico, before his traumatic experience with the Lobos, has a message worth noting. He hit close to the truth when he said, while President of Idaho State, that:

Some college and university presidents I have known have looked upon intercollegiate athletics much in the same light as they would regard the illegitimate son at the family reunion. On a good day and in the right company, it might be played down or charged off to one of those nuisances or accidents of life. And, in some company, the subject simply is avoided altogether (Nelson, 1977:1).

In 1973 Harold L. Enarson, President of Ohio State University where the athletic budget was $4 million a year, made two observations. He said that the goal of winning has become "close to obsessive," and the growing intensity of intercollegiate competition is "tragic." He added that, "an unhealthy kind of interaction was developing" between communities and teams. Sportsmanship has become lost in an atmosphere of "emotional super stimulation" (Starnes, 1973 8). However, Mr. Enarson said it was "simplistic nonsense" to contend that de-emphasizing athletics would automatically emphasize academic excellence.

The same year, President Maurice Mitchell of the University of Denver bluntly attacked college athletics when he said: "Up to now, you couldn't even get a preacher to look at the immorality involved in athletics; they must be afraid God is an alumnus. I love sports, but I despise what's happening. Sports today are rooted in detested fraud" (1973: 8).

John Silber, president of Boston University, made his part in governance quite clear when he stated: "One myth is that football builds loyalty among alumni. In my experience this simply isn't true. We've done a survey that shows the friends of the library among alumni have produced $5 for every $1 produced by friends of football. We are putting the alumni to the test with football at Boston U. If it doesn't become self-supporting within three or four years, it will be abandoned" (1973: 8).

A. Whitney Griswold, former president of Yale, represented the Ivy presidents' governance philosophy of intercollegiate athletics by saying that athletic scholarships are "the greatest swindle ever perpetrated on American youths" (Underwood, 1979: 204).

During his ten years as USC president, John R. Hubbard, who preceded the incumbent president, James H. Zumberge, called college sports "a glue that holds the university together" (Kirshenbaum, 1980: 19). In August, 1980, USC was disqualified from the season's PAC-10 football championship because of "unwarranted intrusions into academic processes." After an in-house study charged that 330 "academically marginal" athletes had been admitted "based on athletic prowess as judged by the athletic department and without normal admissions office review," President Zumberge responded: "The potential exists for gradually undermining the integrity and credibility of the educational enterprise as a whole."

One school, two different directions in governance.

Administrators of intercollegiate athletic programs, especially college presidents, have a touch of schizophrenia because they view the non-academic programs in one light and the academic programs in another. Justice Byron "Whizzer" White, addressing the National Federation of State High School Associations in 1965, said: "The problems in controlling athletic programs come about because we are dealing with human nature in a specialized context" (White, 1965: 7). White advocated following the advice of Dr. George Norlin, long-time president of the University of Colorado, who was well aware that intercollegiate problems were old problems. Dr. Norlin's words were:

Lo, all these centuries human nature remains unchanged . . .

Perhaps we had better accept this unflattering fact and make the best of it. Perhaps the time may come when college students will hold pep meetings to stir the philosophy department to do or die or will root with enthusiasm when the department of chemistry discovers a new element, but that time has not come nor will the Carnegie report on athletics (or others like it) bring it about in our day or our generation (1965:7).

Considering the governance alternatives, administrators should probably take Dr. Norlin's advice and reinforce it with Justice White's conclusion: "Human nature and athletics, as Shelley said about another subject are 'through time and change, unquenchably the same' " (1965: 7)

# REFERENCES

**Davis, Park H.**
1911 *Football: The American Intercollegiate Game.* New York: Charles Scribner and Sons.
Harvard University
1885 "Athletics at Harvard." *University Magazine.* (n.d., n. p.).
Hyman, Mervin D. and Gordon S. White, Jr.
1977 *Big Ten Football.* New York: MacMillan.
Kirshenbaum, Jerry
1980 "USC: The University of Special Cases." *Sports Illustrated* 532(October 27): 19.
Nelson, David M.
1962 *Football Principles and Play.* New York: Ronald Press.

1977 "Football is Alive." Paper presented at the meetings of the National Federation of State High School Association. Biloxi, Mississippi. (January).
Sage, George H. (ed.)
1970 *Sport and American Society.* Reading, Pa.: Addison-Wesley.
Shea, Edward J. and Elton G. Wieman
1967 *Administrative Policies for Intercollegiate Athletics.* Springfield: Charles W. Thomas.
Starnes, Richard
1973 "Abuses in Bigtime College Sports Spur Mounting Criticism." *The Chronicle of Higher Education.* (December 10):8.
White, Byron R.
1965 "Athletics: . . . Unquenchably the Same?" Paper presented at the meetings of the National Federation of State High School Athletic Associations. Williamsburg, Virginia (June).
Wilson, Kenneth J. and Jerry Brondfield
1967 *The Big Ten.* Englewood Cliffs, N.J.: Prentice-Hall.
Underwood, John
1979 *The Death of an American Game—The Crisis in Football.* Boston: Little Brown

# ATHLETICS AND ACADEMICS: A CASE STUDY IN REASSESSMENT

By
Gregory F. Lucey

In recent years, the vitality of the higher education system in the United States has been seriously challenged by double-digit inflation, recession-stagnation, a saturated job market, and a decline in the number of prospective college students in the traditional age groups. Attitudes of growth and expansion characteristic of the 1960's and 1970's have changed to ones of retrenchment, reassessment of programs, and re-establishment of priorities. Current economic realities necessitate the development of economic strategies capable of ensuring the survival of quality education in the United States.

It is our belief at Seattle University that the starting point for such review is the educational mission statement of the institution. With this statement, which identifies the school's purpose and outlines its objectives as its premise, the institution can set appropriate priorities and allocate resources to effectively meet established goals. Each department or activity can also be evaluated in terms of its contribution toward achieving the institution's objectives. Given that fiscal limitations exist on the number and variety of programs which can be offered, evaluation criteria must take into account both educational priorities and economic limits. The programs of greatest priority will be those which contribute towards fulfilling the institution's mission to a degree which makes them cost-effective.

While intercollegiate athletics has long been accepted as an integral part of most college campuses, its role has been quasi-educational. It has been argued that while only a few students benefit directly, intercollegiate athletic programs indirectly serve all students by providing examples of fitness, good sportsmanship, leadership, self-discipline, and teamwork. The monies (e.g., gate receipts and alumni contributions) generated from inter-collegiate athletic competition can be used to finance other activities.

The cost of intercollegiate athletics in United States' colleges and universities has increased from $300 million in 1974 to $500 million in 1979. Continually escalating operational costs coupled with the fact that successful intercollegiate athletic programs must prioritize income generation, and thus put the public's entertainment desires and interests ahead of the participation interests of students, underscore the need for a fundamental reassessment of the role of intercollegiate athletics in higher education. Seattle University has just completed such a reassessment.

This article is written in the hopes of providing assistance for those of you who are, or may be, reviewing the form, function, and relevance of your institution's athletic program in relation to your school's mission and financial constraints. I am going to describe how Seattle University, a small, private institution, raised questions about the relevance of its intercollegiate athletic program. The dynamics of the decision-making process, and the insights gained as a result of the whole assessment procedure will be brought out in the ensuing discussion.

# BACKGROUND

Seattle University is a small, urban university with a 45-acre campus located in the heart of the city. It is one of the 28 Jesuit-sponsored, independent colleges and universities in the United States. Over the past 90 years, this institution has evolved from a liberal arts college into a university with eight major divisions: The College of Arts and Sciences, the Albers School of Business, the School of Science and Engineering, the School of Education, the Institute of Public Service, Matteo Ricci College, and the Graduate School. With more than 4,000 graduate and undergraduate students, 600 employees and a $20 million dollar annual budget, Seattle University is a viable, regional university committed to meeting educational needs in the Pacific Northwest. The university has maintained its traditional liberal arts orientation while developing strong, value-oriented professional programs. Since 1976 the university has steadily improved its internal management systems, maintained a balanced budget, and strengthened its overall financial position.

In the 1950's, Seattle University gained national recognition and even prominence through a very competitive basketball program of which Elgin Baylor is perhaps the best-known product. The school has never had a football program. By the 1970's, however, the athletic program was not paying its own way and, by 1979, its rapidly escalating deficit was becoming a major financial problem. Rampaging inflation, especially in team travel costs and salaries, was compounded by the need to comply with Title IX of the Education Amendment of 1972. Also, since the university did not have an adequate spectator facility for its revenue-producing sport, basketball, Seattle played home games four miles from campus at the Seattle Center. This adversely affected even student attendance to the point that, by 1980, it was estimated that only 4 percent of the students attended home games.

During 1979-80 (its last year of "major" competition), Seattle University basketball averaged less than 1,500 paid attendance per game. It should also be noted that Seattle University and other Puget Sound area schools have been forced to compete increasingly with professional sports teams. Competition in the area for the public's discretionary dollar has grown fierce with teams in major league soccer, baseball, basketball, and football. High school and college attendance figures have dropped greatly in the last few years.

Another important factor in Seattle University's situation was a growing lack of interest and participation on the part of students in the athletic program. Mens' basketball was the only program which seemed to attract some student following, and even that was minimal. There seemed to be a sense of alienation between the student body and those students participating in the athletic program. Full-scholarship students who came to Seattle University to participate in the athletic program became increasingly interested in gaining an entree into professional careers in athletics rather than in attaining an academic education

Seattle University's projected athletic program deficit for fiscal year 1981 was 75 percent of the total. In dollars, this amount translated to a deficit of $323,000 out of an athletic budget of $428,000. This deficit was projected, assuming the continuation of a level of funding which the Director of Athletics, the head basketball coach, and the Vice-President for Student Life already believed was inadequate for a level of recruitment which would successfully attract top athletes. There was also a deficiency in funding for promotions that would enable the athletic teams to draw and increase gate receipts. A brief review of comparable programs indicated that a doubling of funding would be required to provide a first-class Division I program!

A final factor for consideration was that other departments of the university were also experiencing inadequacies in their funding. Thus, the question was raised as to whether other educational and academic programs would be deprived of adequate funding in order to provide for an even higher level of funding for the athletic program. In light of these circumstances, Seattle University's administration recommended to the university's Board of Trustees that approval of the portion of the budget pertaining to intercollegiate athletics be withheld and that a task force be established to review the athletic program to determine what the role of intercollegiate athletics should be at Seattle University. On February 27, the trustees had an extensive and thorough discussion as to whether or not to approve the athletic budget as presented or to engage in the review. One of the major issues addressed was the question of timing. Because an athletic program is ongoing and is either involved in the season itself or in recruiting and gearing up for the next season, there is really no time that an evaluation, which involves the continuation or non-continuation of the program, can be scheduled without in some way jeopardizing the future of that program. Additionally, if the study is to be a prolonged one, a choice has been made to, in effect, commit to at least the year during which the study occurs; this means the possible loss of another several hundred thousand dollars. Seattle University's trustees decided that the study should be intense, but of short duration, and to reassemble prior to the deadline for the recruitment letters of intent for male students. (It was already too late for letters of intent for female students.) A period of five-six weeks was available for the study and for a recommendation to come from the president to the trustees.

# THE REVIEW PROCESS TASK FORCE FORMATION

On the morning following the trustees' meeting, the president met with several of the vice-presidents and staff advisors to establish the task force. It was decided that a representative group of no more than eight should be identified, and that this group should be representative of students, faculty, alumni, and the Seattle community-at-large. A desire was also expressed that the representation include men, women, and minorities. Two students, two alumni, two faculty, one representative of the general community of Seattle, and one administrator who would serve as a chairperson comprised the task force. The member would be appointed by the president after sufficient consultation with the appropriate constituencies.

The task force then consisted of seven: six whites, one black; four men and three women; three alumni and four non-alumni, two of whom were students and would-be alumni. What was lacking was an administrator, a Jesuit (in the case of Seattle University, a Jesuit-sponsored institution), and a chairperson. Several of the vice-presidents were considered; I was selected because of my skills in group process, my availability, and my position as Vice-President for Educational Planning.

The task force was charged with the responsibility of examining thoroughly all aspects of athletics at Seattle University in light of its stated educational mission, the context of fiscal constraints, regional economic and demographic projections, and related issues in higher education. The charge was expressed in terms of an investigation of three options: (I) continuation of Division I competition, (II) continue intercollegiate athletes but at a competitive level less than NCAA Division I, or (III) discontinuation of intercollegiate athletics and the adoption of a "life-sports" program of instruction and intramural competition. From the beginning, these options were understood by the task force not as an exhaustive listing of the acceptable alternatives but as examples of the range of options to be considered.

This study was perceived from the outset by the task force as a summative evaluation. That is, the purpose of this study was to offer direction to the president and the Board of Trustees for a major decision regarding the athletic program at Seattle University. The underlying issue was perceived to be university priorities in the allocation of limited educational resources. Within that context, the fundamental issue was always that of a quality: a high caliber intercollegiate program versus a diverse program designed for optimum participation. The task force, therefore, focused its study on the major issues of collegiate athletics in the 1980's and the question of feasibility of the various options for a small, independent university. Questions of implementation were explored only as required for the more general feasibility question. The task force was aware from the beginning that the major constraint on its study was time. At the expense of other obligations, the members individually resolved to devote whatever time was required to meet the demands of the task; within 24 days, the task force met 22 times for a total of 85 hours.

## Data Collection

Two types of data were perceived as necessary for this study: factual data and judgment data. Most of the factual data were available from the various university offices and from the finance or athletic offices of other universities. The factual data centered around expenditures and revenues, actual and projected, from 1975 to 1985, at Seattle University. Expenditure and revenue data of other institutions in various divisions were also secured as was information on scholarship policy and practice, conference and athletic organization regulations, and problems of governance at individual schools. The collection of judgment data, that is, data on the perceptions and opinions of people on the various issues, took several forms:

1. **Semi-private interviews with select people and groups:** In all, 50 people were interviewed by the task force, including the athletic director, each coach, and players from each team.

2. **Surveys:** (1) A survey instrument, designed by Dr. Robert Larson, Professor of Sociology and member of the task force, was distributed on March 10 to all classes at 10:00 a.m. and 5:35 p.m. with a potential of canvassing 2,000 of the university's 4,100 students. Several adverse circumstances limited the return to 817, or roughly 20 percent of the students. (2) The same survey intrument, with some minor alterations, was distributed to all 480 full time faculty, staff, and administrators in the university. Nearly 50 percent, or 220 responded. (3) From a population of 4,600 active alumni, a random sample of 450 who live in the greater Puget Sound area was drawn for a telephone survey. On March 17 and 18, the task force members, with some outside assistance, interviewed 304 of the 450 alumni, asking them eight key questions from the survey instrument used for the other groups. (4) The Tomahawk Club, an athletic booster club, on its own conducted a telephone survey of its members and of season-ticket holders. The results and analysis of this survey of 114 people were supplied to the task force.

3. **Open forums:** To provide university students, personnel, alumni, and friends the opportunity to address the task force, open forums were held on two dates. Roughly 300 people attended, with slightly over 50 persons speaking. The second forum was widely publicized through the media and through advertisements in the newspapers.

4. **Written statements:** Letters to the task force were encouraged in preference to phone calls. Approximately 100 letters were received and shared by the task force.
5. **Consultation:** The task force consulted with knowledgeable people regarding physical recreation and life sports as well as the issues related directly to intercollegiate competition. This consultation was done primarily by telephone. Several institutions were identified which were studying or had studied these same issues. In all, 12 individuals were contacted at least once. Most of these people provided both factual data and recommendations. Dr. Will Holsberry, executive secretary of the National Intramural Recreation Sports Association, and Dr. David Olson, athletic director at Pacific Lutheran University, addressed the task force.
6. **Literature:** Literature related to the issues was reviewed at the outset of the study by Dr. Donna Orange, a faculty member of the task force. Selected articles were then shared by the task force.

# Data Analysis

**Financial data.** The relevant financial data were interpreted in diverse ways by those addressing the task force, whose members made every effort to understand the fiscal data relating to the intercollegiate athletic department. The data were viewed in the context of the fiscal constraints of the university and in comparison with fiscal data from other universities who participate at various levels of intercollegiate competition. With the data provided, a projection of expenditures and revenues for the athletic department through 1985 was developed. The projection was made at minimum and optimum levels of operation.

Several observations might be helpful in understanding these data and the conclusions: (a) A "deficit," as used by the university, refers to the difference between direct revenue to the department from gate receipts, guarantees, etc., and expenditures of the budget for the direct costs of the program; (b) revenue does not include major grants to the university nor tuition paid by student-athletes; (c) fringe benefits, insurance, and the use of university athletic facilities are absorbed by the university in other budgets; (d) gift income from the booster clubs and other sources are permitted as funding "above budget," safe by assuming that these gifts did not exceed $50,000 annually. Analysis of the projections revealed that projected increases in gift income and revenue would not offset the projected operating cost of even minimum funding for the program at Division I level. Comparison of the athletic budgets of other institutions with the university's budget showed that competition at Division II level would reduce expenses only minimally and would reduce revenues. Thus, competition in Division II would probably also mean increased deficit spending.

**Scholarships from Institutional Funds.** Seattle University allocated institutional funds for student scholarships through: (a) need-based financial aid, (b) merit scholarships, and (c) athletic scholarships. The merit scholarships included the honors program scholarships and the alumni merit scholarships. The merit scholarships may or may not be part of the need-based package. Athletic scholarships varied from a full-ride (tuition, room and board, and books) to a partial remission of tuition. In a few cases, athletic scholarships were part of a need-based financial package.

The nature of athletic scholarships was a focal point of much of the task force's discussion. Some members viewed partial tuition scholarships as a source of new revenue to the university; some viewed all athletic scholarships as an inappropriate charge to the department, based on the "empty chair theory;" and others maintained scholarships were not a real cost to the university. However, the administration of Seattle University considered a scholarship as a real cost. In fact, the tuition revenues covered only about 75 percent of the educational and general expenditures in the university budget. Complete agreement was not reached on the accounting procedures within the task force. However, this became a moot question when it was decided to include a recommendation in the final report to discontinue athletic scholarships.

## Survey Results

The response to the three surveys conducted by the task force was more than adequate to provide useful data. Although the survey of the student population was a partial canvas, the responses were representative of the major demographic divisions within that population. A number of items on the surveys were valuable in the nuanced reflection they evoked in the discussions. The most significant data for the final decision were the responses to the question of which option the respondent would recommend to the task force. Because a similar question was asked of those surveyed by the Tomahawk Club, a comparison of the responses of six different groups was possible: (a) Season ticket holders and Tomahawk Club members, (b) alumni, (c) students, (d) staff, (e) faculty, and (f) administrators.

With the exception of those surveyed by the Tomahawk Club, there was a strong preference in the university community to discontinue participation in Division I. On the other hand, there was a strong desire among both students and alumni for some kind of intercollegiate program. Among both of these groups, more favored Division II than either Division I or intramurals-life sports. These results were interpreted to mean that a majority wanted to have both participatory and spectator intercollegiate sports at an affordable level. The support for continuation in Division I ranged from 88.6 percent in the Tomahawk survey to 8.3 percent among the administration; 29.2 percent of alumni surveyed favored this course of action as did 29.8 percent of student, 15.9 percent of staff, and 9.5 percent of faculty.

The support for Option III, the expanded intramural and life sports programs, ranged from 3.5 percent in the Tomahawk survey to 80.6 percent for the administration. Between these extremes, Option III was favored by 29.2 percent of alumni, 31.9 percent of students, 52.3 percent of staff, and 58.1 percent of faculty. Division II participation was the preference of 7.9 percent of those surveyed by the Tomahawk Club, 41.5 percent of alumni, 38.2 percent of students, 31.8 percent of staff, 32.4 percent of faculty, and 11.1 percent administration.

These numbers were combined in two different ways: Those who wanted to continue in Division I and those who desired that Seattle University have some form of intercollegiate athletics. Such a desire was expressed by 96.5 percent in the Tomahawk survey, 70.8 percent of alumni, 68.1 percent of students, 47.7 percent of staff, 41.9 percent of faculty, and 19.4 percent of administration. The percentages of those who favored Division II were added to those who favored Option III to find out what share of these groups believed it was time for some kind of change from Division I. This attitude was evident in 11.4 percent of those in the Tomahawk survey, 70.7 percent of alumni, 70.1 percent of students, 84.1 percent of staff, 90.5 percent of faculty, and 91.7 percent of administrators. From all of these percentages, it was concluded that the survey data indicated a strong desire for change toward a stronger participation emphasis, coupled with a continuing desire for those values potentially achievable by some sort of intercollegiate competition.

## Open Forums and Written Statements

Most of those who spoke at the open forums or wrote letters expressed strong support for continuation of Division I competition. There appeared to be considerable duplication between these two groups and the Tomahawk Club membership. In all, at most 300 persons voiced strong support for the continuation of Division I competition.

# PROCESS OF DELIBERATION

As indicated above, the committee met daily for 22 of 24 days. Much of the time was spent in hearing the opinions of various constituencies and reviewing the factual data. Once the factual data deemed necessary had been gathered and studied and the task force had listened to the various persons it felt should be heard, the task force closeted itself and began its deliberations with an all-day, off-campus retreat. At the outset of the retreat the chairperson presented a series of 14 assumptions considered basic to the discussion of the athletic issues. It was necessary that the group come to an understanding of the basic ideas underlying the decision-making process so that there would be a common vocabulary and starting point from which they might discuss alternatives. Approximately half a day was spend reviewing, modifying, and reaching agreement on the following nine underlying assumptions:

1. That participation in physical recreation, i.e., sports, is an appropriate part of the total educational mission of Seattle University;
2. that competition, whether intramural or intercollegiate, within the

parameters of basic regard for human persons and of good sportsmanship, is an acceptable part of athletic activity and is not in conflict with the educational mission of the university;

3. that quality programs, activities, or achievements under the sponsorship of Seattle University enhance the reputation and expand the
recognition of the university;

4. that recognition and reputation are necessary to the continuation and
development of the university;

5. that the development of a recreational/intramural sports program,
which could include: (a) open recreation, (b) intramurals, (c) outdoor
recreation, and (d) intercollegiate club sports, would enhance the
ability of Seattle University to effectively carry out its education mission;

6. that a quality intercollegiate athletic program at Seattle University
contributes to the image of the university and expands its recognition, besides providing valuable educational experience for those involved;

7. that intercollegiate athletics exist in the United States in varying
forms and levels of competitiveness for men and women: (1) Division
I, II, and III of the NCAA and the AIAW; (2) NAIA; (3) club sports;

8. that the recommendation of the task force must maintain the affirmative stance of the university with regard to minorities and women;
and

9. that the sports program at Seattle University, as currently managed,
structured, and funded, is unacceptable.

Building upon the above assumptions, the task force began to explore
and identify various alternatives which they might consider for their recommendation to the Board of Trustees. The idea in developing alternatives was
not to present an alternative which the member of the task force was advocating, but in a brainstorming fashion to try to lay out before the task
force all the various types of alternatives which might be considered. This
process took the better part of the remaining half-day on retreat. By the end
of the day, it seemed that three alternative recommendations had been
worked out:

1. stay in Division I,
2. participate in intercollegiate athletics, but at a lower level, and
3. drop intercollegiate sports and emphasize intramurals.

The following day, the task force met and articulated these three alternatives in some detail, discussing them at length and coming to an agreement that these three options were those with which they wished to proceed.
A "pros and cons" or "advantages and disadvantages" analysis was made
for each option, and the advantages and disadvantages of the three were
compared. This procedure took the entire second day of the retreat. After
developing a set of conceivably viable options and after an extensive process
of weighing the advantages and disadvantages of each, the task force was to
identify the grounds upon which it built its recommendations. The grounds
are presented in the following statements. The task force recognized:

1. That a quality Division I intercollegiate athletics program has contributed to the growth and development of Seattle University over the past 30 years;
2. that the Seattle University intercollegiate athletics program has in the past had and continues to have a very positive, permanent influence on a good number of students;
3. that a quality intercollegiate athletics program can provide an opportunity for some minority people, especially blacks, to receive a quality education and to achieve leadership status within various communities to which they belong;
4. that the achievement of national recognition by our athletic teams could affect positively both recruitment of students and the acquisition of resources;
5. that significant efforts have been made by several groups to support various university teams resulting in an annual total gift income of roughly $50,000; and
6. that the recommendation of the task force, if accepted, could have a negative effect on some alumni and possibly a few potential donors to the university.

However, the task force also recognized:

1. that Seattle University is a small, independent university, relying almost entirely on tuition, gifts, and grants for its resources. While fiscally stable, the university has very limited resources to meet pressing needs in faculty and staff compensation, library acquisitions, and facilities (maintenance, renovation and replacement), all of which are critical to its central educational mission;
2. that the current funding level for the intercollegiate program at Seattle University is below the minimum needed for the levels of its present competition or even for that needed for Division II;
3. that with an inflation rate of approximately 20 percent and the need to provide equal opportunities in athletics for men and women, there is a multiplier effect in the expenditures for athletics that can only result in an increased deficit in the university budget for intercollegiate athletics at the Division I or the Division II level;
4. that even with a full-time professional fund-raiser coordinating and directing this effort, sufficient funds would not be generated to offset the increased budget needed for Division I competition and/or the increased deficit expected because of inflation and other factors;
5. that the level of "professionalism" in major collegiate athletics makes it extremely difficult for a university to fund a successful first-rate football or basketball team and to maintain its integrity;
6. that a major involvement in sports entertainment is difficult to justify as appropriate to the educational mission of the university;
7. that the physical development and conditioning of the body and the development of skills in several lifetime sports are valued components of the holistic education Seattle University espouses;
8. that students of all ages have a growing interest in physical fitness

67

and physical recreation, i.e., participation in sports;

9. that a diverse athletics program designed for optimum student participation will be an attractive feature for incoming students, a feature increasingly available at other universities;

10. based on the surveys conducted, that the alumni and students strongly support some level of intercollegiate competition and that the alumni, students, staff, faculty, and administration strongly support the discontinuation of intercollegiate competition in Division I;

11. that intercollegiate competition at a level equivalent to Division III of the NCAA can provide: (a) the opportunity for students to benefit from the experience of team work, striving for excellence, competitive sportsmanship, etc., (b) a focal point for other student activities, and (c) a rallying point for the larger university community.

On the third day, the task force set aside all discussion concerning the values which should be operative in their recommendations.

All of the various value concepts for consideration in making this kind of decision were listed on a blackboard. Some of these concepts included fiscal needs, community support, campus spirit, education benefits, physical fitness, and character development. Approximately 25 values were listed and discussed to determine if there was a clear understanding of what was meant by each, which ones overlapped, and what would be the best statement or understanding of each. Each member of the task force then listed privately the five values he or she felt were most important; the list of values was prioritized by the group by indicating the votes for each; this gave the task force a sense of where members were in terms of these values. The task force then returned to the three options developed and asked which option best expressed the values which had been chosen. Each person considered his five values and asked, "The best expression of my first value would be found in Option # ?; the best expression of my second value would be found in Option # ?" and so on.

In a round table fashion, each person presented his or her highest priority value and indicated which option would best express it. Five rounds were made, with each person placing his or her values on one of the options. A group consensus on the options which best expressed the groups' values emerged; a general discussion followed. Then, each person was asked to simply sit back and, without making a final decision or commitment, to express where they were with regard to a recommendation. Would they favor Option #1, 2, or 3 and why? After this process was completed, the task force departed for the evening, allowing time to reflect on what had transpired. Members returned the following day with the understanding that they would repeat the last step of stating for the group where each was individually, and why. This procedure made it evident that a group consensus had been reached; the question then became one of formulating a recommendation which would express it. The following recommendation was developed to incorporate all the values prioritized. The task force recommended:

A. that Seattle University reaffirm its commitment to the value of athletics for its students, but recommend a creative new direction for the program which would optimize the participation of students.

B. that this could be achieved by having an athletic program which includes: (1) an expanded and revitalized program of physical recreation/life sports; and (2) some intercollegiate competition at a level equivilent to Division III of the NCAA.

C. that the regulations of Division III of the NCAA on athletic scholarships be adopted as university policy; that is, "financial aid for student-athletes must be consistent with the established policy of the institution for financial aid for all other students."

D. that in the reallocation of scholarship funds available as a result of this decision, consideration be given to the need for: (a) additional institutional funds for the general support of students needing financial aid; (b) making Seattle University accessible to minorities, especially blacks; and, (c) increasing the alumni scholarship fund.

E. that this total program be placed under the direction of a person committed to optimum student participation, both male and female, in wide variety of sports activities, capable of good management of the program and the athletic facilities at Seattle University; namely, the Connolly Center and the intramural field; and creative in the approach to program development.

F. that the statutes of the university be revised in order to establish an oversight committee for athletics and physical recreation which reports to the Vice-President for Student Life. This oversight committee would replace the Athletic Board as currently structured.

G. that the funding for physical recreation/life sports and intercollegiate competition be sufficient for viable, attractive programs but not exceed a maximum determined as appropriate for an educational institution with limited resources. This funding level can only be determined in practice over a few years.

H. that careful consideration be given to the coordination of the new athletic program with the department of physical education.

I. that the active, ongoing support of the administration for this program be made evident.

J. that the design of these programs include an evaluation process.

The task force submitted their final report to Father William J. Sullivan, S.J., President of Seattle University, on March 31, 1980. Based upon the task force's recommendations, Fr. Sullivan, in turn, wrote a synopsis of the report, added his own endorsement, and submitted the information to the Board of Trustees. On April 3, 1980, the trustees formally adopted the recommendations submitted.

# FOLLOW-UP ACTION

A six-member Transition Committee, comprised of two members of the task force and chaired by the Vice-President for Student Life, was established to implement the recommended changes for the athletic program. Numerous issues had to be considered immediately: selection of sports to be continued or dropped to create a balance in number of men's and women's teams; development of a set of personnel committed to the re-direction of the athletic program; establishment of scholarship policy for continuing athletes; determination of one-time conversion costs; establishment of budget for the new program; realignment with athletic associations; and re-scheduling of events.

Within two months, a new sports director and a complement of part-time coaches were hired. Two male sports teams were dropped, leaving four male sports: basketball, baseball, soccer, and tennis, and four female sports: basketball, tennis, volleyball, and gymnastics. The budget for inter-collegiate athletics was cut by 50 percent. The net deficit was reduced by 75 percent. The elimination of two teams reduced the number of student athletes by 20 percent. However, an increase of 800 percent in the in-tramural program budget has enabled the university to provide the students with the beginning of a good life-sports program.

While it is too early to determine all the ramifications of Seattle University's decision to re-focus its athletic program, early indications have been very positive. Participation in the intramural program has more than doubled; the majority of the student-athletes elected to remain at Seattle University and to continue competing; the women's basketball team finished their first season under the new program in the regional play-offs of the AIAW with a record of 23 - 8; the women's gymnastics team was ranked seventh nationally; and the men's teams had average seasons against regional competition.

Despite the fact that some alumni support of the university has been withdrawn, the overall gift income from alumni is up over last year. Likewise, while the decision may have influenced some students not to enroll at Seattle University, the overall enrollment is at a record level a year following the decision. The institutional fund for merit and need-based grants-in-aid has been increased by $135,000 for the 1981-82 budget as a direct result of the decision to drop athletic scholarships. Plans have been made to continue to monitor the effects of this decision on the university. Evaluations will review the adequacy of budgets, the use of facilities, the level of program participation, and the extent of student satisfaction with the programs.

# THE TIGER DEVOURS THE LITERARY MAGAZINE, OR, INTERCOLLEGIATE ATHLETICS IN AMERICA

By
Allen Guttman

From 1935 to 1942, Louisiana State University sponsored an internationally admired literary magazine, **The Southern Review,** with which were associated such famed figures as Cleanth Brooks, Allen Tate, and Robert Penn Warren. In the dark days of World War II, the financially pressed university had to choose between the **Southern Review** and an adequate supply of fresh meat for the tiger which the school kept as a mascot for its football team. The tiger won. It was an easy victory and one which American professors are likely to find quite predictable, but it is difficult to imagine a similar choice at Oxford, the Sorbonne, or Tubingen. British, French, and German centers of higher learning are seldom characterized by the excellence of their rugby players, cyclists, or soccer team. Only in America can an institution like Notre Dame be perceived as a major university on the basis of its football triumphs. The most remarkable aspect of this situation is that American academics, apart from a bemused or embittered minority, accept this state of affairs as if it were part of the unalterable order of nature. Curiously, the hallowed tradition of intercollegiate athletics, with an emphasis on football and basketball, is little more than a century old.

Intercollegiate athletics began under the sponsorship of students who sought to test their skill and prowess against that of rival colleges despite faculty preference for rivalries of a more intellectual sort. Students in England began the tradition in the early nineteenth century, but contests between Oxford and Cambridge remained more or less in the hands of the students while intercollegiate athletics in America grew rather quickly into an institution governed not by undergraduates but by faculties, administrations, and, in many cases, alumni. Guy Lewis and other sports historians have made the story of the growth of the institution a familiar one. Intercollegiate competitions like the Amherst-Williams baseball game of 1859 led to associations like the Intercollegiate Baseball League of 1879 (Lewis, 1970). Associations formed to promote baseball, football, crew, and track and field laid the ground for a national organization concerned to regularize and administer all intercollegiate athletics. The National Collegiate Athletic Association (originally called the Intercollegiate Athletic Association of the United States) was born amid controversy in 1905-1906, but the controversy was engendered not by the fundamental question of the academic legitimacy of intercollegiate sports but rather by the secondary question of their excesses.

By the beginning of the twentieth century, professors generally assumed that sports were a part of physical education and that physical education was an important aspect of moral education. The question, therefore, was not whether to allow intercollegiate contests but rather how to prevent the bloodshed and mayhem that had become associated with "the big game."

By 1929, the Carnegie Commission has ample evidence to indicate that the quest for athletic glory was attended by distortions and dishonesties that made a mockery of the ideals which colleges and universities supposedly embody. The authors of the report noted mildly that a "system of recruiting and subsidizing has grown up, under which boys are offered pecuniary and other inducements to enter a particular college" (Savage, **et.al.**, 1929:XV). Although recruiting was "the most disgraceful phase" of the problem, the report commented bleakly on the commercialization of college sports and on the special treatment accorded to strapping young men of negligible intellectual ability. The preface to the report expressed the authors' conclusions:

> In the United States the composite institution called a university is doubtless still an intellectual agency. But it is also a social, a commercial, and an athletic agency, and these activities have in recent years appreciably overshadowed the intellectual life for which the university is assumed to exist . . . The question is not so much whether athletics in their present form should be fostered by the university, but how fully can a university that fosters professional athletics discharge its primary function (1929: viii, xii).

(The reference to "professional" athletics was presumably justified in part by the sums of money given to student-athletes and in part by the more important fact that the young men in question devoted the majority of their time to sports.) The response to the widely publicized report was a call for reform, a call which was already forlorn and which has since become ridiculous.

Despite periodic efforts to institutionalize some kind of restraint upon intercollegiate athletics, the evils lamented in 1929 have grown worse. In 1956, Herman Hickman wrote of the crisis in college football and quoted Michigan's Fritz Crisler, chairman of the NCAA Rules Committee: "We have discarded the principles on which college football was established . . . We are nourishing a monster which can destroy us if we admit we are powerless to direct, resist or control it" (Hickman, 1956:7). In 1974, Indiana's Bobby Knight remarked: "When they get to the bottom of Watergate, they'll find a football coach" (Kennedy, 1974:88). The desire for victory has grown even more intense and the pressures brought to bear upon coaches, who are held responsible for the outcome of the contest, have become enormous. The rewards of success (i.e., victory) are psychological as well as economic. A man like Bear Bryant of Alabama or Woody Hayes of Ohio State can enjoy national fame and take satisfaction (politely concealed) in the fact that he is better-known than the governor of the state, not to mention the president of the university. And the results of failure (i.e., defeat) are punitive. Coaches whose teams have losing seasons can expect to be pilloried in print, burned in effigy, and separated from the university. The casualty rate of coaches is high; of 130 head football coaches in the NCAA's university division in 1970, 50 had been fired or forced to resign before the beginning of the 1974 season (Benagh, 1967).

Since intercollegiate football and basketball, and to some extent track and field, attract large crowds of spectators, money from the "revenue-producing sports" has become a regular item in the budget of departments of athletics and physical education. When income from the TV networks is added to the take at the gate and through season tickets, institutions like UCLA or Penn State can become dependent upon income which is, of course, significantly influenced by athletic victory and defeat. An invitation to the Rose Bowl can make the difference between a budgetary deficit and a "healthy" surplus. Indeed, it is common knowledge that alumni and state legislators are invariable more generous to their alma mater or state university when the football team has done well. When Ohio State's football record dropped from 7-2 one season to 4-5 the next, the alumni fund dropped by almost $500,000; Missouri's improvement from 6-5 to 10-1 was accompanied by a 95% increase in gifts (Denlinger and Shapiro, 1975).

Confronted by the stark contrast between success and failure, many if not most coaches are tempted to do whatever needs to be done to win. They justify infractions of the rules with the ancient rhetorical argument, **tu quoque**; in modern form, "Everybody does it." Since professors once were students, they know fairly well what it is that everybody does. Outsiders can discover the facts from a number of recent studies: Kenneth Denlinger and Leonard Shapino, **Athletes for Sale**; Joseph Durso, **The Sports Factory**; or

73

Jim Benagh, **Making It to Number 1.** Bear Bryant of Alabama commands a small fleet of private airplanes to ameliorate the recruiter's hardships. The appeals of football fame at Alabama and the promise of a crack at the National Football League are supplemented by the tangible evidence of Paul W. Bryant Hall, where scores of football players and a scatter of other athletes reside in fully airconditioned comfort. The dormitory has a marble-columned entry and prints of Roman ruins—symbolic suggestions of gladiatorial glory crumbled into dust? At Oral Roberts University, basketball rather than football was perceived as the key to academic identity. Black athletes were recruited and the hypocrisy of their "student" status was refreshingly admitted by an assistant coach; asked how many of his players graduated from the university, he replied, "Do you know what my job is at that school? It's to teach those kids how to use a bar of Dial soap and a tube of Ipana toothpaste. I'm the guy who has to get them to turn down their goddam stereos at three A.M. so my family can get some sleep" (Benagh, 1976:15). Although he had a C average in high school, basketball star Moses Malone received scholarship offers from over 300 colleges (Durso, 1975); talented violinists seldom do as well. The ultimate in debased recruitment may have occurred when Thomas Affinito invented a high school basketball star whom he named after himself, Tom Fini. After sending out a number of faked newspaper clippings and a letter of application, "Tom Fini" was inundated by telephone calls, telegrams, letters, and offers of full scholarships (Cave, 1961).

Recruitment of the academically unqualified has gone beyond the discovery and matriculation of Americans with no marked interest in academic endeavor; it has become common, especially in track and field events, to recruit abroad. The University of Texas at El Paso boasts of a cross-country team made up entirely of Africans; since arriving on campus in January of 1973, track coach Ted Banks has won five indoor and three outdoor championships (Marshall, 1980). Is it possible that these athletes were recruited by idealistic coaches eager to spread the benefits of higher education to Kenya and Tanzania? While informed observers assume that the abuses of recruitment occur mainly at the "big-time" universities and least often at the elite schools which refuse to offer "athletic" scholarships at all, there is good reason to suspect that even institutions like Amherst College will open their doors more quickly for a football player with a C average than for an academically superior student whose talents are exclusively bookish.

Once the athlete has been recruited, in accordance with or in violation of NCAA rules, there is a tendency for him or her to concentrate on sports rather than on the less-spectacular academic activities. As every professor knows, in order to remain eligible, the student must comply with certain rules, e.g., maintain an acceptable G.P.A. Reports of "Mickey-Mouse" courses have been common for decades, but a recent series of comments in **Sports Illustrated** suggests deceptive skills undreamed of by the Carnegie Commission in its 1929 report. During the 1979-80 academic year, thirty athletes from Arizona State, California Polytechnic-Pomona, New Mexico,

Oregon, Oregon State, Purdue, San Jose State, and Utah were said to have received extension-course credits from Ottawa University (Ottawa, Kansas) and Rocky Mountain College (Billings, Montana) for courses they had not taken (Kirshenbaum, 1980A).

Assistant basketball coach Manny Goldstein of New Mexico was accused of bribing Oxnard Junior College's Dean of Admissions, Dr. John Woolley, to falsify a student's transcript by adding to it credits for courses supposedly taken at Mercer Junior College (Papandek, 1979; Boyle, 1980). Meanwhile, the University of Southern California discovered 28 of its athletes enrolled in Speech Communication 380 were attending class. The campus newspaper, **The Trojan,** printed part of an essay by one of these athletes evaluating a debate: "I when went John because He had a point on girl that I couldn't not again, so that made me think girl don't have body for lady unless they wont that why I went with John" (Kirshenbaum, 1980B:7). The University of Southern California seems also to have a 400-meter runner of extraordinary speed; in the fall of 1977 he took Economics I at 8 a.m. at Rio Hondo Junior College in Whittier, Chemistry 22 at 9 a.m. at Pasadena City College, and Literature 1B at 10 a.m. back at Rio Hondo (Kirshenbaum, 1970C). Winning the 1978 NCAA 400-meter championship in 45.33 must have been easier. Summarizing the situation in the late spring of 1980, John Underwood concluded: "From the moment the student-athlete sets foot on campus, the name of the game is 'majoring in eligibility' and it is a vulgar, callous, shameful, cynical—and perfectly legal—exploitation of the system by and for the American college athlete" (Underwood, 1980:43).

Although the Association for Intercollegiate Athletics for Women (AIAW) initially rejected national championships and athletic scholarships for women on the grounds that such scholarships were part of a destructively competitive system of corruption and exploitations, the pressures were clearly too great to withstand. Even though AIAW rules prohibit personal visits for recruitment, many coaches admit that they find such visits "necessary." Coach Marianne Stanley of Old Dominion asks: "What good are rules if they can't enforce them?" Athletic Director (Women's Sports) Donna Lopiano of Texas remarks: "You can't legislate morality" (Hannon, 1978:38).

And what do faculty members think of such a state of affairs? Since most professors at American schools are themselves Americans, it is probable that most of them support the system. They, too, go to the games and talk them over in the Faculty Commons. The more thoughtful among them see intercollegiate athletics as secular rituals in the service of what is loosely referred to as "school spirit." When confronted with evidence of gross dishonesty and comic-opera travesty—like the campus hero who reads at a fourth-grade level—the average professor is likely to develop a bad conscience. When asked to award credit to a semiliterate who has turned in none of the work for his course, the professor is likely to feel that his code of ethics has been violated. The response in such instances is the call for reform.

Suggestions for reform are many and have come from those who know the system best. Feeling that they are trapped in the academic equivalent of the international arms race, coaches and athletic directors have called for stricter NCAA rules and for more sustained effort at enforcement. If **every** coach knew that **no** coach offered sub-rosa cash payments to prospective stars, then **all** coaches would suffer less anxiety. But self-regulation invariably raises the question best formulated by the Roman poet Juvenal, who knew a thing or two about the Colosseum and the Circus Maximus: "Quia custodiet ipsos Custodes? ('Who will watch the watchmen?')" (Humphries, 1959). One answer to the question, offered by a scholar with NCAA experience and a profound sense of the importance of college football, is that the faculty should resume a more active if not a dominant role in the governance of intercollegiate athletics (Cady, 1978). Since faculties proved unable to control sports when sports were, comparatively speaking, in their infancy, it is questionable that the overworked professoriat, torn between teaching, research, and administering, can assert any kind of authority over the athletic leviathan. When Ohio State's faculty council bravely voted 28-25 to decline the Rose Bowl bid for 1962, three nights of rioting followed. "With characteristic objectivity and good taste, the Columbus **Dispatch** published on its front page the names, addresses, rank and salaries of the faculty members who supposedly had voted against the Rose Bowl" (Vare, 1974:117-118). Their colleagues on the faculty responded by electing more pliant representatives. Even if, by some miracle, athletic directors and coaches adhered to every jot and title of NCAA regulations, the system would remain a kind of cartel whose "rules and regulations . . . are detrimental to the athletes" (Sage, 1979:2).

Knowing that reform of the present system is improbable, some critics, like John Rooney and Allen L. Sack, have attempted to cut the Gordian knot; they have suggested that colleges and universities remove the hyphen from student-athlete and separate the academic from the athletic. Let the academy sponsor **professional** football, basketball, etc. Rooney, who has studied recruitment patterns in two important books, calls for "an honest business operation designed to entertain the university community, alumni, and other interested parties" (Rooney, 1980: 160). Using his knowledge of the geography of American sports, Rooney has sketched out his plan in considerable detail.

The proposal is an attractive one. With one stroke, hypocrisy is ended. There is, however, at least one fundamental objection to this call for radical reform through overt professionalism. Should institutions of higher learning be involved in the entertainment business? James Michener, himself a successful entertainer, feels that colleges and universities should provide the nation with athletic spectacles: The universities "are obligated to provide nationwide entertainment and they would be delinquent if they sought to avoid this responsibility" (Michener, 1976: 217). This is a peculiarly American notion that suffers from the inability to imagine an alternative.

There **are** alternative possibilities. The most attractive of them has long been institutionalized in Europe, especially in the Federal Republic of Germany. In the German system, universities devote themselves to education (including physical education and the scientific study of sports), while private clubs provide for both participant and spectator sports. The corruption of the university is avoided by the elimination of temptation. Semiliterate coal miners are not lured to play soccer for Heidelberg, because Heidelberg has no varsity soccer team. This omission does not signify a lack of interest in sports on the part of students and professors; it means that the intense interest in sports has been institutionalized in the private club rather than in the public university.

There is another advantage of the club system over the university-based system. One of the continual complaints against American physical education is that it concentrates on team sports which adults seldom have a chance to play. Americans are familiar with the stereotype of the forty-year-old alumnus, physically unfit, positively unhealthy, still fixed on that inevitably receding moment of glory when he shot the winning basket for State. Private clubs are, however, open to everyone; they presently include approximately one quarter of the **entire** West German population. They include children of elementary-school age and hardy types in their sixties, seventies, and even eighties. While Americans usually abandon serious participation in sports after graduation from high school or college, 55% of the **Deutscher Sportbund's** 11,753,681 members (1976 figures) were over twenty-one (Timm, 1979). German sports clubs field thousands of teams at every level of competition from novice to fully professional. In soccer, for instance, there are 94,903 teams affiliated with the **Deutscher Fussball-Verband,** which is in turn a member of the **Federation Internationale de Football Association** (Gardner, 1976). Among these club-sponsored teams are the professionals organized into regional and national leagues. While these leagues have suffered from corruption and scandal, the bribers and the bribe-takers have not dragged the universities into the mire (Rosen, 1978; Blodorn, 1977).

Is it practical to propose such a system for the United States? In **one** sport, running, the private clubs have already developed to the point where they are probably as important as the university-sponsored teams; millions of Americans of both sexes and all ages are involved in recreational runs and in competitive races at every level of excellence from the neighborhood to the international. Running, of course, is a relatively inexpensive sport. Clubs can spring up at almost no cost. Is it practical to turn the major team sports over to private clubs when colleges and universities have invested billions of dollars in their athletic complexes? The answer is not easy, but the problem may be less formidable than it seems at first glance. Educational institutions will continue to require facilities for physical education and for intramural and recreational sports. Other facilities can be sold or leased to private clubs or even in some cases to professional sports franchises. The fact that stadia are **in situ** on the campus is unfortunate but should not blind us to the possibility of a legal and administrative transfer from the university to another institution which does not pretend to be involved in higher education. Americans have begun, through their legislators, to demand that government officials be free of conflicts of interest; can we not ask as much of our educators?

# REFERENCES

Benagh, Jim
    1976    *Making It to Number 1*. New York: Dodd, Mead.
Blodorn, Manfred
    1977    *Fussballprofis: Die Helden der Nation*. Hamburg: Hoffman and
            Campe.
Boyle, Robert H.
    1980    "A Scandal That Just Gets Worse and Worse." *Sports Illustrated*.
            52 (June 9): 27-25.
Cady, Edwin H.
    1978    *The Big Game: College Sport and American Life*. Knoxville: University of Tennessee Press.
Cave, Ray
    1961    "A Ruse Flushes Some Eager Recruiters." *Sports Illustrated*. 14
            (May 29): 20-23
Denlinger, Kenneth and Leonard Shapiro
    1975    *Athletes For Sale*. New York: Crowell.
Durso, Joseph
    1975    *The Sports Factory*. New York: Quadrangle.
Gardner, Paul
    1976    *The Simplest Game*. Boston: Little, Brown.
Hannon, Kent
    1978    "Too Far, Too Fast." *Sports Illustrated*. 48 (March 20):38.
Hickman, Herman
    1956    "The College Football Crises." *Sports Illustrated*. 5 (August 6):6-11,
            59-60.
Humphries, Rolfe (Trans.)
    1959    *Satires of Juvenal*. Bloomington: Indiana University Press.
Kennedy, Ray
    1974    "427: A Case in Point." *Sports Illustrated*. 40 (June 10):86ff.
Kirshenbaum, Jerry
    1980    " 'As Bad As Anything That's Ever Come Along.' " *Sports Illustrated*. 53 (February 25):11.

    1980    "The 28-Credit Dash." *Sports Illustrated*. 52 (March 24): 7-8.

    1980    "Inside A Trojan Course." *Sports Illustrated*. 52 (March 31): 7.
Lewis Guy
    1970    "The Beginning of Organized Collegiate Sport." *American Quarterly*. 12 (Summer): 222-229.
Marshall, Joe
    1980    "Little Sister Wins A Race on Her Own." *Sports Illustrated*. 53
            (December 8): 75-76, 79.
Michener, James A.
    1976    *Sports in America*. New York: Random House.

Papandek, John
  1979    "Now New Mexico Feels the Heat." *Sports Illustrated.* 51 (December 10): 32-41.
Rooney, John F.
  1980    *The Recruiting Game.* Lincoln: University of Nebraska Press.
Rosen, Charles
  1978    *Scandals of '51: How The Gamblers Almost Killed College Basketball.* New York: Holt, Rinehart and Winston.
Sage, George H.
  1979    "The Intercollegiate Sport Cartel and Its Consequences For Athletes." *ARENA Review* 3 (October): 2-8.
Savage, Howard J., Harold W. Bentley, John T. McGovern and Dean F. Smiley
  1929    *American College Athletics.* New York: Carnegie Commission.
Stagg, Paul
  1947    "The Development of the National Collegiate Athletic Association in Relationship to Intercollegiate Athletics in the United States." Unpublished in Ph.D. dissertation. New York University.
Timm, Waltemar
  1979    *Sportvereine in der Bundesrepublik Deutschland.* Schornderf: Karl Holman Verlag.
Underwood, John
  1980    "The Writing on the Wall." *Sports Illustrated.* 52 (May 19): 43.
Vare, Robert
  1974    *Buckeye.* New York: Popular Library.

# CUI BONO?
# CONTRADICTIONS
# IN COLLEGE SPORTS
# AND ATHLETES'
# RIGHTS

By
**Allen L. Sack**

The problems plaguing college sport are not new ones. There is ample evidence (Deming, 1906; Hanford, 1974; Savage, 1929; Underwood, 1980) to demonstrate that illegal payments to athletes, grade tampering, unethical recruiting practices, lowering of academic requirements for athletes, and a variety of other abuses have been cause for concern for over a century. Only recently, however, has there been a growing awareness that these problems are the result of structural contradictions in the organization of college sport; they are not caused by a handful of unscrupulous coaches or deviant athletes. This shift of focus from the individual to the organizational level of analysis (cf. Santomier et. al., 1980) is one of the most promising developments in current discussions of college athletics.

The purpose of this paper is twofold. First, an attempt will be made to identify the deep-seated organizational contradictions in college sport which make certain abuses predictable, if not inevitable. Secondly, I will describe the types of governance structures which, on organizational grounds, seem most appropriate to the various levels of intercollegiate competition. In the final section of the paper, a newly emerging organization, the Center For Athletes' Right in Education (CARE), will be discussed as an alternative to present structures which supposedly protect the rights of college athletes.

# A Typology of College Sport

Blau and Scott (1962) have argued that organizations vary considerably in structure and in the problems they must confront depending on who are the prime beneficiaries.[1] Because this question of "cui bono?" (who benefits?) is often raised relative to college sport (Berryman, 1976; Sack, 1979; Santomier, 1980), a brief discussion of Blau and Scott's typology of formal organizations seems in order. Depending on the prime beneficiary, Blau and Scott delineate four organizational types: business concerns, service organizations, mutual benefit organizations, and commonwealth organizations. The first three types have definite relevance for this discussion of college sport.

Many people benefit to a greater or lesser degree from a business concern. Employees receive wages, customers consume desired products, and society as a whole at times benefits from general business prosperity. However, the **raison d'etre** of a business concern is not social welfare nor employee satisfaction. Rather, the prime beneficiaries of business are owners and managers who are in rational pursuit of profit. According to Blau and Scott, "the dominant problem of business concerns is that of operating efficiency—the achievement of maximum gain at minimum cost in order to further survival and growth in competition with other organizations" (1962:49).

In service organizations, on the other hand, considerations of administrative efficiency must not jeopardize the quality of professional service. Professionals may have to engage in activities from time to time which are not profitable in a purely business sense in order to meet the needs of their clients. It may be economically rational, for instance, for poorly endowed private universities to increase significantly the class sizes of instructors and to cut a number of vital academic programs. However, as service organizations, universities must risk going into the red in order to insure high-quality education to their student clients. When economic concerns consistently take precedence over service to students, universities are transformed into business, and radical changes can be expected in the nature of administrator-faculty, and faculty-student relationships.

Mutual benefit organizations, according to Blau and Scott, exist primarily for the benefit of the general membership. Labor unions, political interest groups, voluntary organizations, and clubs are composed of people seeking to meet their special needs by joining together with others with mutual interests. Because of member apathy and other factors discussed by writers like Robert Michels (1962), mutual benefit organizations often have difficulty maintaining democratic governance structures. Nonetheless, the survival of such groups ultimately depends on active and voluntary participation by the membership.

The structure of club sports at many colleges and universities closely approximates the mutual benefit organization. Rugby clubs, for instance, are often organized by the players themselves, and have as their major goal the fun and recreation of their members. Club sports are truly amateur in nature in that they are participant rather than spectator-oriented. Generally, club members elect their own captain and officers, provide their own equipment, and schedule their own games. Like other clubs on campus, athletic clubs may receive some funds from student governments or other university sources. For the most part though, clubs maintain considerable autonomy, preferring democratic self-governance to university oversight.

Intercollegiate sport takes the form of a service organization when its prime beneficiaries are students in pursuit of an education.[2] The underlying assumption of this "educational model," as Berryman (1976) has labeled it, is that sport participation, when kept in proportion, can be a vital component of a student's total education. Colleges and universities in America which most closely approximate the service model of athletic organization are those which grant no scholarships based on athletic services rendered. Generally speaking, this group consists of a number of elite private colleges and universities, a larger number of small colleges (e.g., NCAA Division III), and women's athletic programs which do not make financial aid dependent on athletic performance.

In the Ivy League, for instance, need-based scholarships guarantee that student athletes can give education higher priority than athletic performance without jeopardizing their continued financial aid. Yale football players miss practice when this interferes with a scheduled class. They can give up athletics altogether if their roles as students are unduly compromised by the demands of their sport. Yale's nine-game football schedule, refusal to participate in post-season bowls, and attempts to recruit athletes by the same criteria as other students, reflect at least a partial commitment to the service or educational model.

In athletic programs where student athletes are in fact the prime beneficiaries, governance structures take the same form as other university committees which are responsible for academic life. A board of athletic control composed of faculty, administrators, and perhaps students can be quite effective in universities committed to the service model of sport. The major function of such committees is to insure that decisions concerning athletic policy always give priority to the educational needs of student athletes and that athletic competition be limited to schools that are equally committed to the educational model of sport. Regulatory bodies like the National Collegiate Athletic Association (NCAA), the Association of Intercollegiate Athletics for Women (AIAW), and the National Association of Intercollegiate Athletics (NAIA) are important at this level mainly as facilitators of intercollegiate championships of various sorts. Otherwise, their role in defining the relation of athletics to education is fairly limited.

Although the service organization model of college sport still survives in higher education, it is clear that this model has been eclipsed in importance by sport organized as a business concern. To quote Santomier (1980: 6), "in big-time intercollegiate athletic programs, athletes are not the primary beneficiaries of the organization. The primary beneficiaries are the owners (universities) and managers (athletic administrators and coaches)." This, of course, is not to say that other people do not benefit from highly commercialized college sport. Fans are provided with first-rate entertainment and athletes receive notoriety and a variety of financial and educational benefits. Most big-time athletic programs, however, exist primarily to attract students, prestige, and revenue to universities.

When college sport is organized as a business concern, winning becomes an economic necessity. Spectators pay to see a winning team, not one that is foundering; and to win, considerations of managerial efficiency and economic rationality must take precedence over service to clients. When Penn State's football coach Joe Paterno was asked his views on the freshman eligibility rule, he responded that he strongly believed that it was not in the best academic interests of athletes. He went on to say, however, that he does not argue the point because doing so "would hurt recruiting and our team" (1980: 39). When faced with the decision of either serving players' academic needs or winning, those who run the college sport business must choose the latter or place their programs in jeopardy.

In the business model of college sport, the student athlete is transformed into a paid entertainer. This redefinition of the student athlete's role is necessitated by demands imposed by the business model. To win games and fill stadiums, skilled athletes must be recruited from throughout the country. In return for athletic services rendered, these athletes receive a contract, or scholarship, entitling them to such things a room, board, and tuition. At many universities, athletes also receive money from alumni and other sources. Compensating athletes for their services is rational and equitable. However, the knowledge that this scholarship and other financial benefits are dependent on athletic performance is likely to lead an athlete to view academic demands as secondary.

# Contradictions in the Business Model

From an organizational standpoint, it is clear that many colleges and universities in America are in effect supporting their own professional athletic teams. Although commercialized sport and higher education are fairly strange bedfellows, the mere presence of professional sport in academia need not produce the corruption, exploitation, and unethical conduct which have prompted so much criticism and debate over the years. In other words, given the proper organizational framework, professional college sport could continue to perform vital economic, social, and other functions within higher education while at the same time operating with the integrity that characterizes so many other business concerns in America.

The fundamental contradiction in big-time college sport is not that universities are in the business of mass commercial entertainment. Rather, the problem is that universities and the regulatory bodies that represent their athletic interests refuse to acknowledge this fact. To return to Blau and Scott's typology, it can be argued that big-time athletic programs are run like business concerns where owners, i.e., universities, are the prime beneficiaries. Yet college administrators, governance bodies, and the public at large persist in the illusion that highly commercialized college athletic programs are service organizations where the education of student athletes has priority.

The imposition of a service or educational ideology in what is clearly big business produces role conflicts which in turn almost guarantee various forms of deviant behavior. Many college coaches, as Edwards (1973: 133) has argued, are judged by the same criteria as coaches at the professional level. College administrators and governing boards demand that coaches win games, fill stadia, and meet the entertainment needs of fans and alumni. A losing coach is fired. From the perspective of the business model of sport discussed above, this is exactly how a coach should be evaluated. The problem is that coaches are hampered in their professional coaching role by an amateur code of ethics which denies that big time-college sport is commercial entertainment and insists that education, not winning, is the major priority. These contradictions lead to predictable results.

If coaches become overly concerned with the academic and human needs of athletes, they may have to accept practices which make winning less likely, thereby threatening their very livelihoods. If they do what is logical and perhaps necessary to win, like recruiting athletes who are poorly prepared for college work, they run the risk of being sanctioned by organizations like the NCAA. Given these contradictory role demands, the ability to skillfully circumvent amateur regulations has been informally incorporated into the role requirements of the college coach. The incompetent coach is not one who violates amateur regulations, but one who is caught. To quote Darryl Rogers (1980), the coach who has taken over Arizona State's scandal-ridden football program, "They'll fire you for losing before they'll fire you for cheating."

The big time college athlete is also subject to contradictory role demands. On the one hand, coaches make demands on athletes which differ little, if at all, from those made on professionals. The athlete who lets academic concerns interfere with his/her role as an athlete runs the risk of losing financial aid. On the other hand, athletes are expected to handle the same course loads and to maintain the same academic standards as regular college students. It is not surprising, given the strains inherent in the scholar-athlete role, that athletes have been found to be more likely than regular students to cheat, take gut courses, and to seek out other academic short cuts (Sack and Thiel: 1979). A recent survey (Horvath, 1981) of athletes in relatively small-time athletic programs in the state of Connecticut found that 48 percent of the male scholarship athletes say they were encouraged by coaches and athletic departments to take "gut" courses; 42 percent felt pressured to take less demanding majors.

Perhaps the greatest contradiction in the business model of college sport is that its major governing body, the NCAA, imposes rules and regulations which presuppose a service or educational model. The following statement, taken from the NCAA manual, is clearly in line with a model of college sport in which student athletes are prime beneficiaries. The NCAA proclaims as its basic purpose "to maintain intercollegiate athletics as an integral part of the educational program and the athlete as an integral part of the student body" (1979: 7). This goal of the NCAA is certainly a worthy one and is perfectly consistent with athletic programs like those in the Ivy League which eschew athletic scholarships and other practices which transform sport into big business.

The irony is that when NCAA principles are applied to highly commercialized college sport, it is the financial interests of universities, and not the educational interests of athletes, that are primarily served. In fact, the more aggressively the NCAA imposes its amateur code of ethics on big-time college sport, the more it exploits athletes both educationally and economically. College athletes in big-time athletic programs work as hard as professionals and generate millions of dollars in revenue. The NCAA's insistence on defining athletes as amateurs allows universities to stage mass athletic spectacles for commercial gain while compensating athletes with salaries below the minimum wage (Sage, 1979). The concept of amateurism also works against the academic interests of big-time college athletes by creating the false impression that there is not inherent conflict between the scholar and athlete roles.

Many writers (Koch 1971, 1973; Sage, 1979; and Atwell, 1980) have argued that the NCAA acts as a cartel which controls wages, restricts competition, and maximizes profits in the area of intercollegiate athletics. The position taken in this paper is that anytime an organization operated as a business concern attempts to pass itself off as a service organization, employees are bound to be exploited. Inasmuch as the NCAA helps to legitimize the amateur myth and imposes rules and regulations which restrict competitive market principles in the college sport industry, it clearly resembles a business cartel.

The Association for Intercollegiate Athletics for Women (AIAW) is the other regulatory body which has had a major impact on college sport. Like the NCAA, the AIAW is publicly committed to the central tenets of amateurism (Hult, 1980). Unlike the NCAA, AIAW institutions until recently have in fact been able to control some of the excesses that inevitably plague the business model of college sport; however, this is changing. In 1973, the AIAW sanctioned athletic scholarships based on athletic ability, and sports like women's basketball and volleyball are beginning to demonstrate their potential as revenue producers.

The results have been predictable. Since July of last year, nine colleges—including Old Dominion College in Virginia, a leader in women's basketball—have been placed on probation by the AIAW for recruiting violations (Lichtenstein, 1981). It would appear that as the emphasis of women's sport slowly changes from education to revenue production, women athletes and coaches will have to deal with the same role strains as their male counterparts. Likewise, there is no reason to believe that the AIAW's amateur ideology will be any less exploitative than the NCAA's when applied to the business model of college sport. Given the growing structural and ideological similarities between the NCAA and the AIAW, it is not at all surprising to find that the latter is being swallowed up by the former and that many business-minded women applaud this development.

# WHAT ARE THE ALTERNATIVES?

The analysis presented above suggests that there are two logical solutions to the problems confronting big-time college sport. One would be to drive revenue-producing sport out of academia altogether. The other would be to free the college sport industry from the facade of amateurism, thereby granting legitimacy to what in most cases already exists, i.e., professional college sport. The first solution can be ruled out as highly impractical. Commercialized college sport has become an indispensable part of college life. The second solution is far more realistic and seems to be gaining support among both critics and supporters of commercialized college sport.

Rooney's (1980) discussion of exactly how the professional college sport industry could be organized seems like an excellent starting point. By openly admitting that college sport is in fact big business, many practices which are presently viewed as deviant or unethical would overnight become normal and legitimate. One way of reducing crime, argue labeling theorists (cf. Becker, 1963), is to define previously criminal acts as socially acceptable. The acceptance of college sport as a legitimate form of business would constitute an extremely important step toward restoring honor and integrity in intercollegiate athletics.

Whether universities take this step or not, athletes must still address themselves to one very fundamental question: Where is the organization or governing body that is most likely to defend the interests of big time college athletes? It has already been pointed out that the NCAA and AIAW ultimately defend the financial interests of management; it is also the case that boards of athletic control are relatively powerless in big-time sports schools. As most cases, they simply rubber-stamp policy set by coaches, athletic directors, and other higher-level administrators. The fact of the matter is that no organization presently exists at the big-time college level which defends the rights and interests of athletes.

# THE CENTER FOR ATHLETES' RIGHTS IN EDUCATION (CARE)

It follows from the logic of this paper that an organization is needed at the big-time college level that is analogous to the players' organizations which presently negotiate contracts for professional athletes. Given the difficulties of organizing college students, it is unlikely that such an organization will emerge in the near future. One organization which has considerable potential for developing as an effective advocacy group for athletes is the Center For Athletes' Rights in Education.– CARE is a joint project of Sports For the People, Inc. (SftP), the National Conference of Black Lawyers (NCBL), and the National Football League Players' Association (NFLPA). Local chapters are composed of former and present college athletes, college factulty, lawyers, and other interested parties.

CARE is presently working on two levels to address some of the most blatant examples of athletic abuse. In the New York metropolitan area, a major "hunting ground" for college recruiters, CARE is undertaking a project to provide counseling to high school students who are contemplating athletic involvement in college. Working with principals, students affairs coordinators, and parents' associations, CARE will conduct workshops and lectures on the athletic recruiting process, athletic grants-in-aids, and problems faced by intercollegiate athletes. Drawing on the resources of the NFLPA, NCBL, SftP, and a number of New York Foundations, CARE will develop a variety of programs to educate high school athletes regarding their rights and responsibilities vis-a-vis college recruiters. This New York City Project will serve as a model for other efforts to counsel high school athletes throughout the country.

At the college level, CARE's focus is more national in scope. The Center's National Advisory Board is composed of athletes, lawyers, and administrators from various parts of the country.

# Functions of The National Center

1. Counseling and informing athletes of their rights.
   a. Provide easy access to information and resources for student athletes in the form of a toll free 800 phone line housed and staffed in the Center's office. Questions about financial aid, NCAA or AIAW regulations, legal rights, etc., will be answered free of charge.
   b. Develop crisis intervention teams to provide immediate negotiating services to athletes facing expulsion, removal of scholarship or other denials of due process.
   c. Publish an athlete's guide to college sports aimed at guidance counselors, teachers, high school coaches, graduates and their parents. Similar in format to college guides like Lovejoy's and Barron's, the athlete's guide will focus on won-loss records, stadium size, graduation rates for athletes, number of athletes who go on to pro ball, recruiting practices of staff, time spent in practice, classes missed because of practice, etc.
   d. Develop a national network of Center For Athletes' Rights on college campuses to be available on a more regular basis to counsel athletes and to perform an advocacy function for them vis a vis faculty, administration, coaches, athletic directors, etc.
   e. Develop a "letter of intent" which athletes would ask coaches to sign prior to the athlete's signing the school's "letter of intent." The Center's letter would specify the university's obligation to the student-athlete, including matters such as course selection, practice time, tutoring, remediation and length of scholarship.

2. Lobbying for reform.
   a. The Center hopes to arouse public sentiment in favor of a whole sale restructuring of the NCAA. This is to be done by writing opinion articles, appearing on TV and radio talk shows, testifying at Congressional hearings on sports and by building a network of concerned parents, educators, and athletes who believe that college sport must be primarily concerned with the educational and human needs of athletic participants.
   b. Lobby to change NCAA regulations which profit universities at the player's expense. The one-year renewable scholarship rule and the transfer rule both must be challenged as restrictions on free trade.
   c. Efforts will be made to pressure universities to commit themselves publicly to either the educational or business model of college sport. The NCAA and powerful institutions it represents can no longer have it both ways.
3. Acting as a clearing house for sports information.
   a. The Center will publish a newsletter which will give updates on court cases, problems faced by athletes at other schools and methods used to meet these problems.
   b. The Center will also help students, faculties and administrators become more aware of alternative models of college sport. The Center will support research to determine whether highly commercialized college sport is as necessary to the survival of universities as many college presidents think it is.
4. Collective bargaining.
   In addition to the functions discussed above, it should be noted that if and when proposals for paying college athletes become a reality, the Center For Athletes' Rights will have developed the kinds of expertise necessary to bargain collectively on behalf of college athletes.

In closing, it should be emphasized that an advocacy group like The Center For Athletes' Rights in Education only makes sense when college sport is run like a business concern. At other levels, faculty-administrative committees, the NCAA, AIAW, NAIA, or even students themselves might constitute the appropriate governance body. Ultimately, it is college presidents, governing boards, and faculties who decide what model of intercollegiate sport should be adopted. If the business model is chosen, universities should not be surprised when union-like organizations begin to emerge to protect the rights of employees, i.e., college athletes.

## FOOTNOTES

[1]For arguements for and against the use of the Blau, Scott typology, see Burns (1967: 121) and Weldon (1972: 76-78).

[2]Education is used here in a limited sense. While learning a trade such as carpentry or even professional football can broadly be conceived as being educational, this is not how the term has traditionally been applied in colleges and universities.

[3]I am indebted to Sports for the People's Executive Director, Cary Goodman, and Board Chairman, Mark Naison, for providing information on the structure and goals of the Center for Athletes' Rights in Education.

# REFERENCES

Atwell, Robert
1 9 7 9"Reflections on College Athletes." *Educational Record.* 60 (Fall):367-373.
Berryman, Jack
1 9 7 6"Historical Roots of the Collegiate Dilemma." *Proceedings of the 79th Annual Meeting of the National College Education Association for Men,* pp. 141-161.
Blau, Peter and W. Richard Scott
1 9 6 2*Formal Organizations: A Comparative Approach.* San Francisco: Chandler.
Burns, Tom
1 9 6 7"The Comparative Study of Organizations," Victor H. Vroom, (Ed.), *Methods of Organizational Research.* Pittsburgh: University of Pittsburgh Press.
Deming, Clarence
1 9 0 6"Mr. Camps Financiering? Extraordinary Facts about Yale's Athletic Monies." *New York Evening Post.* (January 18).
Edwards, Harry
1 9 7 3*Sociology of Sport.* Homewood, Illinois: Dorsey Press.
Hanford, George
1 9 7 4An Enquiry into the Need for and Feasibility of a National Study of Inter-collegiate Athletics. Washington, D.C.: American Council of Education.
Horvath, Joseph
1 9 8 1"Survey to Assess the Need for a Center for Athletes' Rights," Sponsored by Sports for the People, Inc. New York; N.Y.
Hult, Joan S.
1 9 8 0"The Philosophic Conflicts in Men's and Women's Collegiate Athletes." *Quest.* 32:77-94.
Koch, James V.
1971     "The Economies of Big-time Intercollegiate Athletics." *Social Science Quarterly.* 52:248-260.
1 9 7 3"A Troubled Cartel: The NCAA." *Law and Contemporary Problems.* 38:135-150.
Lichtenstein, Grace
1 9 8 1"The Wooing of Women Athletes." *New York Times Magazine.* (February 8): 30.
Michels, Robert
1 9 6 2*Political Parties.* New York: Collier.
National Collegiate Athletic Association (NCAA)
1 9 7 9*NCAA Manual, 1979-80.* Shawnee Mission, Kansas: NCAA.
Paterno, Joseph
1 9 8 0Quoted in Douglas S. Looney, "A Lot of People Think I'm Phoney." *Sports Illustrated.* 52:34-45.
Rogers, Darryl
1 9 8 0Quoted in Mark Asher, "Colleges Show the Seamy Side." *Washington Post Service,* 1980.
Rooney, John F.
1 9 8 0*The Recruiting Game.* Lincoln: University of Nebraska Press.
Sack, Allen
1 9 7 9"Big-time College Sport: Whose Free Ride?" *Quest.* 27:87-96.

Sack, Allen and Robert Thiel
1 9 7 9"College Football and Social Mobility: A Case Study of Notre Dame Foot-
ball Players." *Sociology of Education.* 52:60-66.
Sage, George
1 9 7 9"The Intercollegiate Sport Cartel and Its Consequences for Athletes."
*Arena Review.* 3: 2-8.
Santomier, James P., William G. Howard, Wendy L. Pilty and Thomas G.
Romance
1 9 8 0"White Sock Crime: Organizational Deviance in Intercollegiate Athletics."
*Journal of Sport and Social Issues.* 4(Fall/Winter).
Savage, Howard
1 9 2 9*American College Athletics.* New York: The Carnegie Foundation.
Underwood, John
1 9 8 0*Death of an American Game.* Boston: Little, Brown.
Weldon, Peter D.
1 9 7 2"An Examination of the Blau, Scott and Etzioni Typologies: A Critique."
*Administrative Science Quarterly.* 17:76-78.

# THE ATHLETIC DIRECTOR AND THE GOVERNANCE OF SPORT

By
Fred L. Miller

The present role of a Director of Athletics is one of complexity and contradiction. He is both educator and businessman; he is a policeman, yet a promoter; he is a motivator of coaches, as well as a rules maker and enforcer; he is a public relations man, yet a tough corporate officer; he is a fund raiser and tight budget operator; he is heavily involved in promoting women's athletics, yet must maintain a strong men's program on the same budget; and, he must also have a working knowledge of legal, medical, management, educational, and business skills.

Many see only the highlights of the Athletic Director's job — attending games and frequent social functions, speaking to boosters, alumni, and friends of the university, travel, attending meetings, attaining a high public image, etc. It appears to be the "good life."

But is it? What are the pressures that direct the Athletic Director? To whom is the modern Athletic Director responsible for the governance of sport, and what are the forces that govern sports in the country today?

# MANAGING CROSS PRESSURES

In answer to the above questions, one would immediately think of the institution's President, but that only scratches the surface. In reality, the Athletic Director (hereafter, AD), and the governance of intercollegiate sports in general, is influenced by a multitude of individuals and groups, many of whom do not have the same demands. The modern AD must be the catalyst that brings these entities together into a meaningful direction. If, for example, the AD spends too much time raising outside funds (out of necessity), oftentimes the inner workings of his program go astray. If, on the other hand, the AD spends too much time on the internal administrative functions, the fund-raising activities go lacking. Either way, in today's harsh athletic world he/she will be soon looking for other work if the AD does not strike a successful balance of activities and react intelligently and forcefully to the pressures of a variety of special individuals and/or special interest groups.

Among these entities to whom the AD must respond for the goverance of sport are the institution's president, the athletes, the coaches, the national individual sport rule-making bodies, (e.g., the Football Rules Committee), the university's faculty-controlled Athletic Council (a cross-section of the university community that sets policy for a given program), the university comptroller with whom all athletic administrators must be in concept with respect to fiscal affairs, the medical profession who influence the medical aspect of sport including the well-being of athletes with emphasis upon competitive safeguards, the alumni and boosters whose fiscal involvement is a necessity but whose fiscal clout can also be a definite problem, legislative bodies such as the Congress or state legislatures whose passage of laws exerts sometimes obvious and often subtle pressures, the legal profession whose lawsuits and threatened legal action have an ongoing governance effect, the conferences, and national and international athletic legislative bodies, such as the National Collegiate Athletic Association, (NCAA), the American Sports League, the National Olympic Committee, the Association of Intercollegiate Athletics For Women, the National Junior College Athletic Association, the Sports Federations, and the National Association of Intercollegiate Athletics. The rules and enforcement procedures of these groups can have a great effect on the actions of the AD. Let us examine these groups more closely.

## The President

The chief executive officer is charged with the administrative function of the complex operation of today's university. Athletics is but one part of this multifaceted whole. While most presidents agree that it is a most visible and complex part, they give it varying degrees of attention.

A president will normally charge a faculty-controlled committee to give scope and direction to a given athletic program, and this group will generally set policy. In addition, a faculty athletic representative will oversee the function of eligibility clearances for men's and women's programs. The president will charge the AD with the administrative function of operating intercollegiate athletics, whether it be an integrated program or contain separate men's and women's programs.

An alarming tendency in most major programs is to insert a vice president between the athletic director and the president. Many presidents appear to prefer this buffer because athletics, particularly in many large-scale programs, is often volatile and time-consuming, and to avoid unwanted pressure, many presidents prefer to stay one step removed. Presidents have learned, many the hard and painful way, of their community's lust for winning, and most chief executives choose not to be in the direct "firing line" should athletic problems erupt. The strategy is to assign a vice-president the responsibility for overseeing the athletic program. If the athletic program has separate men's and women's directors, the vice president becomes, in essence, the director of athletics. For those concerned ADs, this is a worrisome trend since many of these vice-presidents have little background in the governance of sport.

Presidents are now being asked to take a more decisive role in the actions of the NCAA and exert more control over their own athletic programs. While at first blush this appears to be sound, in reality it is cosmetic in nature and erodes a more meaningful governance procedure; it is an unrealistic demand. How then can the president be spread. If the NCAA wants more of the president's time, then why not the AIAW? The rationale is the same.

The most meaningful relationship is to have the president become reasonably knowledgeable about intercollegiate sport but give the AD the responsibility and the **authority** to operate the program in accord with well established guidelines and policies. The president should have a direct line of communication with his AD in Division I programs. At this level, the AD should have vice presidential status because the governance of this type of program needs this type of direct communication. Division II or III programs, where the emphasis and subsequent problems are lessened, do not necessarily need this direct communication. Here, the AD may be responsible to a dean of a division head.

## The Athletes

Should the governed have a voice in governing? In this society, the answer is obviously, yes!

But what is obvious is not always practiced. Athletics has, in the past, had the role of the coach and/or the AD cast in the power role of dictator—hopefully benevolent, but not always. Today's athlete takes exception to his or her role of being at the bottom of the athletic power totem pole. He/she feels he has necessary and valid input, and he does.

Coaches and administrators should welcome this input through a type of athletic council composed of athletes (men and women) from all sports. The AD should meet regularly with, and more importantly, listen to this group.

Through an athletic council, the director can receive input of the needs and desires of the athletes. The council, made up of representatives of all sports, may have varying membership numbers depending upon the size of the programs. The athlete should have input into rules changes, budgets, squad size, schedule, travel, etc. It is the wise coach and/or administrator who, within limits, utilizes these data.

When the governed become part of the governing process, procedures are improved and the program is enhanced. The recent changes in the composition of U.S. Olympic Committees where the athletes became voting members of those committees are examples of this concept.

# The Coaches

A common complaint of coaches is that their voice goes unheard; to a large degree this is true. They feel, for example, that they are victims of unrealistic compliance procedures and have had no voice in their development. In an attempt to effect changes in Division I NCAA legislation the College Football Association (CFA) was formed. Unique in this group's lobbying technique was the seeking of advice from the nation's leading football coaches. Meeting annually as a group to effect legislative changes regarding recruiting, visitation periods, grants in aid, financial matters affecting football, etc., the athletic directors, faculty representatives and presidents have begun to solicit the football coaches' recommendations and present them to NCAA meetings as a framework for legislative change where appropriate.

Examples of such recommendations or proposals, some of which have already been approved by the NCAA body and others which will become proposals for future conventions, include: (1) restrict off-campus visitation periods for prospective student athletes, (2) establish normal academic progress rules for enrolled student athletes, (3) eliminate "part-time" recruiting oriented coaches who are not conversant with all applicable rules, (4) eliminate the casual contact ("bump") rule with prospective student athletes, (5) study graduation rates of enrolled student athletes, etc.

Coaches' recommendations for governance in their sport are sometimes self-serving and out of step with economic realities of a total integrated athletic program. By and large, however, when they understand the total picture, their recommendations are sound when utilized within the framework of the College Football Association.

The interrelationships between the AD and coaches concerning rules enforcement in the Division I Football and Basketball programs need obvious improvement. Those who make rules (primarily faculty representatives and the ADs in the NCAA) need to make certain that these rules can be followed by the coaches who must implement the rules in a day-to-day fashion. This fact alone justifies the involvement of coaches in the rule-making process.

If coaches want input on rule-making, then they should have some reponsibility for proper implementation. Thus, all coaches should be tested on rules knowledge which includes national, conference, and institutional legislation and policies. Through a consistent exposure of rules interpretations to the coaches by means of five to six annual seminars conducted by the AD, the coaches should be able to maintain an up-to-date knowledge of what is expected of them in their role in the governance of their sport.

The breakdown in governance normally occurs at this level. The credo that a coach will get fired for losing quicker than he would for cheating is common. In the National Association of Collegiate Directors of Athletics (NACDA) publication of December, 1980, in an article titled, "The Ongoing Athletic Crisis—A Solution, Part II Mechanics," this writer pointed out that five to eight percent of the coaches habitually cheat (Miller, 1980). This affected 50 to 60 percent of the remainder who rationalize thay must cheat to compete. This cheating to obtain competitive advantage is the cancer within the governance of sport and it must be eliminated for college sport to survive! Again, in the NACDA publication, **Athletic Administration,** of October, 1980, this author pointed out in the article, "The Ongoing Athletic Crisis— A Solution," that the current operation for rules compliance within intercollegiate sport does **not** work. Enforcement by the institution, the conference, and the national body (i.e, the NCAA, AIAW, etc.) is always after the fact; hence, compliance is motivated by punishment, not prevention.

Coaches and ADs must realize that they do not currently meet the criteria of being classified as a profession such as legal or medical professions and will not become one until they can evaluate and police themselves. The aboved-mentioned "solution" suggests that an "athletic audit" procedure outside the umbrella of the NCAA would do just that. The "audit" would **prevent** cheating and serve as a tool to assist coaches and athletic administrators to truly become professionals.

# Athletic Audit [1]

The athletic audit is the primary tool to alter the framework of athletics to allow for a productive (as opposed to punitive) enforcement of the rules. It is essential that we establish audit procedures (i.e., similar to accreditation program for law, medicine, etc.) that meet national legislative needs, university needs, coaches' needs, and most importantly, the needs of student athletes. This audit would be a positive and preventative program; it would be a complete review of compliance to existing rules within the athletic program, with emphasis on football and basketball.

The system that we have now just doesn't work! The three current levels of compliance and rules enforcement (which all take place after the fact, doing little good as solution) are: (1) institutional (the AD is held responsible), (2) conference (conference commissioners are held responsible), and (3) national (the NCAA is the primary "heavy" here). None of them work! (1980a)

The concept of institutional integrity and analysis of the problems does not work. Athletic directors today are being "chewed up" like confetti as are head and assistant coaches, in the pressure sports of football and basketball. Within the National Athletic Directors Association there is a 30 percent annual turnover in the mailing lists. Of the 15 past presidents of the National Athletic Directors Association only one is currently involved in athletics. The rest have been fired, have died, or have retired. ADs are so busy managing, scheduling, budgeting, meeting with various groups, doing public relations, and keeping their programs solvent, it is naive at best to hold them personally accountable for the institution's enforcement program.

To have an audit team visit a campus every two years would serve an institution extremely well since the audit would provide objective analysis of rules compliance in a given program. The AD knows the coaches, knows the families, and does not want to look for a wrongdoing. There is an obvious conflict of interest when the athletic director must promote the program and at the same time police the program. Most athletic directors will take action if infractions surface, but most do not look for infractions. They're hoping that these infractions don't exist or will go away. In essence, the institutional program of compliance with rules with the athletic directors serving as the chief investigator is ineffective. The error that most athletic directors make, because of the punitive nature of the present enforcement procedures, is one of nonfeasance as opposed to malfeasance.

The athletic audit, to take place every two years, would be a positive experience for all involved. To obtain the cooperation of all players and coaches, they **must have immunity for a one year-period and not be held guilty for any violations.** Give the entire NCAA Division I coaching staff a fresh start; this is essential for the success of the "audit" approach. If this immunity is not given, we'll have no cooperation from players and coaches, and hence, just another program that will not work. The intent is to get athletic programs back on a correct track, to get our coaching staffs doing the right thing. Most coaches would cooperate with this type of approach since they would not be placed in a competitive, disadvantaged situation with respect to recruiting.

If the audit team finds violations, they would return within one year to insure that these violations are voluntarily corrected. The audit team would hold all information internally. To give the information concerning violations to a university president or athletic director would necessitate a self-disclosure procedure to the NCAA consistent with existing rules. If violations are not corrected by a staff member within the twelve-month period, the data are then given to the institution and the offending coach should be suspended or terminated. The self-disclosure procedures then take place but, in reality, should not be necessary because the problem should have been solved, the coaching staffs remain stable, no one has lost a recruiting advantage, and integrity is restored to athletics.

This type of procedure is similar to the concept of the "voluntary letter of intent" which has proven successful **outside** the NCAA umbrella. The entire thrust of the audit is **preventative, not punitive.** This kind of audit program must be funded separately and apart from the NCAA or any other national group. A small, close-knit, non-profit corporation consisting of skillful attorneys, athletic directors, conference personnel, ex-football and basketball coaches, and possibly CPA's would man such an audit team. They must know what questions to ask. This group would be responsible only to the individual university and not to a national body.

Funding for the audit would be the responsibility of the individual institution, yet it could be augmented by a grant from a national body such as the National Science Foundation. This could well be the most **important athletic stipend a university could make.**

The coaches are the most important level in the governance of sport. If we can achieve compliance here through preventative audit procedures, the system of sport that we have developed in the United States can flourish. If we cannot eliminate cheating the system will self-destruct and governance becomes mute!

# The National Playing Rule-Making Bodies

Inherent within the NCAA and AIAW are a variety of sport rules making bodies such as the Rules Committees for Football, Basketball, Track and Field, Swimming, etc. These committees are necessary for the governance of each and every sport, but they exert direct and sometimes subtle pressures on sport in general. For example, rules are often passed which have direct financial implication for the sport. An added event in track and field has a cumulative effect beyond just program space. A new event could mean more judges, new equipment, addition of an assistant coach, increased recruiting expense, and so forth. The elimination of the "Dunk" in basketball affected those universities which were in competition with professional teams for the entertainment dollar. Fans wanted the excitement of the "Dunk", and it was long overdue to return after more than a decade of absence. The primary reason for the initial rule change to eliminate the "Dunk" was the emergence of the active, big center such as Lew Alcindor (Kareem Abdul Jabbar) at UCLA in the mid-sixties. But, the "Dunk" had significant entertainment value and meant something in terms of gate receipts. This pressure, more than any other, stimulated its return. The adding of a weight class in wrestling, while sound in theory, increased cost seven to nine percent for travel, insurance, and related expenses.

The rules committees are dominated by coaches who oftentimes do not view the financial ramifications of their acts with any priority. But the AD is vitally concerned with these implications. While the delicate financial balance of intercollegiate sport may suffer in the income sports of football and basketball by acts of omission by the respective rules committees, the act of additive rules present similar problems to the AD.

The passage of rules having financial implications needs a check and balance system. While the rules committees act as pseudo-independent agencies in the governance of their particular sport, they do not grasp the overall implications on the tightly squeezed athletic dollar. Athletic Directors need a review procedure, such as the NCAA Executive Committee to explore these areas. Within the NCAA Committee structure, the Executive

Committee, currently composed primarily of ADs and commissioners, wields the most influence in that body, with the exception of the NCAA Council. This committee would meet the check and balance need. Rules committees may view this as a threat to their autonomy; but a check and balance system, while not perfect, is necessary to protect the undermining of the financial structure of sport. Thus, these examples present an additional pressure on the ADs role in governance of sport.

# The Faculty Athletic Council, the Faculty Athletic Representative and the Academic Counselor

The Faculty Athletic Council must be a cross-section of the university community and must have the power (perhaps tempered with the power of a President's veto) to set athletic policy. This group, while faculty-controlled, should contain students (including student athletes), administrators, alumni, boosters, the faculty athletic representative, and the AD as voting members.

This committee's role in the governance of sport is obvious: it should define the limits in which the AD must work; it should approve budgets, capital projects, schedules, ticket prices, policies, etc.; it should meet at least once a month and have active subcommittees to research solutions for new policy implementation. This board exercises institutional control of athletics and should set the policy for both men's and women's programs. It is counterproductive to have two boards since obvious conflict would arise.

The faculty athletic representative is a likely choice to chair such a group. Not only does he/she have sole authority for the determination of eligibility, the faculty athletic representative is also the normal voting representative for the institution at the national and conference meetings. The faculty athletic representative should oversee not only eligibility conformance, but should ascertain that all student athletes are in degree-oriented programs taking legitimate courses that lead to a chosen degree. The concept of just keeping marginal student athletes eligible at all costs with non-degree courses is blatant exploitation and must be eliminated.

In the past, the academic counselor has been responsible to the AD and/or the coaching staffs (particularly in football and basketball). This allegiance has led to problems: specifically, keeping athletes eligible at the expense of cheating, which has led to "bogus courses," non-degree course patterns, and general usurping the role of academics on a given campus. The academic counselor should be responsible to either the faculty athletic representative or the dean of student services to help avoid the athletic cheating scandals.

The role of the AD with relation to the above three entities is one of support and cooperation. Intercollegiate sport is enhanced by this distinction and the sharing of governance in this area.

# The University Comptroller

Athletics suffers from the dilemma of being a business-oriented educational activity housed in an institution solely geared to the cautious expenditure of funds. However, fiscal practices of a university, regardless of the frustration concerning the business type activity of the athletic department, must generally be held constant.

The key here is the concept "generally." A university comptroller's office needs to be sensitive to the expediency of disbursing funds due to the business nature of athletics. The mobility of athletic teams and recruiting needs requires that funds be made available in a more rapid fashion than in other areas of the campus.

The generation of athletic revenues in major athletic programs necessitates a certain amount of flexibility from the comptroller's office. AD's in major universities must have expertise in marketing their athletic programs that are in reality inconsistent with the way business is conducted in other departments. As such, the AD and the comptroller need sound policy agreement in matters of generating and expending large amounts of monies. Naturally, even though athletics may be somewhat unique as a business enterprise in an academic setting they must follow agreed-upon fiscal policies for internal university credibility and consistency.

In summary, with previously agreed-upon flexibility of income generation and expenditure of funds, the AD must yield to the policies of the university fiscal officer. If the flexibility is not present and thoroughly understood by all, chaos will develop, If the Athletic Department does not follow the general university fiscal policies, any fiscal problem will be overly magnified and athletics will suffer. The governance of funds, which directly affects the governance of sport, is thus set by the university's chief fiscal officer and carried out by the AD and his designees.

# The Medical Practitioners

The AD who does not follow the sound medical advice from the team physician or from appropriate medical bodies is lacking in intelligence, and sport could be severely impaired by the threat of lawsuit due to injury and corresponding medical treatment. Written policies for the operation of the training room, medical emergencies, and practices must be well-thought out and presented in standard form for all to follow.

The escalating costs of medical insurance and medical care indicate that the governance of this issue is influenced by the team physician, the university health center, the head trainer, and policies gleaned from national bodies directed at the collective medical problems of all universities. Affordable medical insurance is becoming an ever-increasing problem, especially in the contact and/or high-injury risk sports of football, wrestling, ice hockey, gymnastics, and water polo. Any casual review of excalating insurance rates, particularly as related to product liability litigation, would validate this point. More national athletic injury data need to be collected to provide a data base for rules changes to protect the athlete. Additional data are constantly being brought forward concerning drug abuse in athletics. This problem, international in scope, must be solved initially at the local level, then nationally, and finally, internationally. Exposure of the problem and data collection must be accomplished before meaningful change can result.

The modern AD must not only become aware but must become astute in the areas surrounding the medical aspect of sport. The governance of this issue clearly rests outside his expertise, but his jurisdiction in applying sound medical policies cannot be forfeited.

# The Alumni and Boosters

Gate receipts, television and contest-related revenue are inadequate resources of revenue for a broad athletic program in today's inflationary world. Universities have found that it is necessary to have alumni/booster support to balance the budget effectively. This necessity can be the classic double-edged sword. Those who control the purse strings control, to a degree, a phase in the governance of sport. To counteract this, athletic directors must temper overt booster involvement with a series of checks and balances that can still keep needed dollars coming into the athletic program yet keep will-intentioned boosters from violating rules.

For every university, there is their own distinctive style of organizing booster groups and for raising needed dollars. It is essential that university control be exercised over these funds since, in effect, they are pseudo-university monies. Violations of NCAA rules often take place when university control is not exercised. If the AD or another university official is utilized as the treasurer of the booster club, the bulk of problems can be eliminated if the AD or his designee co-sign the checks and annual university-sponsored audits are conducted.

Coaches often utilize boosters in the recruitment process of prospective student athletes. Normally, this can have beneficial results, but if boosters go beyond NCAA, AIAW, etc., rules, problems develop. Some boosters do not know the complexities of the rules and some do not care if they break them. Obviously, the governance of sport is impaired when either of the above alternatives is allowed to happen. Some of these problems can be avoided if boosters can be constantly informed (because they are a rapidly changing population) as to what their proper role can and should be in the development, operation and governance of an institution's athletic program. This is an additional charge to the AD. Seminars especially for boosters are a good mechanism to instruct these supporters on their proper role and on the rules which govern their activity. Boosters can also be required to record each contract with an athlete and to forward a report of this contract to the AD's office.

# The Impact of Legislation by Elected Bodies

The most obvious impact of a legislative passage of a law has been the effects of Title IX by Congress and the resulting interpretations by the Office of Civil Rights in the Department of Health, Education, and Welfare. It has taken the better part of a decade for most of the interpretations to settle, yet in many areas of the country confusion still exists, and progress has been lacking to provide women in sport their just due.

No informed Athletic Director will quarrel with the equal right of women to compete with similar financial support, use of facilities, and compatible scheduling. Many have been and are frustrated with the rhetoric of many university Presidents that while athletics for men and women are essential educational offerings, they insist that the director of athletics earn or raise the dollars to accomplish the Title IX goal and still maintain a broad-based men's athletic program. Often, this is not possible.

Affirmative action demands, mandated by law, that a university become an equal opportunity employer necessitates the need for a broader personnel management perspective than ADs have exercised in the past. Most universities utilize coaching selection committees who may not grasp the broad perspective of hiring minorities in key positions even though they may not be the most qualified for the job. The influence of the AD must be utilized because any overt charge of racism through lack of hiring and training minorities could seriously neutralize the effectiveness of the institutional athletic program. Athletic programs that have had racist charges leveled at them became less effective basically because the prominent black athletes shy away from such programs. The public visibility of athletics makes this area of campus personnel practices extremely sensitive. The bottom line, however, is that hiring minorities in a balanced fashion makes good sense and is the right thing to do.

State legislative bodies also influence appropriations for travel, facility development, salaries, staff positions, outside uses of university facilities, and a variety of other tasks. Thus, athletic administrators in state-supported universities must be politically active and adept to insure that these governance forces maintain a fair perspective to the continuance of athletics. The utilization of key boosters to act as effective lobbyists (consistent with the overall aim of the university) is a recommended strategy.

# The Law and the Legal Profession

Sport is one of the few "industries" that allows groups of competitors (the athletic conferences and cartels such as the NCAA) to govern themselves. It is essential that this self-goverance protects those that are governed—primarily, student athletes. The law states that people in the area of amateur sport can govern themselves provided that they furnish the people protected (student athletes) due process under the provisions of the constitution. Thus, sport is operated in the least restrictive legal manner, dissimilar to other entities in our society.

However, rules-makers have recently been edging away from these basic concepts, setting the stage for legal confrontations that would erode this least restrictive style of governance. The power of NCAA decisions when they restrict the First Amendment rights of student athletes is a potentially explosive problem.

Further, sport has been beset with product liability lawsuits that have had some effect on the income-producing sport of football. Basically, many helmet manufacturers have discontinued manufacturing helmets because their product liability insurance became too costly and there was little resulting profit in this selling venture. Helmet manufacturers have won most lawsuits, but this legal cloud of product liability is ever-present.

The AD must have access to sound and consistent legal counsel, coupled with a working knowledge of how to act like a reasonably prudent administrator in the most volatile area of education offerings. Law and the legal profession provide constant pressure on the AD and the governance of sport.

# Regional, National, and International Rules-Making Bodies

Many state, with a certain degree of accuracy, that we should suspend all rules-making bodies for five years and work only to eliminate non-enforceable and non-productive rules that are currently in the various rule books. The growth and complexity of sport have caused so many new rules to fit extremely heterogeneous groups that they become bewildering to follow.

Further, contradictions between AIAW and NCAA rules, for example, place the instifition in a "no win" governance procedure. To illustrate this, women under NCAA rules can actively recruit away from campus while women under AIAW rules can only assess talent with no contract being made with prospective student athletes. Men feel that women are wasting funds in the "assessment" process and women prospective student athletes wonder why they cannot receive paid campus visits as the men do. While these disparities are slowly being worked out, the confusion still exists.

Probably the most effective rules-making bodies for institutions are the athletic conferences to which they belong. Basically, these are homogeneous groupings of universities on a regional basis. Many academic meetings are held on these conference guidelines. These schools have similar problems and the governance issues are easier to thrash out.

The national sport bodies such as the NCAA, AIAW, NAIA, NJCAA, possess a much different set of problems. Some legislation obviously meets national needs but legislation passed at this level is the result of compromise or of coalition voting. This may or may not meet the governance needs of a particular region.

If the reader feels there is political maneuvering at the national level, it pales by comparison with international sports governance legislation. A casual review of voting by the various national sport federations and the

Olympic rules bodies indicates the need for expertise in the art of compromise and negotiation. While such maneuvering might not be in the best interest of governance of sport, it is the best vehicle we have, and the astute AD can learn to live with these processes that so obviously affect the rule-making areas in the governance of sport.

# SUMMARY

The reader can see that the athletic director's role in governance is molded by different forces. The athletic director must have direct access to the President and have the background and knowledge to influence the President's decisions. The athletic director must understand the needs of the institution's athletes and coaches. He must be strong and persuasive with coaches as a group as well as the athletic council. His knowledge of the Athletic Department's fiscal policies must have depth and consistency with university fiscal policy. He needs rapport with and understanding of medical, legal, booster and rules-making bodies.

The alarming trend of a President inserting a buffer (a Vice-President) between himself and the athletic director must be reversed. Athletic directors must convince their President of the naiveté of this type of administrative structure. Problems and decisions in athletics quite often need rapid decisions and this "buffer" only delays the process—often to the detriment of the athletic program.

At national meetings of athletic directors, more emphasis must be placed upon the cross-pressures that influence the decisions of the athletic director. Athletic Directors must articulate the need of a broad-based, well-financed program to meet the growth needs of international sport through the American system of sports development, which depends upon interscholastic and intercollegiate sport.

While all of these forces mold the athletic director's view of governance in sport, he must still set his own course. All of the varying publics and individuals that have input into governance only see governance from their particular perspective; they cannot and do not perceive the total picture of athletics as the athletic director must do. He must weave in and out of these pressure groups to achieve a balance in the goverance of sport. He must meet this charge if sport is to flourish in the future.

## FOOTNOTE
[1]The following material is drawn from Miller (1980a).

# REFERENCES

Miller, Fred L.
  1980a "The On-going Athletic Crisis—A Solution." *Athletic Administration,* 15 (October): 7-11.
  1980b "The On-going Athletic Crisis—A Solution." Part II: Mechanics." *Athletic Administration,* 15 (December): 23-24.

# PART III
# BEYOND THE CAMPUS: EXTERNAL INFLUENCES ON GOVERNANCE

# INTRODUCTION

Ever since the first intercollegiate athletic event in the mid-1850's, the course of action of college athletic programs has been dictated by groups which, in fact, do not originate within the boundaries of the campus. That is, a great deal of what happens in intercollegiate athletics is the result of a response to the interests and demands of externally based constitutencies. The contemporary questions of institutional control and academic relevance in athletics can be viewed largely as reaction to a situation where it appears that there external constituencies have more to say about athletics than do campus entities. That is, non-academic groups have usurped control of athletics from campus representatives.

The group which draws the greatest amount of attention in this matter is the National Collegiate Athletic Association (NCAA). This is particularly true with reference to large-scale, NCAA Division I Programs. The first few selections in this section describe the NCAA and its operational style. Ted C. Tow, a member of the NCAA headquarters staff, details the purposes and operational guidelines of this regulatory body. His point is that despite considerable criticism, the NCAA is only acting in accordance with the desires of its membership, some 700 colleges and universities of various sizes and varying degrees of athletic emphasis.

The fact that the NCAA is a cartel, or an association of college and university firms that exists in order to establish and preserve a monopoly over certain activities (i.e., athletic competition), is the point made by the Koch and Sage selections. Koch, an economist, asserts that the NCAA cartel does what any effective cartel does: it sets the prices of labor, regulates the quality and quantity of output, pools the profits, and polices the behavior of its members. Above all, the cartel attempts to maintain competitive equality among its members in order to enhance the attractiveness of its authority and, ultimately, to make sure each member realizes a profit from that activity. Sage goes on to say that in its effort to preserve the structure of the cartel, labor (here, the college athlete) suffers. The athlete is limited in choice of the institution to attend either because of scholarship limitations or transfer restrictions. When he or she does get a scholarship, it is clearly for a lesser amount than the actual worth of the athlete's contribution to the athletic program. Even though Koch and Sage direct their remarks at the NCAA, these comments are applicable to some extent to the organization and operation of other athletic regulatory bodies (eg. NAIA, AIAW).

Originally, the Association for Intercollegiate Athletics For Women (AIAW) was founded on principles which were athlete-centered and educationally focused. Bonnie Slatton, formerly acting Executive Director of the AIAW, asserts in her contribution that those who founded the AIAW did not want to duplicate the NCAA or its operating philosophy which appeared to favor "big-time" programs and corporate procedures. The recent decision of the NCAA to offer championships in women's sports has stirred considerable controversy in womens' athletics and has stimulated many to question the future of the AIAW.

As the NCAA is well-known, the National Junior College Athletic Association (NJCAA) is a mystery, even though one-third of the students in institutions of higher education can be found on the campuses of two-year community or junior colleges. Raepple, Perry and Hohman describe the NJCAA and the athletic controversies that face this type of institution. They note that while the NJCAA system of governance is not as structured as that of the NCAA, it has not been without problems, particularly when it comes to eligibility and financial aid abuses.

The selections by Horrow and Lowell are representative of a concern that is more prominent today than ever before. That is: "What are the legal ramifications of athletic policies and certain occurrences under the umbrella of athletic competition?" Rick Horrow, a lawyer and a leading advocate of the application of normal definitions of legal and illegal behavior to the sports field, asserts that the sponsor of athletic competion, whether it be a professional franchise or college athletic program, can no longer rationalize excessive violence on the field in terms of that old maxim "It is just part of the game." The courts will soon be in the locker rooms, and this means that those who govern athletics will have to be very much concerned about certain types of behavior which heretofore had been defined as "acceptable" but which now could be seen as violations. Lowell, in a broader perspective, asserts that college programs face a potentially great number of legal issues beyond those of violence and Title IX.

The final selections in this section discuss the influence of two significant external constituencies—the community and the alumni. Kjeldsen asserts that contemporary problems in athletics are not the result of the actions of misguided individuals but are due to systematic conditions in athletics such as the win-at-all costs mentality and the economic return available to community interests. Sigelman and Carter offer a statistical analysis which compares alumni giving patterns to the success of various athletic programs. They point out that trying to win for the sake of the alumni may be misguided, since they found no correlation between giving and winning. Just as alumni giving does not seem to be related to the won-lost record, so also should one question the relation of winning percentage and legislative appropriations or private donor giving. These associations may also be more mythical than real.

# THE GOVERNANCE ROLE OF THE NCAA

### By
### Ted C. Tow

The National Collegiate Athletic Association (NCAA), the oldest and best-known of the national governing bodies in intercollegiate athletics, is the organization through which the majority of the nation's four-year colleges and universities speak and act on athletic matters at the national level. It is a voluntary association of more than 880 institutions, conferences, and organizations devoted to the sound administration of intercollegiate athletics in all its facets.

Through the NCAA, its members consider any athletic problem that has crossed regional or conference lines and has become national in character. Since its founding in 1906, its deliberations have dealt almost exclusively with men's intercollegiate athletics, inasmuch as women's intercollegiate athletics did not begin to develop on a national basis until the late 1960s and early 1970s. Since 1975, however, the NCAA membership has considered the provision of programs and services for women's athletics. At the 75th annual NCAA Convention in January, 1981, the membership voted overwhelmingly to provide representation for women throughout the NCAA structure, to sponsor a total of 29 championships for women in all three NCAA divisions, and to provide other programs and services for women's athletic programs at the member institutions.

The Association's involvement in women's athletics came about because a rapidly increasing number of member institutions wanted alternatives for both competition and representation for their women's programs; this occurred at least partially as the result of the emergence of a clear pattern of establishing single structures for athletics at the institutional and conference levels. The vote of the member institutions represented a landmark commitment to the advancement of women's sport and expanded opportunities for female student-athletes, coaches, and administrators.

Approval of that concept would represent one of the most significant developments in the storied history of the NCAA, which was founded, not surprisingly, as the direct result of problems in the sport of football during the early 1900's. The rugged nature of the game at that time, typified by mass formations and gang tackling, was causing numerous serious injuries and some deaths. Many institutions were discontinuing the sport, with others advocating that it be abolished from intercollegiate programs.

President Theodore Roosevelt summoned college athletics leaders to two White House conferences to urge reformation of the game, rather than abolition. Two meetings of interested institutions were held in December, 1905, with 62 institutions forming the Intercollegiate Athletic Association at the second of those gathering on December 28, 1905. The association officially was constituted March 31, 1906, and took its present name in 1910. For several years, it existed as a discussion group and concerned itself largely with playing rules. Although the forerunners of NCAA championships date back to 1883 (tennis), the association did not conduct its first official championship until the National Collegiate Track and Field Championships were introduced in 1921. More championships and additional sets of playing rules followed, but it was not until just after World War II that the NCAA's role in the governance of athletics moved significantly from the areas of discussions, championships, and playing rules to regulatory considerations.

The "Sanity Code"—adopted to establish guidelines for recruiting and financial aid to athletes—was found to be ineffective, as abuses in those areas grew in both number and seriousness. [1] In addition, post-season football games were multiplying rapidly without control or supervision, and member institutions were becoming increasingly concerned about the effects on football attendance from unrestricted television.

The complexity and scope of those problems, coupled with growth in membership and the number of NCAA championships, provided dramatic evidence of the increasing need for full-time professional leadership. The association's activities had been directed by its elected volunteer leadership for years, operating from their own institutions; in the 1940s, the Big Ten Conference had provided office services for the association inasmuch as its commissioners served during that period as NCAA secretary-treasurer. In 1951, Walter Byers, who had been handling NCAA affairs on a part-time basis as an executive assistant in the Big Ten office, was named full-time executive director of the NCAA; shortly thereafter, he established the association's national office in Kansas City, Missouri.

In 1951 and 1952, the association's membership adopted a program of controlled live television, delegated prescribed rules-enforcement powers to the NCAA Council (its policy-making body), and approved legislation to govern post-season football bowl games. The NCAA's regulatory function, as it is known today, had begun.

The functions of the association are reflected in its statement of purposes and services:

# Purposes

•To uphold the principle of institutional control of, and responsibility for, all intercollegiate athletics in conformity with the NCAA constitution and bylaws.

•To serve as an overall national discussion, legislative and administrative body for the universities and colleges of the United States in matters of intercollegiate athletics.

•To recommend policies for the guidance of member institutions in the conduct of their intercollegiate athletic programs.

•To legislate upon any subject of general concern to the membership in the administration of intercollegiate athletics.

•To study all phases of competitive athletics and establish standards therefore, to the end that colleges and universities of the United States may maintain their athletic activities on a high plane.

•To encourage the adoption by its constituent members of eligibility rules in compliance with satisfactory standards of scholarship, amateur standing and good sportsmanship.

•To establish and supervise regional and national collegiate athletic contests under the auspices of the association and establish rules of eligibility thereof.

•To stimulate and improve programs to promote and develop educational leadership, physical fitness, sports participation as a recreational pursuit and athletic excellence through competitive intramural and intercollegiate programs.

•To formulate, copyright and publish rules of play for collegiate sports.

•To preserve collegiate athletic records.

•To cooperate with other amateur athletic organizations in the promotion and conduct of national and international athletic contests.

•To otherwise assist member institutions as requested in the furtherance of their intercollegiate athletic programs.

# Services

To achieve and further its purposes, the association:

•Maintains a central clearinghouse and counseling agency in the field of college athletic administration.

•Enacts legislations to deal with athletic problems when they spread across regional lines and member institutions conclude that national action is needed.

•Conducts research as a means of developing solutions to athletic problems, such as surveys on television, postseason events, athletic and recreational facilities, sports injuries and safety, recruiting, financial aid, playing and practice seasons and the cost of intercollegiate athletics.

•Provides financial and other assistance to various groups interested in the promotion and advancement of intercollegiate athletics.

•Represents the colleges and universities in legislative and regulatory matters on the state and Federal levels, covering topics such as Federal taxes affecting college athletics, antibribery and gambling laws, television, international competition and Federal aid to education affecting sports and physical education.

•Administers group travel and medical insurance programs whereby member institutions can provide catastrophe coverage for student-athletes when they are engaged in practice, play or transport; also, administers a loss-of-revenue insurance program providing games—cancellation insurance for catastrophic losses suffered in the sports of basketball and football.

•Provides a film-television production service (NCAA Productions), which produces special programs for television, conference highlights films, National Collegiate Championships highlights films and television coverage of NCAA championships not carried by a national television network. NCAA Productions also offers a library of more than 100 films and oversees the NCAA Television News Service, which supplies major television networks with material regarding NCAA sports and championships.

•Promotes and participates in international sports planning and competition through membership in the U.S. Olympic Committee, Amateur Basketball Association of the USA, Track and Field Association of the USA and the US Baseball, Gymnastics and Wrestling Federations. The NCAA also has sponsored international competition with Japan, Mexico and the Republic of China.

•Sanctions postseason competition and certifies noncollegiate contests to protect the interests of its members and their student-athletes.

•Compiles and distributes official statistics for intercollegiate football, basketball and baseball and maintains NCAA records for those sports.

•Promotes NCAA championships and all of intercollegiate athletics through planned promotional activities through the NCAA national office and conducts general public-relations activities in behalf of the association, its members and intercollegiate athletics in general.

•Publishes the **NCAA news** 18 times each year and dozens of other publications annually to advise its members and other interested parties of events and information important to intercollegiate athletics.

•Establishes committees to formulate and interpret playing rules in 14 sports.

•Offers 43 National Collegiate Championships for men and 10 for women, with the latter number to increase to 29 if the 1981 NCAA Convention adopts additional proposed women's events.

•Maintains a program of enforcement of the association's legislation.

•Annually offers 80 postgraduate scholarships of $2,000 each to outstanding student-athletes who have excelled academically.

•Conducts an awards program, including the Theodore Roosevelt Award, presented annually to a distinguished citizen of national reputation and outstanding accomplishment who was a varsity athletic award winner in college, and the College Athletics Top Ten Awards, presented annually to five outstanding senior student-athletes and five distinguished former student-athletes on their silver anniversary as college graduates.[2]

No other organization in intercollegiate athletics provides all of those services, and their appeal to colleges and universities has been evidenced in the steady growth of the NCAA. After World War II, the membership totaled 317, including 278 active member institutions in 1949. The next year, those figures jumped to 387 and 362, respectively, the biggest one-year increase in the association's history. With the exception of 1971, when the total membership declined by one, the membership roster has increase each year. In the 1980-81 academic year, it included a record 740 active member institutions, 73 allied members (conferences), 46 affiliated members (coaches' associations and other athletic organizations), and 24 associate members (institutions that do not qualify for active membership), for a total membership of 883, also a record.

While the NCAA offers many programs and advantages not available in other organizations (for example, the association pays all transportation costs and, where possible, per diem expenses for all participants in its championships, as well as negotiating television contracts that provide direct financial benefits to institutions participating in the televised events and indirect services and programs for all NCAA member institutions), its role in the governance of intercollegiate athletics is perhaps best characterized, at least for comparative purposes, by three interrelated precepts: total accountability to its member colleges and universities, the principle of institutional control, and adherence to an extensive and ongoing enforcement program.

# ACCOUNTABILITY

The NCAA, as an administrative organization, is nothing more than its membership; it does only what the membership directs or approves. There is no NCAA rule that has not been adopted by the membership; there is no interpretation of an NCAA rule that has not been, or will not be, approved by the membership; there is no NCAA policy that is not subject to membership approval.

The final authority and governing body of the association is its annual convention, held during the first two weeks in January. Every regulation in the NCAA constitution and bylaws is adopted by the membership in convention assembled; every executive regulation, interpretation and recommended policy, as well as every portion of the association's enforcement procedure, is subject to approval of the convention. Each active and qualified allied member is entitled to one vote on all issues before the convention. In certain bylaws, each of the association's three divisions is enabled to adopt its own legislation (e.g., in recruiting, playing seasons, championship eligibility, financial aid, and division membership criteria); however, such legislation may be rescinded by a two-thirds majority of all delegates present and voting.

In the interim between conventions, the 18-member NCAA Council is responsible for establishing and directing the general policy of the association. Members of the Council are elected directly by the convention itself, and all three divisions and the eight NCAA geographic districts have prescribed representation thereon. The Council meets four times annually, in addition to occasional telephone conferences. It is required to report its actions to the annual convention, and any Council decision is subject to review by the convention upon request by any delegate.

To broaden the representational base in the association's administrative structure, the 1977 convention approved the establishment of division steering committees as subcommittees of the Council. Each division's committee includes the Council members representing the division and an equal number of representatives who do not serve on the Council, the latter appointed on a precise geographic representation formula and specifically taking into account those segments of the division's membership that are not represented on the Council. These committees meet three times annually and submit recommedations to the Council. They can take no action without Council approval.

An Executive Committee of 10 members is charged with transacting the financial affairs of the association and with overall administration of NCAA championships. The NCAA president and secretary-treasurer (elected directly by the convention) serves on this committee (as well as on the Council), and the remaining eight members are elected by the Council, with all divisions represented. The Executive Committee is required to report its actions to the convention, and any such action is subject to review by the convention upon request by any delegate. The secretary-treasurer also presents a complete, printed financial report to the annual convention.

In the interim between meetings of the Council and the Executive Committee, the president, secretary-treasurer and executive director are constitutionally empowered to transact necessary items of business, subject to the approval of the Council and Executive Committee at their next meetings and subject, therefore, to approval of the membership in convention assembled.

The membership directly elects the members of the association's sports committees, which are responsible for conducting the NCAA championships, and in 14 sports, for maintaining NCAA playing rules. In addition, all members are urged repeatedly to submit recommendations for service on the Council and on all Council-appointed committees.

Therefore, the NCAA's legislative and administrative activities are participatory processes in every respect. Every action is controlled by the membership at the annual convention.

# INSTITUTIONAL CONTROL

The NCAA is, and always has been, an organization of institutions, not of individuals. Institutional control is the association's most fundamental principle. That principle is set forth in the NCAA constitution: "The control and responsibility for the conduct of intercollegiate athletics shall be exercised by the institution itself and by the conference, if any, of which it is a member" (1980-81). The constitution states that administrative control or faculty control, or a combination of the two, constitutes institutional control and specifies that administration and/or faculty must make up at least a voting majority of the board in control of athletics at the institutional level.

Further, the constitution clarifies that the institution's responsibility includes the act of an independent agency, organization or individual when a member of the institution's executive or athletic administration or any athletic department staff member has knowledge that such agency, organization or individual is promoting the institution's intercollegiate athletic program, including financial contributions to the athletic department or an athletic booster organization, or assistance in the recruitment of prospective student-athletes. In short, each member institution agrees as a member of the NCAA to control its own intercollegiate athletic program in accordance with the rules and regulations of its conference and of the NCAA.

In practice, the time-tested principle of institutional control is reflected in a number of ways, all recognizing that the institution's chief executive officer has the ultimate responsibility for all institutional programs, including athletics. For example:

*As noted, the NCAA is directly responsive to its member institutions. The institutional direction comes from the chief executive officer, the athletic board or committee of the institution, the faculty athletic representative or the director of athletics, whichever is designated by the chief executive to act for the institution. It does not come directly from coaches, other institutional staff members, or the institution's student-athletes, whose avenue for expression is expected to be provided via customary institutional channels.

*The chief executive must certify annually the institution's voting delegate(s) to the NCAA convention, thus assuring, to the greatest extent possible, that the votes at the convention represent institutional positions, rather than individual viewpoints. In an increasing number of cases, the chief executive attends and votes for the institution.

*The chief executive is required by NCAA bylaw to certify annually that he or she, or a designated representative, has reviewed with all athletic department staff members the rules and regulations of the NCAA, that the institution is in compliance with those rules and regulations insofar as can be determined, and that it intends to maintain such compliance.

*Only the chief executive, faculty athletic representative, or director of athletics, acting on the authority of the institution, is entitled to submit an amendment for consideration at an NCAA convention or to request waivers or submit appeals as provided in NCAA legislation.

The practical result of these procedures and the constitutional requirement is that an athletic program that is out of control is in that condition because the institution itself has failed to exercise the control it should. Such a condition is not a failure of the NCAA, its regulations, or the other member institutions.

# ENFORCEMENT PROGRAM

In August 1951, the NCAA Council developed a 12-point program to deal with pressures in intercollegiate athletics and forwarded that program to the chief executives of all member institutions, requesting their reactions as the basis for future NCAA legislation. At the subsequent NCAA convention in January, 1952, the membership adopted amendments to the constitution and bylaws dealing with academic standards, financial aid, ethical conduct, and out-of-season practice in football and basketball, all stemming from the response to the 12-point program.

In addition, that convention established a Membership Committee to consider complaints filed with the association charging the failure of a member institution to maintain the academic or athletic standards required for membership or to meet the conditions and obligations of membership. In its April, 1952, meeting, the NCAA Council created the operating procedure for the Membership Committee and its Subcommittee on Infractions. In October of that year, the Council voted to recommend to the 1953 convention that disciplinary action be taken against three member institutions for violations of NCAA regulations; two months later, it forwarded to the membership a 10-point plan to strengthen the enforcement mechanism of the NCAA and its allied conferences. At the 1953 convention, the membership adopted the Council's recommended disciplinary action relative to infractions by the three member institutions. That convention also delegated certain enforcement powers to the Council by authorizing that body to take disciplinary actions (other than termination or suspension of membership) between conventions.

Thus began the NCAA enforcement program, the most extensive and effective self-policing effort of any voluntary membership organization in any field. It is a cooperative undertaking involving the member institutions and allied conferences working together through the NCAA in a unified effort designed to improve the adminstration of intercollegiate athletics. After more than a quarter of a century of refinement and expansion, the enforcement program today works in the following manner: Allegations of violations reported from a variety of sources are referred to the NCAA investigative staff, and a preliminary investigation is initiated to determine if an official inquiry is warranted. The involved institution is notified promptly and may appear in its own behalf before the Committee in Infractions, a five-member body consisting of representatives of member institutions, usually including three or four law professors. Findings of the Committee on Infractions and any resultant penalty are reported to the institution, which may appeal, if it desires, the findings and/or the penalty to the NCAA Council. In such cases, the Council— after considering both the report of the committee and the presentation of the institutional representatives, may accept the committee's finding and penalty, alter either or both, or make its own findings and impose a penalty it believes appropriate. Again, any action of the Council is subject to review by the annual convention.

Penalties available to the committee (or the Council) include more than a dozen alternatives, ranging from a private reprimand to a provision in which the member institution must show cause why its membership in the association should not be suspended or terminated. As a guiding principle, the penalty is broad and severe if the violation(s) reflect a general disregard for the governing rules of the association; in those instances in which the violation(s) are isolated and of relative insignificance, the penalty is specific and limited.

The NCAA membership repeatedly and overwhelmingly has supported the goals of its enforcement program, which perhaps were best summarized in the Committee on Infractions' annual report to the membership at the 1980 convention by Charles Alan Wright, University of Texas, Austin, chairman of the committee:

The committee is well aware that it has dual responsibilities. On the one hand, it must always be sure that those who may be adversely affected by its determinations—institutions, athletes, and staff members—are provided not only the constitutional minimum of due process, but the fairness that one expects from an association whose very reason for being is to ensure sportsmanship and fair play. On the other hand, the committee cannot allow its processes to become so difficult that those who would see a competitive advantage by violating the rules may do so knowing that there is no realistic possibility that they will be held to account (NCAA, 1978-79:46).

The committee and the NCAA membership are in the third decade of an enforcement program that is directly related to the principle of institutional control and balanced by the NCAA's unique and thorough system of accountability to the membership itself. The program, in Professor Wright's words, is "vigorous and fair"—words that serve equally well in describing the National Collegiate Athletic Association itself.

# FOOTNOTES

[2]All references to NCAA goals, services, structure, and constitutional provisions are drawn from the *NCAA Manual, 1981-82.*

[1]The "Sanity Code" was adopted by the 1947 NCAA convention. The code contained a set of five "Principles for the Conduct of Intercollegiate Athletics"—specifically, these were entitled "Principles of Amateurism," "Principles of Institutional Control and Responsibility," "Principles of Sound Academic Standards," "Principles Governing Financial Aid to Athletes" and "Principle Governing Recruiting." These principles had stemmed from a "conference of conferences" held in July, 1946, and subsequently were adopted as permanent NCAA legislation by the 1948 NCAA Convention, by which time the five principles were commonly referred to as the "Sanity Code", inasmuch as they were designed to "bring some sanity" to college athletics. The code in itself was found to be ineffective, as abuses particularly in recruiting and financial aid grew in both number and seriousness. But the code did provide groundwork for the legislative and compliance procedures that were to come.

# THE ECONOMICS OF "BIG-TIME" INTERCOLLEGIATE ATHLETICS*

*Reprinted with permission from *Social Science Quarterly,* 52 (September, 1971): 248-260. Footnotes are renumbered to accommodate a different referencing system.

Organized intercollegiate athletics, long a fixture on the American scene, has developed into an economic phenomenon of considerable importance. The organization and operation of this market[1] is unique and interesting when viewed in the context of economic analysis. The task of this paper is to apply economic analysis to intercollegiate athletics and to highlight several of the most interesting features of that market such as the peculiar market for student-athlete inputs.

The contention of this writer is that the market approximates a cartelized arrangement and that considerable insight into intercollegiate athletics can be gained by taking this analytic viewpoint.

## THE NATURE OF THE MARKET

The dominant force in intercollegiate athletics today is the National Collegiate Athletic Association (NCAA).[2] All of the colleges and universities which operate expensive "big-time" athletic programs are members of the NCAA, and approximately 650 schools are members **in toto.** The NCAA currently conducts 27 national championship sporting events in 18 sports and engages in a host of other activities ranging from record keeping to negotiating television contracts for its members.

Until 1948, the NCAA did little except write playing rules for various sports and conduct occasional tournaments. Since that time, however, the NCAA has assumed great power and simultaneously exercises the legislative, executive and judicial functions necessary to the maintenance of an orderly, collusive intercollegiate athletic market. The structure of the

NCAA and the sources of its power are specified in the Constitution of the NCAA, the Bylaws, including "Official Interpretations," the Executive Regulations, the Recommended Policies and Practices, and the Procedures Concerning Enforcement, all of which may be found in the NCAA Manual (NCAA, 1970). The members of the NCAA are bound by these documents, and their adherence to such makes the intercollegiate athletic market openly imperfect and collusive in nature.

The effective control of the NCAA resides with the colleges and universities which maintain "big-time" athletic programs characterized by considerable scholarship aid to competing athletes, large coaching staffs, and athletic budgets which may exceed three million dollars annually. The annual conventions of the NCAA, where the rules of the intercollegiate athletic market are formulated, are dominated by the "big-time" schools, as are the committees which rule the NCAA between the annual conventions.[3] This is true despite the fact that considerably less than one-half of the total membership of the NCAA could reasonably be classified as maintaining a "big-time" athletic program. The attention of this paper is directed to the colleges and universities which maintain "big-time" programs.

The intercollegiate athletic market is appropriately viewed as being dominated by a national cartel which is frequently administered and modified on a regional or local basis. The national cartel, the NCAA, typifies the usual behavior of a cartel in that it: (1) sets input prices for student-athlete inputs; (2) regulates the duration and intensity of usage of those inputs and their subsequent mobility during their careers as collegiate athletes; (3) regulates the type and particularly the quantity of output of games; (4) seeks to pool and divide portions of the cartel's profits (for example, television receipts); (5) makes information available to cartel members concerning transactions, market conditions, and business and accounting techniques; (6) attempts to police the behavior of the members of the cartel; and, (7) levies penalties against cartel members for infractions of the cartel's rules.[4]

Regional conferences of university-firms may modify the national cartel's rules and regulations. For example, a particular athletic conference may limit any university-firm to dispensing no more than 30 new football scholarships per year, or choose to ban spring football practice, or require home teams to share gate revenues with visiting teams.

We reserve until later a discussion of the success that has accrued to the cartel and its members as a result of their efforts, and instead proceed to examine the production function of the university-firms.

# THE PRODUCTION FUNCTION

The firm in the intercollegiate athletic market is the individual college or university (henceforth "university" for brevity.) The production function of the firm is somewhat unusual in several respects. The unit of output of the firm is the competitive game between its own athletic team and that of a rival university-firm. Each unit of output (game) is differentiated in nature. The exact form and amount of this differentiation is never predictable **ex ante**, since the vagaries of the weather, the physical state of the players, and the tightness of the fight for the title of the league, etc., are not always predictable. Nevertheless, it is easily observed that the customer-fans who purchase one unit of output (for example, a Notre Dame versus Purdue football game), typically view it differently than they do another unit of the university-firm's output (for example, a Notre Dame versus Northwestern game.)

It should be noted that the university-firm is a multiproduct firm, Football and basketbal are essentially different products which may in fact compete with each other. Each of these outputs is capable of generating many different streams of utility which are consumed by many different individuals.

The university-firm's output exhibits a characteristic similar to that of many social goods, viz., the transference of utility to many individuals who do not purchase the output. Fans or even gamblers who follow the progress of the UCLA basketball team be means of the public media need not purchase a ticket to attend a UCLA basketball game; nevertheless, they will still be possible recipients of one of the many different streams of utility emanating from the game. This phenomenon is hardly injurious to the actual purchaser of the ticket, however, since his own utility will not be decreased by the utility obtained by others, and may actually be increased if, for example, public enthusiasm is whipped up for the game for which he has a ticket or has attended. This interdependence of utilities illustrates yet another fact: the number of consumers of the same unit of output is virtually unlimited.

The university-firm's output and the streams of utility which emanate therefrom are strikingly similar to the circumstance of admittedly professional athletics. Indeed, there would be little reason to examine separately the intercollegiate athletic market if the emphasis were to be upon the output of that market. Penetrating analyses of professional athletics and the distinguishing features of its output have already been provided by Rottenberg (1950), Neale (1964), Jones (1969) and Davenport (1969). However, the distinctive and noteworthy features of the intercollegiate athletic market lie not on the output side of the market, but rather on the input side of the market and in the rules and regulations which govern the procurement and use of inputs.

The inputs in the production function include the student-athletes who compete, the stadiums, playing fields and facilities, the coaches, trainers, etc., the equipment and supplies (pep pills, steroids, and amphetamines, some would contend), and the indispensable element of competition personified by the other team. The last-mentioned input, the other team, is essential to the productive process. Without another unversity-firm with which to compete, there can be no meaningful output by the university in question. Indeed, a league or conference of competitors may be necessary if the university wishes to produce efficiently.[5]

It is interesting to note that when competition either is unequal or threatens to become so, the cartel steps in and attempts to lessen the imbalance. Such actions are usually taken, however, in the name of preserving the sanctity of amateurism, or in order to maintain the Panglossian relationship in which collegiate athletics are subservient to the overall academic life of the university.

Yet, such reasons for action are not convincing when one views the rules, regulations, and framework which remain to guide the body politic of the NCAA. The essential attributes of the cartel continue unaltered after each so-called "reform." Historically, the major reform movements in intercollegiate athletics (particularly those in the first and fifth decades of this century) have been preceded by or have coincided with great inequality of competition, brought about by the open exercise of various "abuses." Witness the crackdown in the late 1940's and early 1950's on the open bidding and payment for student-athletes.

It must be emphasized that the continued prosperity of the intercollegiate athletic program of a university-firm depends upon fielding winning teams. Consider the approximately 120 university-firms running "big-time" programs whose major revenues are gate receipts from attendance at home games. In the year 1969, the simple correlation between their average per game football attendance and their won-lost percentage was .40.[6] It is not surprising, therefore, that one football coach has reported that "The people you work for don't appreciate anything but winning," (**Wall Street Journal.** 1970: 1).

Since all teams cannot simultaneously have winning seasons, it is intelligent policy for the cartel either to require sharing of gate revenues among all university-firms (winners and losers alike), or to promote equality of competition. The NCAA has typically emphasized the latter approach.

The rules of the NCAA and of particular collusive groups of universities seldom specify how the universities may obtain, combine, or use the inputs in their production functions except in one case—the student-athlete input. The rules and regulations concerning permissible competition for the student-athlete inputs and the subsequent use of these imputs are voluminous and constitute the major restrictions placed upon the activities of the university-firm in the intercollegiate athletic market.

The market for student-athlete inputs may be characterized as one in which a seller (the student-athlete) with partial monopoly power due to limited supply and product differentiation faces potentially many buyers (universities) who are at least partial monopsonists. The university-firms can influence the price of the student-athlete input, but only up to a certain flexible maximum price. That flexible maximum price allows no payment to a student-athlete in excess of tuition, fees, room and board, books and necessary supplies, and $15 per month for laundry expenses. The maximum is indeed flexible in nature since the value of some of these items (for example, the tuition and fees allowing class attendance) will vary greatly from university to university. Lesser prices can be and are paid for the student-athletic input, particularly if the student-athlete is skilled in a co-called "minor" sport such as tennis or gymnastics, where spectator attendance does not generate great sales revenues.

Not every available Babe Ruth or Joe Namath who is walking the streets may be hired as an input, however. The university-firm must be able to predict at least a 1.60 grade point average (on a 4.00 scale) for its hireling, based upon experience tables provided by the NCAA. Since this predicted grade point average is based upon evidence such as previous academic performance, there is a great temptation for a coach to imitate the recent activities of a basketball coach at a major metropolitan university, namely, to enhance the previous academic performance of a prospective seven-foot center by altering his academic transcript. Needless to say, such activities are not tolerated by the cartel at large and are greeted with indignation and censure.

The university-firm also may not purchase or bid for student-athlete inputs who: (1) currently attend another university; (2) have already engaged in four seasons of athletic competition at the college level; (3) originally entered college more than five years previous;[7] (4) have ever played for pay (other than for the athletic teams of an academic institution).

Such rules are designed to prevent instances such as the proverbial halfback who at one time or another played in the backfield of every team in the Southern Conference. But the rules are most explicitly intended to prevent one well-heeled university-firm from raiding the ranks of another university-firm and hiring away its best student-athletes. It is interesting to note that the universities typically do not apply such restrictions to the coaching input in the athletic productive process. Witness the recent jumping of contract by the head football coach of one major southeastern university for the same position at another university in the same athletic conference.

The structural keystone of the market for student-athlete inputs is the national letter of intent. Once a prospective student-athlete who otherwise qualifies for financial aid signs a letter of intent with a given university-firm, he is bound to that university-firm for the space of one year and he may not sign with, nor be signed by, any other university-firm. This provision effectively forecloses all other university-firms from competing for that student-athlete input. Should a student who signs a national letter of intent at State U. decide after his freshman year to transfer to Ivy U., he must sit on the sidelines without competing for one calendar year.[8] The national letter of intent is properly seen as a cartel contract which, if not fulfilled by either part to the contract, results in substantial penalties being levied by the NCAA.

National letters of intent may not be signed prior to a date late in the spring of the year which is determined by the NCAA. It should be noted, however, that still another submarket exists in the overall student-athlete input market which is not covered by the national letter of intent. There is no national letter of intent for student-athlete inputs transferring from junior colleges. The absence of such a requirement opens wide the floodgates for a strenuous competition in this submarket. Because of the previously mentioned quality restriction on prospective inputs which requires a predicted 1.60 grade point average, some student-athletes cannot be given financial aid for their athletic prowess as a four-year university. Hence, they and many others not in that identical circumstance enroll at a junior college.

The submarket for junior college transfers operates throughout the summer preceding the beginning of the academic year and has been known to terminate only a few seconds prior to the formal registration of a junior college transfer at the university of his choice. So competitive is this market for relatively experienced inputs that many university-firms grouped together in a collusive conference have imposed their own conference letter of intent to lessen the uncertainty and strife. The conference letter of intent is a widely used device to restrict competition for student-athlete inputs and is not limited to the market for junior college transfers.

As noted before, the formal price that may be paid for a student-athlete input is administered. Many conferences of colluding university-firms limit the number of student-athlete inputs that may be purchased during a year, both for any individual sport-product, and in an overall sense for all sport-products taken together. A Chamberlinian result emerges: barred from competing in terms of price, the university-firms instead compete primarily on a non-price basis for inputs. The coach who is a clever and skilled recruiter of student-athlete inputs will emphasize such things as the reputation of the coaching staff and the quality of the conference in which the university-firm competes, the high quality of the academic life at the university-firm, the probability of lucrative summer employment and enviable job replacement after graduation. The coach may even seek to induce the prospective student-athlete to sign a national letter of intent by impressing him with the beauty of the coeds attending alma mater. (The female students who assist in athletic recruiting at the University of Florida are known as the "Gator Getters" because of their considerable success.)

The ease of completing the requirements for a degree at Fudd U. may also be used to lure student-athletes. The world is full of uncertainty, however, and many a disappointed student-athlete input has departed the halls of ivy without his sheepskin. None of the starting five on a recent national championship basketball team of a southwestern university has ever received an earned degree from that institution.

The use of already hired student-athlete inputs in the production function is also regulated. Since the typical input can be used no more than four competitive seasons, but may be used over a time interval of five competitive seasons, a crafty coach may choose to withhold one or more of his inputs from competition in any given year. The student-athlete input continues to receive financial aid and is subject to all the usual restrictions placed upon the mobility of inputs. Although he continues to practice with the team, he does not compete in any games between the university-firms. This practice is known as "red-shirting" and can be used to toughen up the student-athlete input and give him additional experience. It may also be used by the university-firm to distribute its available student-athlete talent more propitiously over the five-year interval.[9]

In general, the rules which regulate the use of the already hired student-athlete input are stacked heavily in favor of the university-firm at the expense of the student-athlete. The previously cited rule requiring transfer students to sit out one full season of competition seriously reduces the mobility of student-athletes as well as the negotiating power that they might have where fringe benefits are concerned. The university-firm is not required to grant assurance of financial aid to the student-athlete for more than one year. Further, the university-firm may wait until July 1 preceding the academic year before it must notify any student-athlete input previously hired that it is or is not going to renew his financial aid.[10] The result has been likened to a mild form of involuntary servitude.

At going market prices for student-athlete inputs, there seems to be more than enough takers of scholarship offers, although the quality of these prospective inputs is far from uniform. Some student-athletes undoubtedly do not receive a wage equal to their marginal revenue products. The worth of O.J. Simpson to the USC football team of recent past was probably greater than the wage that the NCAA rules allowed him to be paid. Unfortunately for "Orange Juice," the worth of his next best alternative was also visibly shrunk by the impact of an agreement between the NCAA and the professional football teams which forbids a professional team to sign a student-athlete until that student-athlete's regular college class would have graduated.

As a result, it is not unfair to speculate that a few student-athlete inputs earn positive rents inside the field of intercollegiate athletics. Their next best alternative, athletically, is usually not substantial in nature. Of course, when non-athletic alternatives are considered, then the rent probably disappears and may become negative. At any given point in time, the student-athlete must weigh the capitalized worth of the training and education he is receiving against the primary cost of his education that he actually bears—the negative rent.

It is the availability of non-athletic alternatives that is the primary source of the student-athlete's negotiating power and which enables him to earn a positive rent, athletically speaking, even though he may be earning a negative rent with respect to all markets. This negotiating power is greatly reduced, however, by the considerable social pressure on prospective student-athletes to attend a university and to excel there. Many student-athletes may not seriously entertain the possibility of non-athletic, non-collegiate employment. This may be true for three reasons. First, due to the relative isolation of the intercollegiate athletic market from other markets, the student-athlete may suffer from a lack of knowledge about his worth as an input in alternative productive processes. Second, the student-athlete may attach such great utility to his intercollegiate athletic activities that he is willing to earn the negative rent implied by the availability of more lucrative employment elsewhere. Third, the capitalized value of the training and education he is receiving may be more than enough to overcome that negative rent.

# THE SUCCESS AND PROFITABILITY OF THE CARTEL

The success of the cartelized arrangements, national and regional, is less than complete. Decisive evidence of a truly effective cartelized arrangement is usually the pooling and dividing of the profits of the cartel's members. The NCAA and the regional conferences have taken only minor steps in this direction. Instead, the NCAA has concentrated upon regulating the market for inputs and upon restricting output. These attempts have met with greater success.

The reasons why the NCAA and the regional conferences have been unable to perfect the cartelized arrangement are to be found primarily in the structure of the intercollegiate athletic market. The cost functions of the uni-university-firms are dissimilar and their revenue possibilities unequal. The outputs are differentiated. These factors cause a fundamental divergence of interest among cartel members and militate against continued joint action. Further, the number of university-firms is large and the transactions of the cartel, particularly on the input side, are not public knowledge. As a result, it will usually be profitable for at least one member of the cartel to violate the cartel's rules because the small risk of discovery increases the expected profits to be reaped from that violation. Whereas in the usual business cartel this often takes the form of secret price chiseling in order to obtain the most talented of those inputs. Rumors of under the table payments and gifts to student-athletes are legion, but few can match the documented case of a western university which paid a football star a weekly salary to see that the stadium was not stolen. Whatever the frequency of such episodes, it can be said that violations are a direct outgrowth of the cartelized market structure. While over 100 university-firms were penalized by the NCAA for rule violations during a recent 15-year period, most observers believe that only a small fraction of the actual violators is ever apprehended.''

Finally, the NCAA and the regional conferences have always upheld the principal of the ''. . . amateur student-athlete . . . who engages in athletics for the physical, mental, social and educational benefits he derives therefrom, and to whom athletics is an avocation'' (NCAA **Manual,** 1970-71: 1). The NCAA asserts that it seeks to "develop educational leadership, physical fitness, sports participation as a recreational pursuit . . ." (NCAA **Manual,** 1970-71: 1). Actions which might conceivably increase the joint profits or well-being of the cartel are not always taken if these actions might tend to tarnish the above self-images. To the extent that such statements are actually subscribed to by the NCAA and its members, deviations of the cartel from absolute profit-maximizing behavior might be explained by attributing the deviations to the maximization of utility and psychic income. Alternatively, the threats of governmental regulations, possible loss of privileged tax status, and antitrust suits may be sufficient to curb certain profit-maximizing tendencies of the cartel in favor of an outward devotion to the concepts of amateurism, physical fitness and the like. Calculation of the accounting profits or losses earned by university-firms is hardly an exact science. Revenue figures reported by university-firms are generally unrepresentative in that winning (losing) teams generate many side effects. It is alleged but not clearly demonstrated that alumni contributions soar when Tech caps a successful season by an appearance in the Prune Bowl. An appearance in a well-known and prestigious post-season bowl will, however, usually result in a direct payment of several hundred thousand dollars to each participating team. [12] Enrollment applications are said to climb when the university-firm's athletic teams win and community relations are undoubtedly smoother when State U. finds it possible to reward Senator Snort for his faithful legislative support by giving him a coveted 50-yard line seat.

Winning teams appear more often on the nationally televised series of games sanctioned by the NCAA. In 1970, the NCAA split an estimated $12 million between university-firms and conferences whose teams appeared in televised games. [13]

In sum, the revenue figures reported to the national cartel by the individual university-firms are less than perfect. The cost figures reported to the NCAA are also deficient since debt service charges attributable to athletics and capital expenditures for buildings and stadia are not included. As a result, it is not proper to subtract reported costs from reported revenues and thereby obtain accounting profits.

There is reason to believe, however, that "big-time" collegiate athletics has not in general become the economic liability that many would have the public believe. Table 1 lists the recent revenues and costs of intercollegiate athletic programs reported to the NCAA by the universities operating a Class A ("big-time") program. Note that the ratio of revenues to costs has remained a favorable one and has not fluctuated greatly.

Why, then, do we hear the continual complaint that "big-time" intercollegiate athletics constitutes a drain upon the universities' budgets? (Padwe, 1970). Several explanations have appeal. First, as previously indicated, the cost figures which the universities report to the NCAA are understated by virtue of not including some relevant expenses.

Second, the university-firm produces multiple outputs and some of these outputs do not generate sufficient revenues to cover the cost of producing these outputs. Typically, these outputs are minor sports such as gymnastics, tennis, or golf which do not attract revenues sufficient to defray the expense of maintaining a program which includes maximum allowable scholarship aid and lengthy spring warmup tours. Both the much-ballyhooed devotion of the university firms to a "rounded program" available to all students, and the prestige associated with fielding athletic teams in many sports, combine to prevent the university-firm from dropping an unprofitable sport.

Parenthetically, however, it should be made clear that major sports such as football are typically 'profitable" in the sense of generating attributed revenues greater than attributed costs. Seventy-five percent of the universities maintaining an NCAA Class A athletic program reported revenues to be greater than costs for football in 1969 (NCAA, 1970: 226). It is of interest to note that this represents an increase of 7 per cent over the comparable 1960 figure (1970: 226).

A third factor of some import has been the increase in the size of student bodies at many universities. Upon payment of a small activity fee, the students at most universities are entitled to a seat in the stadium or fieldhouse, with the end result that there are fewer seats available for sale to the public. Only at universities where students are charged a special fee destined for use in the intercollegiate athletic program can it be said that the growth of the student body is an unmixed blessing.

Finally, those who are impressed by the costs of maintaining a "big-time" intercollegiate athletic program frequently fail to recognize that the opportunity cost of these expenditures is not comparable to the opportunity cost of the typical expenditure by another area of a university such as a Department of Economics. Well over 90 percent of the revenues used for intercollegiate athletics are generated directly by that program so that these revenues would not be available except for the existence of the athletic program (1970: 316). Hence, the foregone alternative of an expenditure on the intercollegiate athletic program is small when compared to an expenditure of the same magnitude by a department of Economics.

## TABLE I

The Relationship Between Average Revenues and Average Costs Per
University Operating "Big-Time" Programs[a]

| Year | Revenues (000's) | Costs (000's) | Revenue/Cost Ratio |
|------|------------------|---------------|--------------------|
| 1960 | $ 672 | $ 635 | 1.06 |
| 1961 | 723 | 685 | 1.06 |
| 1962 | 749 | 717 | 1.04 |
| 1963 | 804 | 769 | 1.05 |
| 1964 | 853 | 817 | 1.04 |
| 1965 | 945 | 887 | 1.07 |
| 1966 | 1,086 | 998 | 1.09 |
| 1967 | 1,176 | 1,094 | 1.07 |
| 1968 | 1,246 | 1,187 | 1.05 |
| 1969 | 1,397 | 1,322 | 1.06 |

[a]The revenues and costs are the arithmetic means of the figures reported to the NCAA.

# PREDICTED FUTURE BEHAVIOR

If the characterization of the intercollegiate athletic market as a loosely knit cartel is apt, and further, if the legal barriers to the cartel's actions remain minimal, then the cartel will probably react to its current problems in a predictable fashion. The members of the cartel currently suffer from the hiring of student-athlete inputs, may be avoidable given certain actions by the cartel. A plausible way to reduce the expense of hiring student-athlete inputs is to impose a further restriction upon the quantity of student-athlete inputs that may be purchased by any unversity-firm. Alternatively, the members of the cartel could adopt as their own version of the Ivy League model and progressively lower the permissible price that might be paid to a student-athlete input.

Either of the above solutions will inspire secret chiseling. Ultimately, therefore, one might expect the development of a draft system for inputs similar to that successfully employed by professional baseball. Such a system would give each university-firm the exclusive right to negotiate for the services of a given regional conference. One can envision, for example, the situation where (within the Big Eight Conference) only Nebraska has the right to negotiate with a given prospect. The draft system would greatly reduce recruiting costs and could lead to a uniform reduction by the cartel members in both the stated maximum price that can be paid to any student-athlete input and in the actual price that is paid for student athlete inputs. The conference letter of intent may be viewed as a first step in this direction since it has the effect of insulating a given university-firm from competition for inputs by other university-firms in its conference.

Currently intercollegiate athletics serves as a training and proving ground for athletes who may later play for professional teams. The cartelized system maintained by the NCAA has developed into an inexpensive and riskless source of qualified inputs for professional teams. Cartels do not willingly assume the costs of other cartels without receiving compensation in some form. The NCAA has been slow to recognize the fact that professional teams have benefitted mightily from the cartelization of intercollegiate athletics although they have assumed only a very minor portion of the costs of the system. The NCAA as a monopolist may seek to impose costs upon the increasingly dependent professional teams by means of an agreement mutually acceptable to both parties. The prospects for such are not favorable.

It is more likely that in the long run university-firms or the NCAA may sign student-athletes to long-term contracts for their services. These contracts will extend beyond the period of the student-athlete's eligibility with a given university-firm and will force the professional teams to buy the contract of that individual from the university-firm or the NCAA in order to obtain the individual's services. The cartel would in effect be installing a variant of the reserve clause which sustains much of professional athletics today.

A problem which plagues many universities and especially their athletic departments is the underutilization of capacity. Costly stadiums sit idle except for a few Saturdays per year. The rules of regional conferences such as the Big Ten generally forbid the unversities to rent these stadiums to professional teams without special permission. One can expect to see such rules fall by the wayside in the future. One can anticipate a general attempt by the cartel to allow its members to get fuller utilization of existing capacity; the current move by the NCAA to allow its members to play 11 football games each year is an example.

Movements to share revenues in the classic fashion of cartels will gain strength, both at the national level and at the regional conference level. It is reasonable to expect that the cartel will react to the unprofitability of some of the products in its line by making agreements to terminate scholarship aid in the unprofitable minor sports. Over the long run the NCAA and its regional conferences will apply marginal analysis to each sport and write the rules accordingly. Restrictions by the cartel may be necessary in this case since many university firms exhibit a desire to offer a multi-sport program if others are also doing so. Inexpensive "club" teams will continue to appear in the unprofitable minor sports.

In general, the new rules and regulations of the cartel will tend to equalize competition, revenues, and costs. This will be true regardless of how many fervent paeans are sung to the virtues of amateurism. Violations of the cartel's rules will be made as unattractive as possible by means of lessening any expected gains as to be had from violation and by increasing the expected penalties associated with violation.

# SUMMARY

The major conclusions of this paper are: (1) the intercollegiate athletic market may be usefully viewed as being a cartelized arrangement; (2) the uniqueness of the intercollegiate athletic market is a function primarily of the numerous rules and regulations which operate in the input side of the market; (3) the basic structure of the market has limited the success of the cartel, but not so much that most universities operating "big-time" programs fail to generate a surplus of revenues over costs; and, (4) the pressure of costs against revenues and lack of legal opposition to the cartel's action will lead to predictable future behavior by the cartel.

## FOOTNOTES

[1]It would be more accurate to say that many submarkets exist in intercollegiate athletics due to geographic location, conference rules, differential emphasis upon particular sports and athletics in general, etc. In a very real sense, however, there is a national market for skilled student-athlete inputs, for prestige and ranking, and other factors.

[2]An alternative and in some respects rival organization which operates in the collegiate athletic market is the National Association of Intercollegiate Athletics (NAIA). The NAIA, however, is composed of inexpensive "small-time" athletic programs. The NAIA does little except conduct tournaments and does not engage in the extensive rule-making and practices which so clearly stamp the NCAA as a collusive combination.

[3]The Council of the NCAA, which is largely responsible for governing the NCAA between the annual conventions, is composed of 16 members. Eleven of these members come from colleges and universitites that maintain "big-time" athletic programs.

[4]Alchian and Allen have suggested that the threat or the actual imposition of punishment by the NCAA because of rule infractions by the universities is effective primarily because the NCAA punishments and penalties are related to the academic standing and accreditation of the universities involved. Alchian and Allen contend that the financial support given state universities by their respective legislatures is adversely affected by NCAA sanctions and penalties. However, there is little evidence that NCAA sanctions and penalties have caused any state university to lose academic accreditation or financial support. The major exception to this general lack of evidence appears to be the case where NCAA punishment and penalties cause the university's teams to endure losing seasons and consequently eliminates or reduces alumni contributions which are sensitive to win and loss records (1969).

[5]Almost 90 percent of the approximately 120 universities maintaining a University Division ("big-time") football program in the year 1969 had a conference affiliation.

[6]Statistically significant at .01 level. Data obtained from the NCAA.

[7]Military service, missionary work, and Peace Corps service are permissable reasons for an extension of the five year rule.

[8]This rule is usually not applicable to a transfer student from a junior college.

[9]Several athletic conferences do not permit the practice of red-shirting.

[10]The restrictive rules of the NCAA concerning student-athletes extend well beyond the regulation of price that student-athletes may be paid, methods of competition for their services, etc. In a statute known as the serious misconduct clause, the NCAA also effectively regulates the extracurricular behavior and even the politics of the student-athletes. The serious misconduct statute allows any university-firm ". . . to terminate the financial aid of a student-athlete if he is adjudged to have been guilty of mainfest disobedience through the violation of institutional regulations or established athletic department policies and rules applicable to all student-athletes." (*NCAA Manual,* 1970-71, p. 16). This clause has been used to discourage the participation of student-athletes in peace marches, the growth of Afro-type hair styles, etc.

[11]Data supplied by the NCAA

[12]In an interesting example of cross-subsidization, the considerable monies generated by the University of Notre Dame football team in its 1970 Cotton Bowl appearance were pledge to use as financial aid to disadvantaged students on the South Bend campus. Ostensibly, this was the reason that Notre Dame terminated its long-standing opposition in post-season football bowl games.

[13]Data supplied by the NCAA.

# REFERENCES

Alchian, Armen A. and William R. Allen
    1969      *University of Economics.* Belmont, CA: Wadsworth.
Davenport, David S.
    1969      "Collusive Competition in Major League Baseball." *The American Economist,* 13 (Fall): 6-30.

Jones, J.C.H.
1969        "The Economics of The National Hockey League." *Canadian Journal of Economics,* 2 (February): 1-20.
National Collegiate Athletic Association
1970        *NCAA Manuel, 1970-71.* Kansas City, Missouri: National Collegiate Athletic Association.
1970        *An Analysis of Revenues, Expenses and Management Accounting Practices of Intercollegiate Athletic Programs.* Kansas City, Missouri.
Neale, Walter C.
1964        "The Peculiar Economics of Professional Sports." *Quarterly Journal of Economics,* 78 (February): 1-14.
Padwe, Sandy
1970        "Bigtime College Football is on the Skids." *Look.* 34 (September 22): 66-69.
Rottenberg, Simon
1956        "The Baseball Players' Labor Market." *Journal of Political Economy,* 64 (June): 242-258.
*Wall Street Journal*
*1970        Vol. 50 (September): 1.*

# THE INTERCOLLEGIATE SPORT CARTEL AND ITS CONSEQUENCES FOR ATHLETES

By
George H. Sage

The National Collegiate Athletic Association (NCAA) is the organization that protects and preserves order among colleges and universities engaged in intercollegiate athletics. It is a highly successful business conglomerate whose main function is the production of competitive sports events. Because of its unique structure and a public image that it has fostered, the NCAA is able to exploit its major labor force—student athletes—to an extent that would be impossible in other American industries. Almost all of the rules and regulations of the NCAA benefit the management levels of the organization and are detrimental to the athletes. [1]

While characterization of the NCAA and its activities applies most directly to the universities that sponsor "big-time" football and basketball programs, i.e., the approximately 130 universities that are Division I of the NCAA, it applies in varying degrees to all of the institutions that hold membership in the NCAA. The focus of this paper is on the "big-time," commercialized programs; my comments throughout the paper should be interpreted by the reader to refer to these programs.

# Growth and Development of the NCAA

The NCAA was founded in 1906[2] with a membership of 38 colleges. Its original objective was "the regulation and supervision of college athletics throughout the United States in order that the athletic activities of the colleges and universities of the United States may be maintained on an ethical plane in keeping with the dignity and high purpose of education." The actual control of collegiate athletics was under the jurisdiction of individual member institutions, according to the original charter. Thus, the original purpose of the NCAA was to serve in an advisory capacity to colleges (Stagg, 1946).

Until the late 1940's, the NCAA was not a regulatory body, but at this time it began to deviate from the traditional role as passive observer and consultant in the issues of collegiate sports and undertook a program designed to force member institutions to conform to the policies of the Association under threat of expulsion from membership, if found in non-compliance with these policies. In effect, the NCAA made fundamental changes in its organization to the extent that it became an inspection and accreditation agency with the authority to employ sanctions against member institutions who violated its policies.

The growth in the size of the personnel working in the NCAA and its power in controlling collegiate sports coincided with the increasing commercialization of college athletics, especially football and basketball, after World War II (cf. Scott, 1951). Moreover, it brought with it the concentration and centralization of power and capital. The growth of the NCAA is a textbook example of bureaucratic evolution. Its development involved the growth of a complex administrative network with its own rules, justice, laws, and bureaucrats.[3] Today, the NCAA is the most powerful and prestigious organization regulating intercollegiate athletics in the United States. It has an operating budget of over $22 million (**NCAA News,** September 30, 1980). Income is generated primarily from four sources: television rights; paid admissions to NCAA national championship events, particularly basketball tournaments; sale of publications, and membership dues. About 740 colleges and universities hold active membership in this organization, and all universities which operate "big-time" athletic programs are members of this Association.[4]

Membership in the NCAA is institutional, and its legal authority comes from the colleges and universities which make up its membership and formal structure. While NCAA rules and regulations are formulated at the annual conventions where the institutional representatives come together to vote on policy, the formal authority of the NCAA is highly centralized. This centralization is physically represented by a headquarters located in Shawnee Mission, Kansas, with a full-time staff of over 65 members. It is also represented by the 10-member Executive Committee which transacts the business and administers the affairs of the Association (**NCAA Manual,** 1980-81:33).

# The NCAA As A Cartel

The official public posture of the NCAA is that it is organized only for the promotion of "amateur student-athletics" whose athletes participate in sports "for the educational, physical, mental, and social benefits" they derive therefrom "and to whom participation in . . . sport is an avocation" (**NCAA Manual**, 1980-81:9). The NCAA has always insisted on defining its work force—student athletes— as amateurs. For those who control inter-collegiate athletics, "the amateur ideology helps to validate claims for social status. Commercialism in any form has always been viewed as inconsistent with received and cherished academic values" (Sack, 1980: 5). In fact, the NCAA is a business organization which is part of the entertainment industry whose product is competitive intercollegiate sports events. Sociologist Allen Sack (1980: 5) notes: "By clinging to the myth that big time college athletes are amateurs and that sport is educational, universities can give an air of respectability to what is obviously 'crass' commercial entertainment." Attorney Burton F. Brody (1978: 35) argues that every NCAA rule "exists for one of three purposes: (1) to create the product the Association markets, (2) to maintain the Association's exclusive control of the product, or (3) to keep the cost of producing and selling the product at a minimum."

In order successfully to enforce the last two types of rules that Brody identifies, the NCAA is organized in the form of a cartel, an organization of independent firms which has as its aim some form of restrictive or monopolistic influence on the production and/or sale of a commodity as well as the control of wages of the labor force.[5] Economist James V. Koch (1973: 129) has persuasively argued that the NCAA is a "business cartel composed of university-firms which have varying desires to restrict competition and maximize profits in the area of intercollegiate athletics." For example, the NCAA sets wages that can be paid the largest single group of employees in the industry, the athletes; regulates the mobility of athletes during their career as collegiate athletes; regulates the duration which athletes may be employed; pools and distributes profits of the cartel earned from such activities as televised intercollegiate athletic events and polices the activities of cartel members and levies penalties for infractions (cf. Koch, 1971). Colleges and universities join the NCAA voluntarily, but if they are four-year schools with a "big-time" program, there is no other organization they can join. At a recent Congressional hearing on the NCAA, University of Minnesota President C. Peter Magrath testified: "Membership in the Association is as free-willed and spontaneous as . . . complying with the regulations of the Internal Revenue Service . . . the NCAA regulates the athletic market with the immunity of a protected monopoly" (cf. Good, 1979b: 36).

There are additional ways in which the NCAA functions in a cartel-like manner. All national championships are held under its auspices; indeed, the only national collegiate championships for which individual athletes or teams may compete are those conducted by the NCAA.[6] The Association is the sole negotiating agent for colleges in making TV contracts. The advantage of this monopolistic arrangement is that it gets a lot more money for fewer games. In 1977, it signed a $118 million pact with ABC for the years 1978-81 (cf. Van Dyne, 1977). As noted above, the **NCAA Manual** is the source of power; members are bound by the rules and regulations to this document, and adherence to such makes the big-time athletic industry openly collusive in nature. The power of the NCAA is so great that in the case of Associated Students, Inc. of California State University, Sacramento vs. NCAA 493 F.2d 1251 (9th Cir, 1974), the NCAA was permitted to prevail over a university's own admissions standards and in the face of documented unsatisfactory academic perfomance by the athletes involved.

Evidence of the commercial business nature of "big-time" university athletic programs, standing in much the same relation to commerical sports entertainment as the National Football League (NFL), the National Basketball Association (NBA), etc., is easy to document. The NCAA has a total budget of some $22 million, over $18.5 million of which comes from money earned from sports events, i.e., basketball tournaments, television assessments, etc.; in other words, almost 85 percent of the NCAA's total revenue comes from the staging of commercial sports contests (**NCAA News,** September 30, 1980).[7] Sack (1980:1-2) has noted: "While the NCAA has dedicated itself to stamping out professionalism among athletes, it has never questioned a university's right to stage mass athletic spectacles for commerical gain."

The individual firm in collegiate athletics is the college or university. Over 60 university firms[8] within the NCAA have annual working budgets in excess of $4 million.[9] The formal rules and regulations governing the Association are found in the **NCAA Manual** and it is in this document that the NCAA unwittingly acknowledges that collegiate athletics is a business and that the athletes are wage laborers. On page nine of the 1980-81 **NCAA Manual,** an amateur athlete is defined as one "who engages in a particular sport for the educational, physical, mental, and social benefits he derives therefrom . . . ." The amateur athlete, therefore, does not accept money for sport participation. In its Constitution, also published in the **NCAA Manual,** the Association declares that one of its purposes is to "comply with . . . standards of . . . amateurism." But, as incredible as it may seem, beginning on page 17 of this same **Manual** is a section on "Financial Aid," the key provision of which is: "Financial aid . . . may be awarded for any term . . . during which a student athlete is in regular attendance . . . ." So much for the NCAA as an amateur athletic agency! Let's not kid ourselves, college athletes are professionals as soon as they sign an athletic grant-in-aid. The "grant" is a work contract, and the collegiate athlete is a worker who sells his labor power—that is, his ability to produce and athletic spectacle that draws crowds—to an employer. As Brody (1979:15) noted: "[T]he NCAA is not concerned that an athlete has received pay for his skill; but rather, it is only concerned that the source of the payment be one authorized by the Association. Only payments from unauthorized sources professionalize."

is promoted by the Association is largely a myth promulgated to conceal its real structure and functions and to rationalize its domination. Lewis Cole (1976: 42) noted: " . . . to consider . . . [the NCAA] as merely a regulator of intramural contests is like regarding the directors of General Motors as consultants who merely advise the company on safety precautions."

# CONSEQUENCES OF THE NCAA CARTEL FOR COLLEGE ATHLETES

The actual consequences of cartelized industries are varied and complex, depending upon such factors as the commodity produced and sold, the amount of the market actually under the control of the cartel, etc. But in most cases the negative consequences impact most heavily upon labor and consumers, since cartels typically restrict production and sale through, for example, wage and price fixing. Space limitations preclude a comprehensive analysis of the consequences of the NCAA on trade restraints; instead, I shall briefly examine how cartel-wide policies of the Association protect and raise profits for the Association itself and for the individual university-firms while holding down costs of wages and restricting the mobility and other activities of the largest employee group in intercollegiate athletics, the athletes. The areas in which NCAA regulations impact most adversely on athletes involve payment for labor (scholarships), recruitment, and transfer from one college to another.

In the absence of an open, competitive market, which is the case with intercollegiate athletics, a cartel is free to pay its employees whatever it wishes. The **NCAA Manual** very specifically prescribes the payment that a collegiate athlete may be paid by any university-firm in exchange for his athletic performance. The athlete may be paid a sum not to exceed his educational expenses, i.e., tuition and fees, room and board, and required course-related books (**NCAA Manual,** 1980-81: 12.)[10] At 1981 prices, the cash value of this payment averages about $5,000; of course, the value of these educational expenses is not the same at all university-firms, and this does introduce an element of differential wages into the market. However, the rules which regulate the salary of athletes are stacked heavily in favor of the university-firms at the expense of the student-athlete.[11]

It should be obvious who the beneficiaries are to this cartel-wide limitation on the salary that can be paid to athletes by university-firms. Stripped of the rhetoric used to convince the athletes and the public that athletic scholarships are philanthropic "free rides" and that athletes are living in the best of all possible worlds, the NCAA scholarship is first and foremost a conspiracy to hold down athletes' wages. College athletes are caught in the clutches of the NCAA. They cannot sell their skills on the open market to the highest bidder because there is a wage limit that all cartel members observe. This works to the great disadvantage of athletes, some of whom are very highly skilled, and to the advantage of the NCAA cartel.[12] Some

Perhaps the best sources for an accurate assessment of the nature of "big-time"collegiate sports are university presidents, athletic directors, coaches, and athletes, the persons who are most closely involved with these programs. By and large, they have no delusions about the program. When a football coach was fired at Purdue, the President of the university justified this action by saying: "The main thing is keeping gate receipts at the games as high as possible" (**Rocky Mountain News,** November 27, 1976a; 107). In explaining dismissal of the football coach at Oregon, the athletic director explained: "Economic realities make it a necessity that Oregon establish a competitive program" (**Rocky Mountain News,** November 27, 1976b: 107). One of the most perceptive insights into the relationship between "big-time" collegiate athletics and higher education was made by the Ohio State University President: "I take great comfort in the keen awareness that football and . . . this university tend to be totally separate" (Scorecard, 1979: 7). At the University of Michigan the athletic department is incorporated; it is an independent corporation. Michigan's athletic director, Don Canham, with respect to "bigtime" collegiate athletics, said: "This is business, big business. Anyone who hasn't figured that out by now is a damned fool" (cf. Denlinger and Shapiro, 1975: 252). Eddie Crowder, athletic director at the University of Colorado, echoed Canham's remark: "The difficult thing for the public to understand is that we're a business" (cf. **Rocky Mountain News,** December 12, 1979: 98). Exalted Alabama football coach, Paul "Bear" Bryant, (1974: 325) makes it clear that he is running a commercial business: "I used to go along with the idea that football players on scholarship were 'student athletes,' which is what NCAA calls them. We are kidding ourselves . . . . We don't have to say that and we shouldn't. At the level we play, the boy is really an athlete first and a student second." Frank Kush, former football coach at Arizona State, said: "My job is to win football games. I've got to put people in the stadium, make money for the university, keep the alumni happy and give the school a winning reputation" (cf. Michener, 1976: 260). Denny Crum, basketball coach at Louisville, noted: "We're . . . in the business of filling the gym" (cf. McDermott, 1977: 22). Frank Maloney, football coach at Syracuse University, said: "The sole concern in big-time college sports is money and winning" (cf. **Sport,** 1980: 13). The inescapable impression that these statements convey is that the system of "big time" intercollegiate athletics is organized to manipulate 18-to-21-year-old men to come to a university and provide it with a winning team, some money, and, perhaps, fame.

The athletes themselves acknowledge that they are in a business and they realize what their job as an athlete really is. UCLA basketball player, Andre McCarter declared: "There's no rah-rah stuff about the game . . . . We look at it like a business, like a job . . . . It's like the pros, except you don't have any income" (cf. McDermott, 1974). Oakland Raiders quarterback, Kenny Stabler, had no delusions about college football: "I went to college to play football, not for education" (ef. Jones, 1977: 92).

It is clear that a number of indicators convincingly show that the NCAA has many of the characteristics of a business and that the official image that collegiate athletes generate 10 to 20 times as much income as their scholarship is worth to a school; a few generate as much as 100 times what they receive. The benefits of this wage-fixing to the NCAA and the university-firms are quite evident: the lower the total wage bill paid by the employer, the greater will be the profits. In effect, then, intercollegiate athletics make the labor of the many the wealth of the few. At a recent Congressional hearing, attorney Lana Tyree charged: "The NCAA can market products and use the athletes' images to do so. By restricting the amount of scholarships ...and by restraining the athlete, they have cornered the market . . . Why should the athlete generating a financial empire be singled out for restraint?" (cf. Good, 1979b: 38).

The actual market value of many collegiate athletes is demonstrated by the salaries that are paid them when they are signed to a professional sport contract; a professional contract paying 20 times the college salary is not uncommon. The extent to which the NCAA restricts athlete's salaries is vividly illustrated in the average salaries of college athletes, about $5,000, and the salaries of professional athletes: $78,000 in the NFL, $140,000 in the NBA, $130,000 in Major League baseball, $96,000 in the NHL. Granted that the athletes in the professional leagues are more experienced and more highly skilled, on the average, than collegiate athletes, it is likely that collegiate athletes could command a much higher salary if they were able to sell their skills in an open market.[13]

The athletic scholarship is only one of the many NCAA regulations designed to reduce competition among university-firms for athletic talent. An athlete who enrolls and participates in sports at on NCAA institution and then subsequently transfers to another university is ineligible for athletic competition at the latter institution for one full year. Requiring all transferring students to sit out one full season of competition seriously reduces the interorganizational mobility of collegiate athletes, thus stabilizing the labor market within college athletics and undoubtedly saving the NCAA cartel untold dollars which might otherwise be spent by institutions competitively bidding for the most highly skilled workers. Koch (1971: 252-53) has eloquently described the purpose behind the "transfer rules;" " . . . the rules are most explicitly intended to prevent one well-heeled university-firm from raiding the ranks of another university-firm and hiring away its best student-athletes."

Here again, it is easy to see who are the major beneficiaries of this restriction on college athletes' mobility. On the one hand the NCAA promotes and sells competition through sports, but severely restricts competition for wage labor within its own industry because the complex set of rules and practices that the NCAA has adopted all but eliminates business competition among its members. Athletic directions and coaches are fond of explicating the virtues of competition, but they have formulated cartel-wide regulations to avoid competing for the employees who actually produce the product of collegiate athletics, the sports event. Ironically, it is only the athlete-employees whose mobility is restricted. The NCAA does not apply such restrictions to others in the athletic productive process—the athletic directors and coaches. Indeed, the "jumping" of contracts by college coaches is common. Between 1975 and 1978, Washington State University had three head football coaches leave with time remaining on their long-term contracts; each coached at another university the following year. As Paul Good (1979a: 62) noted, in examining the feelings of betrayal felt by the athletes when a coach resigns after recruiting them: "Student-athletes are exhorted to demonstrate loyalty to their schools and are penalized by losing a year's eligibility if they transfer to another school. But if the Astro-Turf looks greener on the other side to the coach, he's gone without penalty."

In addition to policies limiting athletes' wages and mobility potential, there is the "letter of intent" regulation which prevents an athlete from further shopping for a university to attend after he has signed the "letter"; there is the "scholarship limitation" policy which limits the number of grants-in-aid a university-firm may grant; and there is the recently enacted policy which makes freshmen eligible for varsity competition. The effect of these rules, and others too numerous to mention here, is to restrain competition and reduce costs among cartel members, to the disadvantage of collegiate athletes.'' When one analyzes the NCAA rules and regulations that are applied to athletes from the standpoint of—who benefits?—it is readily apparent that the prime beneficiaries are the NCAA and its member firms, major universities.

It seems rather clear, then, that while the official ideology of the NCAA proclaims its promotion of amateur sports, its operative goals involve the maximization of power and oppression over student-athletes. As a structure of domination, the NCAA is organized to achieve the commands of those who control it. Student-athletes are expected to comply with the formally rational expectations of their roles. At the same time, they are excluded from participation in substantive decisions and are not even privy to information about them (cf. Weber, 1968).

# THE PROSPECTS FOR CHANGE

One might wonder why the public and the athletes themselves do not object to the conditions which exist that enable the NCAA to exploit collegiate athletes. The answer basically lies in the ability of the NCAA to manage the impression that people have about it. Administrative secrecy and selective misinformation exclude the public from accurate knowledge of the goals of the NCAA. Those in control of the NCAA use its resources, such as its publicity and communications machinery, executive staff, and financial resources to delude the athletes and the public about its real interests; moreover, they have the organizational skill to wrap themselves in an aura of "do gooding" so that criticisms of the NCAA can be interpreted as unpatriotic or "traitorous" attacks upon a pillar of American society.

There is a reluctance on the part of people to believe there is anything wrong with the NCAA and collegiate athletics because the public has been duped to believe the good of the NCAA by an elaborate publicity program that masks the reality of those who profit from it. By and large, the American people cherish the illusion that collegiate athletics are merely "fun and games."

As for the athletes, by design and default, they are weak in influence; they constitute a disorganized majority without a common will or impulse, and this isolation and apathy lead to powerlessness. The dice are loaded in favor of the NCAA, since it owns and controls collegiate sports' productive assets. Equally important, though, athletes are expected to view the oppressive conditions as valid, and most athletes do. They consider the athletic authorities as legitimate and competent sources of authority, and they submit readily to the authoritarian and nondemocratic policies of the NCAA. The result is that the NCAA has a stable work force which is faithful both to the conditions and relations of production.

This situation should not be surprising since athletes are the products of a series of social institutions which initiate youth into the formation of a consciousness. These institutional relationships tailor the self-concepts, aspirations, etc., that help legitimate hierarchically structured organizational and economic inequality. Family experience has a significant impact on the personal consciousness of children, and there is a tendency for parents to reproduce in their offspring a consciousness about society roughly comparable to their own (cf. Henry, 1965; Kanter, 1972). Youth and high school athletic programs socialize the participants into "sports world's" collective beliefs, a major pillar of which is the acceptance of a hierarchy of authority. Finally, the orientation of the U.S. educational system reduces discontent over the hierarchical division of labor; the entire apparatus of American education foster a consciousness that validates respect and submitting readily to authority (cf. Bowles and Gintis, 1976). There is considerable evidence that collegiate athletes have been socialized into a basically conservative perspective. Thus, the athlete does not challenge the NCAA because those who direct college athletics control the physical means of force, i.e. eligibility, and also because they accept as justified the "basic legitimations of domination" (cf. Gerth and Mills, 1958: 78).

What are the chances for change within the intercollegiate athletic enterprise that would redress the enormous inequalities and allow the athletes a more equitable share of the revenues which their labor generates? The prospects are not bright. So long as the illusion persists that intercollegiate athletics are just "fun and games" and have primarily an educational function, there will be no perceived need for change on the part of the general public or the athletes.

But if reform is to come about in the NCAA, it will most likely have to start with the athletes. A first step would be in their recognition of belonging to a group with similar grievances and aspirations. This recognition would involve divesting themselves of many current delusions about the NCAA and would also include the development of a cohesiveness that would bind them together in opposition to the current NCAA structural arrangements. To be sure, this would be an extraordinary achievement, and there are few signs that such a movement has ever begun. The isolation that collegiate athletics forces upon its athletes makes the very notion of shared interests difficult to imagine.

The most promising potential for the protection of student-athletes' rights and interests would be the creation of some agency similar to the "player" associations found in professional sports. At present, collegiate athletes have no one looking after their interests, protecting and defending them against exploitation and abuse from the intercollegiate sports cartel. There are agencies in America who speak for and defend the right of wildlife, migrant farm workers, Indians, Blacks, poor Appalachian whites, and various and sundry oppressed and exploited animals and humans, but so far, no agency or individual has emerged to champion the civil rights of some 180,000 student-athletes participating annually in NCAA-sponsored athletic programs.[15]

The only effort that has been made to address the inequalities on collegiate athletics and help athletes gain control over their educational and athletic experiences is the recently created Center For Athletes Rights and Education (CARE) (Sports for the People, 1980). Organizers of CARE plan the Center to provide the following services to athletes: (1) Counseling about scholarships, tutorial programs, and the quality of medical care available at various colleges; (2) legal services to athletes; (3) protection of athletes from abuses by coaches; (4) a guide to help athletes in the selection of a college. Although CARE is not an athletes' union, if successful with its early projects, it may well evolve into a union or "players organization" of some kind. It is too early at this time to predict CARE's course of action; it has the potential to help the athletes see through the institutional myths perpetrated by the NCAA—to demystify the structure by which the NCAA is governed, the arbitrary rules, and the absence of initiative allowed the athletes themselves. CARE's task will not be an easy one; we can only wait and watch the consequences of this experiment. One thing seems clear, though, the most long-term, general, and rational interest of collegiate athletes lies in some agency evolving which can overturn the exploitative relations which keep them, individually and collectively, from sharing in the revenues that their labor produces.

## FOOTNOTES

[1]Former University of Southern California football coach, John McKay (quoted in Underwood, 1976) has noted that every piece of legislation passed recently by the NCAA has been against the athlete.

[2]The original name of the organization was the Intercollegiate Athletic Association of the United States; this name was changed to the National Collegiate Athletic Association in 1910.

[3]For an excellent network analysis of the transformation of the NCAA from a loose confederation of colleges created for mutual support and dissemination of rules into a powerful agent of control capable of bringing serious financial loss on its members caught violating its rules, see Stern (1979).

[4]Its only serious rival to men's athletics, the NAIA, claims as members only those colleges operating small-time programs. The NAIA has no television contract. The AIAW controls collegiate women's sports; this paper is not addressed to women's programs although trends in the AIAW suggest that comments made in this paper may soon apply to the AIAW.

[5]The notion that the NCAA approximates a cartelized arrangement is not original with this paper (cf. Koch, 1973)

[6]The NAIA does hold championships, but its champions are not recognized by the general public to be the "real" national champions.

[7]It should not be surprising, then, why the NCAA division I basketball tournament has been expanded four times between 1974 and 1980. The logic is clear enough: the NCAA and major universities need money to operate and will use hired employees (athletes) to raise it. In 1980 net receipts of the basketball tournament were $11,348,724. Each of the final four teams in the Division I received payments of $326,377, plus expenses; even first and second round losers each received $81,594, plus expenses (*NCAA News*, August 31, 1980). But not one cent of this additional financial windfall that was generated by the athletes went directly to the athletes themselves (other than inexpensive memorabilia)!

The same financial principle applies for football bowl games. It is little wonder that their number has increased over the years to the present 15 post-season bowls. In 1979-80 the 15 bowl games generated a record $23,445,035 in gross receipts. The 30 participating universities received $18,051,932, but the athletes received no increase or bonus in their wages (athletic scholarship).

[8]I am indebted to Koch (1971, 1973) for this accurately descriptive term.

[9]In 1977 the Internal Revenue Service office in Dallas, Texas informed the Cotton Bowl Association, Texas Christian University, Southern Methodist University, and the University of Kansas that the income earned from radio and television broadcasting rights constituted "unrelated business" income and does not have a purpose of the institutions. The IRS indicated it planned to tax that income (cf. *NCAA News*, May 15, 1977).

[10]The whole issue of whether college students should be awarded "scholarships" based solely on athletic ability, and if so what form it should take, i.e. need, will not be addressed in this paper. My personal preference would be for all collegiate financial aid to be based on need, but if scholarships are to be based on talent, i.e., athletic ability, then the athletic talented at an institution should receive only the same proportion of scholarship aid that is awarded for other forms of talent.

[11]Allen Sack (1977) has written eloquently on this issue.

[12]Even if an athlete is extremely poor, he cannot receive financial aid exceeding "commonly accepted educational expenses," and the NCAA has the federal courts in its corner on this issue. In May 1980 the Supreme Court turned away arguments by world class sprinter Clifford Wiley that NCAA limits on other aid to students on athletic scholarships is unconstitutional. Wiley, one of nine children from what the courts described as "desperately poor," received an athletic scholarship to the University of Kansas in 1974 worth $2,621. He also obtained a federal Basic Educational Opportunity Grant of $1,400. Since Wiley was receiving aid totaling some $200 more than accepted educational expenses at Kansas, he was declared ineligible for NCAA competition. (*Rocky Mountain News*, May 13, 1980: 85).

[13]It is not suggested that professional sports is a completely open market. Each of

the professional leagues has cartel-like characteristics.
[14]See Koch (1973) for a fuller discussion of the consequences of these policies for athletes.
[15]There are perhaps twice this many college athletes, when athletes participating under the auspices of the NAIA and the AIAW are considered.

# REFERENCES

Bowles, Samuel and Herbert Gintis
1976        *Schooling in Capitalist America.* New York: Basic Books.
Brody, Burton F.
1978        "Rights, Regulations, and Responsibilities in Physical Education and Competitive Sport in College and Universities." *Proceedings of the NAPE CW/NCPEAM.* Chicago: University of Illinois at Chicago Circle.
1979        "Toward Meaningful Due Process for NCAA Student Athletes." *Arena Review* 3(October): 9-16.
Bryant, Paul W. and John Underwood
1974        *Bear: The Hard Life and Good Times of Alabama's Coach Bryant.* Boston: Little, Brown.
Cole, Lewis
1976        "The NCAA: Mass Culture as Big Business." *Change,* 8 (September): 42-46.
Denlinger, Kenneth and Leonard Shapiro
1975        *Athletes for Sale.* New York: Thomas Y. Crowell.
Gerth, H. and C. Wright Mills
1958        *From Max Weber: Essays in Sociology.* New York: Oxford University Press.
Good, Paul
1979a       "I Feel Betrayed." *Sport,* 68 (June): 62-68.
1979b       "The Shocking Inequities of the NCAA." *Sport.* 68 (January): 35-38.
Henry, Jules
1965        *Culture Against Man.* New York: Vintage Press.
Jones, R. F.
1977        "Gettin' Nowhere Fast." *Sports Illustrated,* 47 (September 19): 88-102.
Kanter, Rosabeth Moss
1972        "The Organization Child: Experience Management in a Nursery School." *Sociology of Education,* 45: 186-211.
Kennedy, Ray and Nancy Williamson
1978        "Money: The Monster Threatening Sports." *Sports Illustrated,* 49 (July 17): 29-88.
Koch, James V.
1971        "The Economics of 'Big-Time' Intercollegiate Athletics." *Social Science Quarterly.* 52: 248-260.
1973        "A Troubled Cartel: The NCAA." *Law and Contemporary Problems,* 38: 129-150.

McDermott, Barry
1974        "After 88 Comes Zero." *Sports Illustrated.* 40 (January 28):
1977        "Dunkers Are Strutting Their Stuff." *Sports Illustrated,* 46 (March 14): 20-27.
Michener, James A.
1976        *Sports in America.* New York. Random House.
National Collegiate Athletic Association (NCAA)
1980        *NCAA Manual, 1980-81,* Shawnee Mission, Kansas: NCAA.

*NCAA News.* (May 15, 1977); (August 31, 1980); (September 30, 1980).

*Rocky Mountain News*
1976a       "Purdue coach Alex Agase is Fired." November 27: 107.
1976b       "Oregon Dismisses Coach Don Read." November 27: 107.
1979        Quote of Eddie Crowder. December 12:; 98.
1980        May 13: 85.
Sack, Allen I.
1977        "Big time College Football: Whose Free Ride?" *Quest,* 27: 87-96.
1980        "Amateurism as an Exploitative Ideology." Paper presented at the annual meeting of the American Alliance for Health, Physical Education, Recreation and Dance, Detroit.
Scorecard
1979        *Sports Illustrated.* 50 (January 8): 7.
Scott, Harry A.
1951        *Competitive Sports in Schools and Colleges.* New York: Harper Brothers.
*Sport*
1980        Quote of Frank Maloney. 71 (December): 13.
*Sports for the People*
1980        "The Center for Athletes Rights and Education." Press Release.
Stagg, Paul
1946        *The Development of the National Collegiate Athletic Association in Relationship to Intercollegiate Athletics in the United States.* Doctoral dissertation, New York University.
Stern, Robert N.
1979        "The Development of an Interorganizational Control Network: The Case of Intercollegiate Athletics." *Administrative Science Quarterly,* 24: 242-266.
Underwood, John
1976        "Football's Dilemma: Bowls or Playoffs." *Sports Illustrated,* 44 (January 19): 26-29.
Van Dyne, L.
1977        "ABC Will Pay $118 Million to Televise College Football." *The Chronicle of Higher Education.* (June 27): 6.
Weber, Max
1968        *Economy and Society.* New York: Bedminster Press.

# AIAW: THE GREENING OF AMERICAN ATHLETICS

## By
## Bonnie Slatton

The format of this book reflects the continued belief that there is SPORT
. . . and then there is "women's sport." Issues affecting governance of intercollegiate sport ostensibly affect female as well as male athletes. Factors
such as the value of athletics to campus life, athletes' rights, economics of
big time intercollegiate athletics affect female as well as male athletic structures. However, because of basic differences in philosophy and stages of
development of men's and women's programs, perhaps a separate chapter
is warranted.

Ten years ago, with the exception of professional members of the National Association for Girls and Women in Sport (NAGWS) and the
American Alliance for Health, Physical Education, Recreation and Dance
(AAHPERD), interest in creating national championship opportunites for
female athletes did not exist.[1] Despite an indifferent and apathetic society
and the leadership of AAHPERD and NAGWS, the Association for Intercollegiate Athletics for Women (AIAW) was born in 1971.

In the early years of AIAW, the basic philosophical foundations were
built. The concepts were simple. The idea was to create an intercollegiate
athletic model which was educationally sound, financially prudent and concerned primarily with the welfare and the enrichment of the student athlete.
This commitment to educationally focused programs was a normal
outgrowth of the evolution of a women's program. Having been carefully
controlled by professional physical educators, intercollegiate athletics for
women began primarily in the form of play days and sports days, with emphasis on participation rather than competition, and only recently evolved
into highly competitive programs. The Division for Girls and Women in
Sport (DGWS) was the controlling body in the 1950's, and recognizing the
need for expansion of national championship programs, the Commission
on Intercollegiate Athletics For Women was formed in the 1960's. The need

for an institutional membership organization finally resulted in the creation of the Association For Intercollegiate Athletics For Women in the 1970's. This change in governance structure was functional rather than philosophical, as will be discussed later in this chapter. For a thorough analysis of the historical development of governance of women's intercollegiate athletics, the reader is referred to a study by Hunt (1976). Simultaneously, under the legislative edict of Title IX, there was a commitment by institutions to provide equal opportunities for all student athletes. While striving for equal opportunity for female athletes, it has often been difficult to maintain steadfast commitment to the philosophical tenets of AIAW. In an effort to provide immediate quantitative benefits to female athletes similar to those afforded male athletes, some have lost sight of the struggle to establish an alternate model of intercollegiate athletics. A case in point was the leadership issue, AIAW moving from a no-scholarship policy prior to 1972 to an attempt in 1976 for tuition-only scholarships and finally to a position of full-athletic scholarships. Indeed, some critics of the women's sports movement have charged that "Title IX will leave intact a socially acceptable, and essentially sexist, definition of sports and women's place in them." (Boutillier and San Giovanni, 1980: 12). While there is concern that in the struggle for equal opportunity, women's programs are simply duplicating the status quo, there is strong evidence that AIAW, through its governance structure and its policies and procedures, still has the potential for creating radical change in intercollegiate sport. An examination of the consistency between the goals of AIAW and its current rules and regulations provides the necessary evidence.

The question is: to what extent is the philosophical foundation reflected in the rules and regulations of the Association? Any organization can list goals and objectives which would warm the heart of any true educator. But the test occurs only when the actual practices are analyzed in the light of goals and objectives.

What does an educationally sound athletic program mean? It means that student rights are as important as institutional rights; and, it means that athletes where possible are treated like other undergraduate students. It means that an athlete's life ought to permit her to attain her academic goals as well as her athletic goals.

AIAW, through its organizational structure and its rules and regulations, has sought to foster broad programs of women's intercollegiate athletics which are consistent with the educational aims and objectives of the member schools and in accordance with the philosophy and standards of NAGWS. Through direct involvement of student athletes in policy-making and with the guarantee of due process to all student athletes and institutions, AIAW has created an alternative to existing intercollegiate governance structuures. As AIAW representatives strive to maintain a reasonable balance between institutional and student athlete rights, it is clear that their regulations have consistently **favored rights of students over the rights of institutions.**

# Institutional vs. Student Rights

Considerable confusion exists in both the NCAA and AIAW with regard to institutional rights vis-a-vis student rights. Prior to discussing this topic, the following analogy if given to clarify separation of rights and powers, with the federal government being analogous to a national governance organization (AIAW), the state government to an institution (a given college or university), and the citizen to a student athlete. While states are permitted to have restrictive laws, e.g. liquor laws, the citizen in that state loses the right to appeal, since the federal government has transferred that authority to the states and/or counties. On the other hand, there are certain rights which belong to an individual citizen which cannot be infringed upon by more restrictive state policies, e.g. freedom of speech. The citizen, therefore, never loses the right to appeal an infringement in this area. Clarification on the matter is currently being sought by those in AIAW. Most assuredly the AIAW has paid considerable attention to the rights of student athletes since one of the cornerstones of the basic philosophy has been to place the welfare of the student above all other considerations. When little was financially invested in a student, the principle mandating student rights was easy to endorse. However, as financial investments in students have significantly increased, so also has the call to increase institutional rights. The crucial question in each AIAW piece of legislation is: Should the regulation give the power of decision to the institution (institutional prerogative) or to the individual student athlete (student athlete prerogative)? For example, current AIAW legislation permits a student to participate in no more than four intercollegiate seasons of play in any one sport. Should an institution have the right to determine that a student may participate in only two or three seasons of play? If so, this would indicate an area where the institutional prerogative prevailed. If not, then the prerogative would lie with the student athlete as to whether she wished to avail herself of the opportunity to compete in four seasons of play.

All regulations should be approached in an identical manner to clarify the right of an institution to impose more restrictive rules in specific areas. Upon clarification of each rule institutions and student athletes will be able clearly to identify instances in which an institution may be allowed to apply more restrictive rules than those stated by AIAW. It is important to note that in all instances where restrictive rules may be permitted, the student athlete will lose the right to appeal directly to the AIAW for violation of her student rights. In other words, in areas where AIAW permits the institution to impose a more restrictive rule there can be no recourse from the student to AIAW because the institution has elected to exercise that option.

## Student Involvement in Governance

Perhaps one of the most significant departures from intercollegiate governance patterns has been direct involvement of student athletes at all levels of AIAW. At the executive board level, students serve as voting members and thus are able not only to vote on proposed policies and procedures but to initiate legislation. State and regional AIAW's involve students as voting representatives, thus guaranteeing voice throughout the governance network. Since the AIAW membership form requests the name of a student athlete representative, institutions are encouraged to involve students at the campus level. In fact, many institutions have a governance board for women's athletics consisting of equal representation of student athletes and coaches. As voting members of the Ethics and Eligibility Committee, student-athletes have direct input for policies ranging from eligibility requirements to serving on Appeals Boards. As members of the Appeals Board, students participate in decisions as to whether penalties shall be mitigated. Every Sport Committee in AIAW has a 20 percent representation of students. The involvement of student athletes at committee as well as board levels should be an effective measure in avoiding exploitation of student athletes. Each year prior to the AIAW Delegate Assembly, the student representatives meet to discuss proposed legislation and its impact on student athletes. As they have become more informed and more knowledgeable about parliamentary procedures, students have begun to speak out at state, regional and national delegate assemblies, taking positions on proposed legislation and fighting for its adoption or rejection. One significant issue on which the assembly was persuaded by the appeal of student athletes was that of the transfer policy at the 1980 Delegate Assembly. Student delegates appealed to the assembly to be considerate of their basic right to participate and to find a compromise which would simultaneously protect the institution and the student athlete. Such a compromise was reached at the 1981 Delegate Assembly and the resultant policy basically states that if a student athlete gives fair warning of intent to transfer and the institution has adequate time to find a comparable athlete, neither the institution nor the student athlete is penalized. However, if the student athlete fails to provide the institution with adequate time to find a replacement, the student loses the right to participate immediately at the new institution.

AIAW's commitment to student athletes' involvement in the governance structure is consistent with the Amateur Sport Act of 1978, which requires that at least 20 percent of the voting representatives on each national governing board be athletes. Being a multisport organization AIAW is not required by the Act to meet the 20 percent athlete requirement, but it is interesting to note that AIAW has established this as a goal prior to the Amateur Sport Act. Indeed, the guarantee of student athlete voting power throughout the governance structure of AIAW is consistent with the 1974 Position Paper on Intercollegiate Athletics For Women which stated in part:

 ".... The enrichment of the life of the participant is the focus and reason for the existence of any athletic program. All decisions would be made with this fact in mind.

 The participants in athletic programs, including players, coaches and support personnel should have access to and representation on the policy-making group or campus and in sport governing organization . . . " (AIAW, 1980: 80).

It is the belief of those in AIAW that if the exploitation of student athletes is to be avoided, adequate voice and power must be assured to those who are governed.

**Student Rights: Due Process.** Focus on student welfare and student rights is most apparent through policies and procedures which guarantee due process to every student athlete and to each institution. Failure of NCAA to provide adequate appeal procedures and due process to student athletes has been well publicized and led to the investigation by the Subcommittee on Oversight and Investigations of the House Government Operations Committee. As a result of these hearings the congressional committee recommended over 150 changes in NCAA policies and procedures to ensure due process and fairness. As stated by John Underwood ". . . what stood out consistently was how ineffective the NCAA is in clarifying its own procedures" (Underwood, 1979: 213).

While certainly not perfect in its procedures, the AIAW has ensured that both the institution and the individual student athlete can utilize the due process and appeal systems in AIAW. Even after exhausting the due process system, mitigation of the penalty can be sought by the institution and/or the student athlete. In short, both the student athlete and the institution are judged innocent until proven guilty rather than the reverse.

The dual obligation of AIAW to protect the rights of institutions and student athletes and to promote fair due process and appeals systems is in tune with general societal standards but is well ahead of its time in athletic governance. The impact of this system on the regulation of intercollegiate athletics should not be underestimated, however. By guaranteeing student athletes and institutions direct appeal procedures, every decision affecting an individual student or a given institution may be questioned. If student athletes utilize these procedures in addition to exercising their power as voting representatives on policy making bodies, there should be virtually no opportunity for exploitation of student athletes.

**Student Rights: Significant Rules.** In addition to a carefully planned organizational structure which answers athlete and institution rights and powers through direct participation, AIAW has established rules and regulations which offer alternatives to rules and regulations established by other collegiate governance organizations. Since women have been denied access to programs in the past, some rules such as "no tainting" allowing intercollegiate athletes to compete with professionals without loss of eligibility, maximizes the participation of all women athletes. In addition, student athletes are encouraged to participate on national and international teams and when such participation has an effect on eligibility, a waiver is generally granted. Although many rules differ from those of other governing bodies, possibly the most noteworthy are those in the areas of recruitment and transfer.

# Recruitment

In an attempt to protect a student's right to privacy, AIAW coaches and athletic personnel are prohibited from off-campus recruitment efforts which involve direct contact with prospective student athletes, their families or coaches. The harrassment of prospective male student athletes has been well documented and has led many prominent male coaches to call for considerable reform in recruiting regulations. In addition to the protection of student athletes, colleges and universities retain the services of personnel who would otherwise be engaging in time consuming and financially costly recruiting trips. Again recent comments by major college coaches attest to the demoralizing experience of recruiting, for both the athlete and the coach. In the November, 1980 NCAA Newsletter, Johnny Majors, football coach at the University of Tennessee stated:

"I just don't think it's very realistic. I'm running around the country, running into the same coaches at the airport, running into each other outside the high school coaches' office and passing each other on the kid's doorstep. It's ridiculous the way we hang around, the way we're spending the time and money recruiting.

And if it's not screwing us up—and it is, because if we spent more time on campus we wouldn't be having so many kids getting in trouble academically—it's screwing the kids up; recruiting is the only time they'll ever have so much attention. I don't see that it prepares them for much in particular. They're never going to be treated so special again" (Majors, 1980: 2).

AIAW regulations also prohibit subsidized visits to campus unless such benefits are a regular part of the admissions practice for all disciplines at the institution. While this regulation is consistent with the commitment to treating student athletes as students first as well as the commitment to financially reasonable programs, concern has been expressed that economically disadvantaged students are severely restricted by this policy. AIAW is currently considering a plan whereby the needs of these students will be addressed and solved.

Of all problems besetting intercollegiate athletics, there is none more visible than those in the area of recruitment, which contributes not only to a financial crisis but an ethical crisis for this nation's intercollegiate programs. The duplication of such procedures for women's athletics would be the ultimate folly of our times.

# Transfer Rule

The transfer rule vividly illustrates two significantly different approaches to athletics. While under NCAA rules, a transferring student athlete may receive financial aid based on athletic ability but may not participate during the year of transfer, the AIAW rule permits participation (if adequate warning is given of intent to transfer) but generally denies athletically based financial aid for that year, unless the institution from which the student athlete is transferring supports the student's appeal for financial aid. This rule reflects AIAW's commitment to provide participation opportunites for a group which has been severely disadvantaged in this area. It also reflects the belief that student athletes ought to be treated where possible as all other undergraduate students. It would be inconceivable for those in higher education to prevent an outstanding musician from participating in an extra curricular activity when she/he transferred to a new institution. The question comes once again to the fair balance between the rights of an institution and the rights of a student athlete.

## Broadly Based Programs

From its inception AIAW has been committed to a broadly based program, the assumption being that to the participant, all sports are major and provide valuable experience. Throughout the development of sport programs for girls and women, a recurring theme has been "a sport for every girl, a girl for every sport," and in many ways that view continues to be promulgated. Although we have moved substantially away from the "playday" and "sports day" concept, there remains a commitment to equal emphasis on all sports. This basic belief is reflected in the financial aid limits established by AIAW, numbers being based on players necessary to field a team rather than the revenue potential of the team.

Commitment to broadly based programs is further reflected in AIAW television contracts, a requirement being that all sports be given some exposure. Since major networks and cable television are generally interested in one or two sports with established spectator appeal, this basic requirement in contract negotiations not only enhances development of current "lesser known" sports but also through exposure may give impetus to development of more varied sport programs for future generations.

The commitment to the development of a broadly based program becomes more feasible when viewed simultaneously with the AIAW commitment to develop for each sport a financially prudent model. This approach also reflects societal determination to become participants as well as spectators. The move being made by some institutions to eliminate so called "minor sports" and to allocate all current institutional resources to two or three sports strongly conflicts with society's demand to participate. The retention of a broadly based sports program, however, is contingent on the ability of the national governing organization to create a financially prudent model for each and every sport, **based**, perhaps, on AIAW's recruiting approach and tuition-only scholarships.

It should not be surprising that those in women's athletics would elect to develop programs with many sport options at minimal cost to the institution, since the opportunity to participate was largely denied to women prior to the 1970's. While women's programs are at vastly different stages of development from men's, the flexibility to meet the competitive level of each team through a divisional declaration for each sport is important to the institution for financial reasons and important to the individual student athlete for competitive reasons.

While an institution joins NCAA with its entire program generally designated in one division, AIAW permits an institution to place a particular sport in any of its three divisions. Hence it is possible that a single institution could have sports in all three AIAW divisions. The fact that institutions can declare divisions by sport leads to another characteristic of women's governance which is different from existing structures. All AIAW member institutions vote on policies and procedures for the regulation of intercollegiate sports for women. The structure, which was not accidental, reflects a concern for the needs and opportunities of student athletes in all women's intercollegiate programs throughout the nation. Policy and procedural processes established by the entire membership rather than by members of each division mean that AIAW member institutions will be less inclined to consider spectator appeal above the welfare of the student athlete. By placing all policies affecting student athletes and institutions before the enire membership, athletic directors, coaches, and athletes are forced to consider ramifications for all athletes, thus discouraging the development of the narrow self-interest of the wealthy and dominant institutions.

Commitment to all institutions is reflected in AIAW's television plan which distributes monies throughout the membership, avoiding the "rich get richer, poor get poorer" syndrome. It is noteworthy that John Underwood lauds the equitable sharing plan of the Big 8 Conference, since that plan is very similar to the existing AIAW television plan.

## Institutional Conerns

While the foregoing discussion has focused on the effect of women's athletics at the national governance level, similar effects are evident at the institutional level. Rather than being absorbed into the existing male athletic structure on the individual campus, women's athletics have frequently created their own governance boards or councils. Student participation in establishing rules ranging from training to award systems is ensured on many campuses. Again, this open communication system allows students to exercise some control over their lives as student athletes on the individual campus. Since the source of funding for women's programs is more likely to be nonrestrictive (nonlegislative) university funds rather than gate receipts or donations, women have a better chance of maintaining an educational focus than do males, who are forced in some instances to rely heavily on outside sources. As noted by AIAW President Christine Grant, "Control of the purse strings results in eventual involvement of private or public interests which may conflict with the basic focus of higher education. Loss of some degree of institutional autonomy is the inevitable price of dependence upon external largess" (Grant, 1979:409).

One effect of the explosion of women's programs has been the seeking of new sources of funding. For example, some states such as Minnesota have successfully requested the appropriation of state funds for their women's programs. In Florida a model has been established whereby the state legislature will match the funds that an individual institution will allocate for women's athletics in order that the institution will be in compliance with Title IX. While these new sources of funding have been sought as a result of the emergence of women's programs, the results offer a ray of hope to those in men's athletics who currently are caught under the yoke of maintaining self-supporting programs.

# AIAW: Agent For Change

AIAW had its genesis through the leadership of women physical educators under the auspices of what has become the NAGWS. With its roots in NAGWS and AAHPERD it is not surprising that its growth has been carefully planned and that it has maintained a commitment to the enrichment of the life of the participant. With its roots in academic departments, and its mentors being faculty in those departments, AIAW inevitably placed emphasis on educational rather than commercial values of sport. Although, as with the development of any organization, changes have occurred, there has remained a commitment to the initial goals of the association. The separation of AIAW from AAHPERD/NAGWS in 1979 was viewed by some as a significant shift from its educational focus, but this has not occurred. On the contrary, through its memorandum of understanding with NAGWS, AIAW has ensured a continued commitment to the original goals of its parent body. Fear that the AIAW would somehow suddenly abandon its heritage as it became an autonomous body was addressed by Peg Burke at the 1978 Delegate Assembly. As a former AIAW president, she made the following comments:

> "Undoubtedly, there will be some who will disagree with AIAW's request for a special affiliation agreement with AAHPER and will fear such a change might result in loss of educational focus for AIAW's program. Are AIAW's educational values so shallow that they can only survive under direct AAHPER control? Are AIAW's members so devoid of historical perspective and imagination that they can neither perceive the strengths and weaknesses of other governance systems nor envision solutions unless their decisions are subject to review and possible reversal? There is nothing in AIAW's history of decision making to support these fears or indicate anything other than a deep commitment to the educational values of intercollegiate athletics. These values will remain whether AIAW's relationship with AAHPER is required or voluntary" (Burke, 1978).

There remains an atmosphere of mutual respect and a dedication to the continued development of women's athletics programs. This is perhaps best reflected in the struggles for effective Title IX implementing regulations and in the more recent resolution whereby AAHPERD/NAGWS have taken strong positions supporting continued governance of women's athletics by AIAW rather than by NCAA or NAIA.

Having sought and failed to receive greater autonomy with the structure of AAHPERD, for financial, personnel and governance decisions, AIAW was forced to establish itself as an independent organization. Additionally, AIAW needed to gain representation to national sport governance groups in its own right rather than through AAHPERD. As national governing bodies are restructuring to be consistent with the requirement of the Amateur Sport Act, it has become even more critical that AIAW have representation equal to other collegiate governance bodies.

The current struggle among intercollegiate governance bodies is not simply a power struggle between men and women. The struggle is over whether an alternate model for intercollegiate athletics will be permitted to evolve further. The ethical, moral and financial bankruptcy in today's big time athletics programs mandates significant change. AIAW is certainly not perfect, and along with NCAA and NAIA, certainly has not created a model devoid of problems. However, AIAW has within its current structure some alternatives which could revolutionize intercollegiate sport. Some of these ideas have been approved but not implemented. For example, the attempt to change financial aid based on athletic ability to tuition and fees only rather than full rides was passed by AIAW in 1976 but was rejected by NCAA in 1977; however, renewed efforts are on the horizon for reconsideration of this significant change. While AIAW could have made a unilateral decision to limit financial aid to tuition and fees for female athletes, there was reluctance on the part of its members to have the principle tested in court. The point is, however, that as NCAA was giving lipservice to cost cutting measures while maintaining its scholarship limits, AIAW was offering an alternative. Perhaps the answer lies somewhere between these alternatives, but a commitment to change is necessary if solutions are to be found. Proposals for change in men's athletics range from drastic revision of recruiting procedures to changes in competitive conferences. In addition to the alternative model for recruitment of athletes discussed earlier, qualifying routes for national championships in AIAW are through geographical regions rather than through arbitrary conferences. This generally means significant reduction in travel costs and in time coaches and students are away from on-campus responsibilities. Moreover, it largely av oids the criticism leveled against men's athletics that teams frequently bypass worthy opponents in order to play traditional rivals. It is ironic that some of the ''radical'' proposals for change in the restructuring of men's competitive units are very close to the current AIAW structure.

In addition to guarantees of student rights and student participation in governance, AIAW has established goals for minority involvement. Having created a standing committee on the status of minority women, AIAW has recently set a goal of at least 20 percent minority representation on all appointments to committees and to outside groups such as USOC and national governing bodies. This action could well serve as a catalyst to other organizations to implement an affirmative action plan which truly guarantees policy making power to members of ethnic minorities.

AIAW does offer viable alternatives in the governance of intercollegiate athletics. Over the past decade, it has become the largest single intercollegiate athletics association. With this growth has come the demand to duplicate existing models. This has not occurred and need not occur if chief executvie officers, athletic administrators, coaches, athletes and the national governing organizations will strive for **real** solutions to complex problems.

## FOOTNOTES

¹One notable exception was a national golf championship which has existed since 1941.

# REFERENCES

1980        *AIAW Handbook*. Washington, D. C.: AIAW Publication.
Boutelier, M. and L. San Giovanni.
1980        "Women, Sport and Public Policy". Paper presented at the First Annual Conference of the North American Society for the Sociology of Sport, Denver, Colorado, October.
Burke, N. P.
1978        "AIAW/NAGWS/AAHPER Relationship". Position paper prepared for AIAW Delegate Assembly.
Grant, Christine.
1979        "Institutional Autonomy and Athletics", *Educational Record*, 60 (Fall): 409-419.
Hunt, Virginia.
1976        *Governance of Women's Intercollegiate Athletics: A Historical Perspective*. Unpublished doctoral dissertation. University of North Carolina, Greensboro.
Majors, Johnny.
1980        "Opinion Out Loud," *NCAA News*, September 30.
Underwood, John.
1979        *The Death of an American Game*. Boston: Little, Brown and Company.

# ATHLETICS IN COMMUNITY AND JUNIOR COLLEGES

By
Roger Raepple
Donn Peery
Howard Hohman

More than one-third of all students enrolled in institutions of higher education attend two-year community or junior colleges. More than one of every two students enrolling in college for the first time chooses a community or junior college (**Chronicle of Higher Education, May 12, 1980: 8**). Of all these students, approximately one-third are interested in securing a two-year degree which they then use to transfer to a four-year institution, one-third seek training in technical/vocational programs not typically available at four-year institutions, and the remaining students, many of whom are adults, are enrolled for job-enrichment purposes and variety of other reasons. The average student age is 27 years old (Gilbert, 1980a:1).

Junior and community colleges are an American invention of the early twentieth century which experienced phenomenal growth during the 1960's and 1970's. Today there are more than 1,200 such colleges, more than four times as many as in 1960 (Gilbert, 1980b: 1). As the philosophy of the junior college expanded beyond the function of university-parallel programs and included occupational programs and adult and community services, a national move to reidentify two-year colleges as community colleges rather than junior colleges developed. These colleges emphasize low-cost, serve commuter students (i.e., few dormitories), practice "open-door" admissions policies, offer a wide range of courses at many different times in a variety of locations to accommodate the many working students who attend, and are typically controlled by a local governing board.

These colleges field more than 4,000 athletic teams in an extensive array of sports for both men and women (**NCAA Manual,** 1980a: 211, 225). Competition among these teams is coordinated and regulated by national, regional, state, and local organizations.

# THE NATIONAL JUNIOR COLLEGE ATHLETIC ASSOCIATION

## History and Development

As the junior college movement in the United States grew, it was only a matter of time until the interest in intercollegiate athletics developed into a desire to conduct athletic championships, particularly national championships. In 1938 the National Junior College Athletic Association (NJCAA) was founded by a group of 13 California junior colleges. The first major activity of the group was to sponsor the 1939 National Junior College Track and Field Meet in Sacramento.

While the organization was founded exclusively by west coast colleges and its growth was slowed by World War II, by 1947 colleges from other regions of the country were expressing interest in a national basketball championship tournament. In 1949, the National Championship Basketball Tournament for junior colleges was held in Hutchinson, Kansas, and included colleges from around the country. Also in 1949, in recognition of the expanding national interest in junior college athletics, the NJCAA divided the nation into 16 geographic regions and the **NJCAA Bulletin** was established as the official publication of the association.

The national junior college movement expanded rapidly in the 1950's, and the growth of the NJCAA reflected this expansion. The association produced new and expanded official publications and became affiliated with a variety of other national organizations such as the American Association of Junior Colleges, the National Federation of State High School Athletic Associations, the National Association of Intercollegiate Athletics, the People to People Sports Committee, and President Eisenhower's Physical Fitness Commission. The affiliations also reflected the growing importance of intercollegiate athletics in junior colleges.

In the 1960's, the NJCAA continued on its course of increasing prominence at the national level when it entered the national federations for three sports: basketball, gymnastics, and track and field. In 1963, the NJCAA became a member of the Board of Directors of the United States Olympic Committee and since that time has been actively involved in all facets of America's Olympic program. The organization continued to grow by adding many new national championships and undergoing periodic reorganizations to accommodate increasing growth and complexity. It employed a full-time executive director for the first time in 1969.

The NJCAA had been an organization devoted exclusively to men's athletics; however, in 1975, a major organizational change occurred when the Women's Division was created and three national championships were authorized: volleyball, basketball, and tennis. By 1979-80, the NJCAA had 489 institutions as members of its Women's Division and 564 in its Men's Division, and the Board of Directors was comprised of one representative from both the Women's and Men's Divisions for each of the 22 geograpic regions (NJCAA, 1980a: 16-19).

While the vast majority of community colleges participating in inter-collegiate athletics are members of the NJCAA, some colleges are not, and at least in one state, California, the decision has been made to confine competi-tion to within the state and, therefore, not to hold membership in the NJCAA.

## Purpose and Functions

As stated earlier, the conduct of national championships in various sports was one of the principal purposes that caused the charter members to organize the NJCAA. In 1980-81, the NJCAA conducted 21 national cham-pionships, 12 for men and 9 for women. In addition, it sponsored 5 national invitational tournaments for men, 5 for women, and a variety of junior col-lege football bowl games (1980a: 9-12). In order to regulate this series of na-tionwide championships and special activities, the NJCAA has adopted rules with which all member institutions must comply. The rules cover four general areas: (1) student-athlete eligibility; (2) scholarships and grants-in-aid; (3) general policies concerning the awarding and conduct of national championship and invitational tournaments, meets, and games; and (4) specific rules governing each sport.

## Structure

The NJCAA, as previously mentioned, is organized into 22 geographic regions. Within each region, the member colleges (one vote per member) elect a men's region director and a women's region director to two-year terms of office, each to represent men's and women's athletics respectively. All activities related to men's comprise the men's division and similarly, a women's division constitutes all women's athletic activities. Together, the 44 region directors (representing the 22 men's and women's programs) con-stitute the Board of Directors, which is the ultimate policy-making body of the NJCAA. The board of directors is responsible for amending the NJCAA constitution and bylaws which govern the conduct of junior and community college athletics.

The Board of Directors elects officers (President, two Vice-Presidents, and two Secretary-Treasurers) who along with two region directors elected at-large, comprise the Executive Committee, which operates under the direction and on the behalf of the Board. The Board also employs persons to conduct day-to-day business. These employees include: executive director, administrative assistant, office manager, financial advisor, attorney, and others as needed.

The 44 individual region directors are the primary points of contact be-tween the NJCAA and its member colleges. The individual directors have an extensive number of responsibilities which include the direct regulation or coordination of such activities as: eligibility determination, interpretation and enforcement of financial aid and related rules, planning and operating region tournaments, membership recruitment, conducting investigations, presiding at annual region meetings, and proposing changes to the constitution and bylaws.

The NJCAA also relies heavily on a committee structure that acts across geographic regions. In 1980-81, 40 standing committees existed. Of these, 28 are sport committees, each proposing policies dealing with a specific sport (e.g., men's baseball, women's volleyball). The remaining 12 committees are responsible for reviewing and making recommendations and, in some cases, implementing policies related to a variety of other issues such as: membership and dues, publications, districting, medical aspects, etc., (1980a:13-15).

The NJCAA rules and regulations which govern junior and community colleges are adopted by the Board of Directors and can be proposed by individual member colleges through their Directors, the Directors themselves, or by the various standing committees.

In addition to the formal NJCAA structure, the coaches of many sports have formed coaches' associations which serve a variety of purposes related to the promotion of their sport and the overall development of junior and community college athletics.

## Finances

In order to become a member of one of the two divisions (men's and women's) of the NJCAA, and institution must meet several eligibility criteria and must pay annual membership dues. The amount of dues is based entirely on the college's level of student enrollment and the range of charges is from $100 per year (0-500 students) to $200 per year (2,001 students or more). The combined membership dues of $149,245 comprised approximately 44.5 percent of the total revenues to the NJCAA in the fiscal year ending on July 31, 1980. Other significant revenues sources included: subscriptions to the Association's magazine, **JUCO Review** ($25,050; 7.5 percent of the total revenue), and receipts from tournaments and meets ($95,896; 28.6 percent). Other revenue sources include: coaches associations' dues, interest on investments, merchandise sales, and donations (NJCAA 1980b: 20-21).

NJCAA funds are expended almost exclusively for national activities such as the operation of the central office, the publication of official documents, and support of national committees and organizations. Almost no funds are expended to support the functioning of the 44 region directors who work closely with member colleges.

## NJCAA Regions: Variety and Flexibility

By comparison with the national rules imposed by other associations which govern intercollegiate athletics in higher education (e.g., the National Collegiate Athletic Association and the Association of Intercollegiate Athletics For Women), the NJCAA rules are less encompassing, less complex, and less limiting in their impact on the operation of each college's athletic program. For example, at the junior college level no national rules exist which establish limits on the number of scholarships junior colleges can offer in a given sport. Hypothetically, a junior or community college could offer 25 basketball scholarships without violating any NJCAA rule. Also, no national letter-of-intent exists for two-year colleges. The only NJCAA rule governing recruitment is one which limits a college to providing a given prospective athlete a single visit to the college campus. A student-athlete may visit as many colleges as he or she wishes and may be contacted an unlimited number of times by a single college.

The individual NJCAA Regions are delegated the authority to establish additional, more restrictive rules if they so choose. The regions, therefore, exhibit a variety of structures and levels of rule-making. Some regions are content to develop a system which carries out and enforces the national rules while adopting few, if any, additional rules for themselves. In these cases, the Regional Director's role is limited to the responsibilities assigned to him or her by the NJCAA, some of which were previously discussed and may not include additional duties established at the region level.

Other regions have established athletic conferences or similar organizations which are responsible for regulating and coordinating intercollegiate athletics among its members through a series of additional regulations adopted by the conference. The state of Florida utilizes such a system.

# THE FLORIDA MODEL

Region VIII of the NJCAA comprises all two-colleges in the state of Florida. Given the flexible system used by the NJCAA, Florida has organized a statewide activities association which, among other functions, regulates and coordinates intercollegiate athletics. Florida's community college Presidents have chosen to adopt a system which employs a number of rules and regulations beyond those established by the NJCAA. For example, Florida has adopted additional financial aid regulations, a statewide letter-of-intent, and limits on the number of athletes who can be provided financial assistance in each sport (e.g., women's volleyball—12; men's tennis—8).

All regions of the NJCAA are responsible for establishing the system whereby a regional champion in each sport is identified. Regional champions, once identified, are then eligible to participate in the national championship tournament or meet conducted by the NJCAA. In Florida, the system for identifying regional champions varies with the sport. For example, in all team sports (e.g., volleyball, baseball, basketball, and softball), the four geographic conferences in the state established by the statewide association identify a limited number of representatives, which then participate in an end-of-year championship tournament. Sports committees, one for each sport, comprised of a representative from each of the four conferences, develop and propose rules to govern their respective sports. These rules are then submitted for adoption to a statewide committee.

Officers of the association are elected by the colleges' Presidents and the NJCAA region directors for men and for women serve as the athletic commissioners for men and women, respectively. The officers, athletic commissioners, and representatives from non-athletic areas serve as the Executive Committee which governs the affairs of the organization. To fund the central office, sport committees, athletic commissioners, tournaments, rules enforcement, promotion, and other statewide activities, each member college pays an annual dues based primarily on enrollment.

Florida, therefore, has elected to operate a system of control and coordination of intercollegiate athletics which extends beyond the national rules enforced by the NJCAA. Other regions, as mentioned earlier, have chosen a less formal system with far fewer additional regulations and limitations. In addition to this self-imposed system of the colleges at the state level, many state legislatures have imposed a variety of laws regulating the conduct of intercollegiate athletics at the campus level. Given this national, regional, and state governance mechanism, individual colleges establish their own internal governance system.

# ATHLETICS ON THE CAMPUS: THE BROAD PICTURE

One of the basic advantages of the junior college easy adaptability to change, has brought about may types of governance models within the junior college movement. There are junior colleges with enrollments of a few hundred students to multi-campus community colleges with over 50,000 students.

Athletic departments reflect the wide range of governance structures. In the small junior college, it is not uncommon to find the athletic director also serving as physical education chairman, teaching classes, and coaching a varsity team. In the large multi-campus colleges, there may be an athletic director at each campus and in some colleges a director of collegewide athletics located within the central administration.

Coaches in junior colleges are most often hired as teachers who receive either release time from teaching or a salary supplement for coaching a varsity team. Most junior college coaches, therefore, are either tenured or on a tenure track as teachers with professional rank. Only recently has this practice come under review because retired, tenured coaches are filling funded positions, thus making it very difficult to find the money for new positions for the incoming replacement coach.

## Funding

Athletic funding in junior colleges generally comes from many sources. In some colleges where physical education and athletics are combined in one department, the physical education budget for the instructional program may supplement the athletic budget by purchasing equipment common to both programs. Many colleges involve students by having some expenditures of the athletic budget controlled by the student government association. This practice varies with the philosophy of the college.

It is usual practice to provide the athletic director with a budget from the college's general fund. This allocation serves to provide equipment and materials common to all varsity teams in order to avoid duplication. Many junior colleges also have developed booster clubs in support of their athletic programs. NJCAA rules permit such clubs, providing funds generated are controlled by the college. Most booster clubs are small and local in nature, comprised of supporters within the community served by the college. Booster clubs serve as excellent vehicles to involve the community in the junior college athletic program.

Ticket sales or gate receipts generally do not represent a significant financial income for junior college athletic programs. Junior college students are usually not charged for athletic programs on their campus, and gymnasiums and stadiums are frequently not large enough to accommodate large revenue-producing crowds.

## Student Characteristics

As stated earlier, the junior college is a unique type of institution in higher education. The student who attends a junior college is also often a distinct type of student. Dickenson (1979: 499) writes that the traditional college population of 18-24 year olds will decline by 20-30 percent in the next decade, and the number of women and minorities will increase. These trends will significantly change the overall campus community and the pattern of participation in college athletics.

The junior college "open door" concept also provides entrance opportunities to many students who would not qualify for admission to a university. Among these students are many athletes. By enrolling in a junior college, they have the opportunity to continue participating in athletics, furthering their education, and then transfering to an upper-division college. Many upper-division colleges recognize the benefit of this avenue and assist junior college coaches in locating athletes who do not have adequate grades to enter a university. Junior colleges provide these athletes with an opportunity to develop their skills in highly competitive, visible competition while improving their grades in classes that are usually small and structured with the student's progress the main objective.

## Institutional Controls

As discussed earlier, the junior or community college is primarily a local institution with a local governing body that has a rather large degree of autonomy. Also, the NJCAA provides for a significant degree of local control in developing athletic policies to comply with national rules.

Recruiting is one area with which each college deals independently. The NJCAA rule is concerned only with the duration of a prospective athlete's visit on campus, when the visitation shall occur, and provisions of paying for the visitation. Each college decides how many visits will be allowed and how the athletes will be compensated for their travel. Florida, for example, will not permit tax dollars to be used for transportation of prospective athletes. Therefore, it usually falls to the booster club to support this activity.

While it might seem that the junior college does not place much importance on recruitment, such is not the case. The successful athletic program demands an active recruitment program. As the women's programs become more competitive, the need for more recruitment funds will be evident and is, in fact, being felt now.

The athletic scholarship is another major area left to the control of each institution. There are no national rules relative to the number of scholarships to be offered in a varsity sport. In some states, however, a maximum number of amount is established. Scholarships vary greatly, then, in what they offer to the student athletes. Scholarships range from tuition waivers only to full grants providing for tuition, books, meals, and lodging.

The allocation of scholarship funds is controlled in various ways. It is not uncommon to find the students, through the student government associations, voting on the number of scholarships provided and the amount to be awarded. This approach requires a concerted, continuous effort in communication with the student body which, because of the two-year nature of the college, promotes annual change in campus student leadership and attitudes towards athletics.

The size of the athletic program is also left to the discretion of the college. The NJCAA does not provide for different levels of competition. There is not a minimum number of teams required in order to permit the school to compete in the NJCAA. In fact, if a school so desires, all athletic funds can be allocated to one team to promote that team to national competition.

The place, role, and importance of athletics in the community or junior college is difficult to assess and report. Athletic importance varies with the perceptions of the administration, trustees, and students on each campus. Most institutions emphasize the academic priority of the athletic program through the student control of funds and teaching role of coaches. Many colleges readily accept the high visibility brought to the campus through the athletic program, even though funds generated from community support usually do not pay for the programs.

Community colleges are finding their athletic programs undergoing rapid change and are making urgent attempts to deal with the complex problems facing the rest of the college in identifying missions, philosophies, and goals while at the same time justifying their existence during budgetary consideration. Through all of the diverse and complex issues concerning community college athletics today, most college administrators maintain that the only justification for intercollegiate athletics is their contribution to educational objectives. Unless athletics sponsored by the college are truly a part of the college education process and support and promote the goals of the institution, then the entire mission of the institution is in jeopardy and the athletic program has no basis for existence.

# GOVERNANCE OF ATHLETICS IN COMMUNITY AND JUNIOR COLLEGES

As we have seen, the hierarchical governance structure of athletics for two-year colleges is characterized by a substantial amount of delegation of authority from the NJCAA to the regions and subsequently to individual colleges when compared to the governance structure for athletics in the other sectors of higher education. The NJCAA has a comparatively small staff which enforces a smaller, less complex body of regulations (eligibility rules being the exception) and exercises control over far fewer financial resources. This system provides greater flexibility and self-control to the organizational units below the national-level structure, namely: NJCAA regions, conferences, and individual colleges.

## Advantages of Current System

1. **Cost.** The direct cost of administering all the functions of the national office is reduced. The fewer rules and regulations to enforce, the smaller the staff, the less the direct cost.
2. **Consistent Philosophy.** As described earlier, a significant characteristic of the two-year college movement is its emphasis on local control and community orientation with flexibility given each college to respond to the unique characteristics and needs of the community it serves. The fewer the restrictions imposed at the national level, the more flexibility provided to each college, the more supportive college administrators are to such a system, and the more encouraged they are to establish and maintain athletic programs over which they exercise substantial control with minimal external interference.
3. **Accessibility.** Region directors are granted substantial authority to carry out the functions of the NJCAA. Because the Directors are physically located in the region and because each is a college employee, they generally are considered to be readily available for consultation and understanding of a college's situation. In Florida for example, the region directors/athletic commissioners are in frequent, daily contact with athletic administrators who seek their opinions and advice concerning rules and regulations. This informal, speedy system appears to reduce greatly the need for more costly, formal contact and review.
4. **Ease of Change.** Again, for other than the national eligibility rules and rudimentary financial aid rules, the NJCAA has delegated substantial rule-making authority to the regions. Consequently, many changes (i.e., those concerning region or conference rules) may be made quite quickly because amendatory authority resides within the regions, not the national office. Such flexibility permits fairly quick

responses to changing circumstances and new needs at a level close to the colleges.

Certainly, the above advantages are not mutually exlusive; they all occur to some degree as a result of the flexibility maintained in the system due to the delegation of authority. Other advantages of a similar nature also exist.

# Disadvantages of Current System

1. **Undetected Violations.** The limited size of the NJCAA central staff hampers its capacity to identify violations among its member institutions. While the NJCAA eligibility rules are both lengthy and complex (almost eight pages of the NJCAA **Handbook** detail eligibility rules), and the review system tends to reduce violations in this area, many junior college athletic personnel believe that violations of financial aid rules can occur without detection. Unlike eligibility where a detailed reporting and review system exists, no such system exists for financial aid. The rules governing financial aid are less detailed (they comprise barely more than a page in the NJCAA **Handbook**), the awards to athletes are not systematically reviewed or accounted for, violations can go undetected, and if they are detected, the size of the NJCAA staff hampers earnest and adequate enforcement.

2. **Inequality of Competition.** The flexibility of the governance system manifests itself by encompassing in a single championship competition colleges with vastly different enrollments, financial resources, numbers of sports offered, numbers and amounts of athletic scholarships offered, and levels of involvement in and support of the intercollegiate athletic program. For example, a large community college which places all of its substantial resources in a single sport competes in the same national championship tournament as the smaller college which competes with fewer resources in several different sports. While each college can make its own choices, the lack, for example, of a rule limiting the number of scholarships for a given sport does tend to make some modicum of equality of competition difficult to achieve. It is perhaps for this reason that in excess of 80 percent of the colleges responding to a recent survey indicated an interest in establishing such national limits (Florida Community College Activities Association: 1981).

3. **Greater Recruitment Costs.** The lack of a national letter-of-intent causes community college coaches who are recruiting to contact a larger number of prospective athletes, over a longer period of time, and more frequently than would otherwise be necessary. Regardless of the size or level of a community college's athletic program, greater costs and more time are consumed in the recruitment efforts than would be necessary if a national letter-of-intent existed. More than 70 percent of the respondents to the survey mentioned above indicated an interest in establishing a national letter-of-intent (Florida Community College Activities Association: 1981).

While other disadvantages exist, these are indicative of the problems inherent in the current system which emphasizes flexibility and a lack of central control and regulation at the national level.

## Developing Issues

As colleges and governing bodies seek a balance to these often conflicting objectives (e.g., flexibility vs. conformity, cost savings vs. adequate enforcement, local control vs. equality of competition), they must also deal with an array of other significant issues, some newly emerging and some of long standing. As described previously, community college coaches have usually been hired as teachers and have been placed on a tenure track. Today, more and more of these teacher-coaches are giving up their coaching duties and retaining the teaching positions for which they are tenured. Their career changes are severely restricting the staff decisions being made by athletic directors—the teacher-coach who gives up coaching retains the staff position and the dollars to support it.

Compounding this staffing/budgetary problem are the demands to provide women's athletic opportunities as mandated by Title IX in an environment on many campuses where available resources are becoming more scarce. This is due to inflation and a reduction in the growth of funding as fewer new students reach college age. As the pressures for funding become greater, many colleges increasingly turn to booster-type organizations which, because of their external nature, are less susceptible to direct control and review by college administrators and thus can create a new array of administrative problems.

Appropriately, perhaps the dominant problem facing community college athletic administrators today is the need to insure the academic integrity of their programs and of the student-athletes who participate in them. Altered transcripts, inappropriate pressure on teachers to change grades, enrollment in non-existent courses or in giveaway "correspondence" courses are examples of the more flagrant, obviously unethical practices which can occur. Of at least equally great concern is the practice, hopefully not widespread, of enrolling student-athletes in legitimate college courses which are individually appropriate but which collectively do not lead to a degree or the the development of skills which are meaningful to the student. Recently, there have been a number of publicized cases of athletes who maintained their eligibility through four years of college but who fall far short of meeting graduation requirements. While not as publicized, similar cases occur at community colleges. During the coming years, the attention of all those involved in community college athletics should become focused on the problem of insuring that student-athletes make reasonable academic progress towards the attainment of college degree.

During the upcoming years, the resolution of these problems will be shaped by and, in turn, shape the system of athletic governance in community colleges.

# SUMMARY

The two-year community or junior college, an American development in higher education, is unique in both concept and function. It provides extensive opportunities for a range of students. Among these opportunities is varsity athletics.

The administration and regulation of community college athletics reflects the mission of the community college itself. Local college control dictates the extent of institutional participation. Interest and support are generated by students and community followers and seldom extend beyond local constituents.

National regulations are designed to provide equality in the application of eligibility, limitations on the maximum benefits of scholarships, conduct of national championships, and coordinating rules for specific sports. The area of enforcement, letter-of-intent, and scholarship limits are, for the most part, not addressed by the NJCAA. The NJCAA provides many publication and record-type services to their membership.

Beyond the flexible and tractable controls of the NJCAA, many states have developed their own organizations to aid in the promotion and regulation of community college athletic programs. The Florida organization is provided as an example of one state's efforts to promote continuity and fairness within a state's programs.

Community college athletic programs, like most programs in higher education today, face some of the most serious problems of the past few decades. Athletic funding, negative public image, recruiting scandals, staffing, Federal requirements, and changing NCAA regulations affect the role of community college opportunities for athletes.

The community college has and will continue to provide a very important bridge between the high school and four-year university for those students who wish or need to explore an alternative method of obtaining a college education and participating in varsity athletics. As long as the community college provides this alternative and the athletic programs maintain integrity in their own governance programs, the community college and varsity athletics will be viable institutions in the American educational and sports scene.

# REFERENCES

Dickenson, D.B.
  1979    "The Future of Collegiate Athletics." *Educational Record*, 60(Fall): 499-509.
Florida Community College Activities Association
  1981    "Summary of Responses to Presidents' Athletic Survey." Tallahasse, Florida.

Gilbert, Fontelle
  1980a   *Learners in Two-year Colleges.* Report for the American Association of
          Community and Junior Colleges.
National Junior College Athletic Association
  1980a   *1980-81 Handbook and Casebook.*
  1980b   *Fact Sheet on Two-Year Colleges.* Report for the American Association
          of Community and Junior Colleges.
  1980b   "Financial Statements." *JUCO Review.* (November): 20-21.

# VIOLENCE IN INTERCOLLEGIATE ATHLETICS: CAUSES, EFFECTS AND CONTROLS

By
Richard B. Horrow

The Harvard-Yale football game in 1895 was described in Europe by the **Munchener Nachrichten** in the following way:

> The football tournament between the teams of Harvard and Yale, recently held in America, had terrible results. It turned into an awful butchery. Of twenty-two participants, seven were so severely injured that they had to be carried from the field in a dying condition. One player had his back broken, another lost an eye, and a third lost a leg, Both teams appeared on the field with a crowd of ambulances, surgeons and nurses. Many ladies fainted at the awful cries of injured players. The indignation of the spectators was powerful, but they were so terrorized that they were afraid to leave the field (National Collegiate Athletic Association, 1979: 8).

While the newspaper report of 85 years ago may have been slightly exaggerated, the problem of violence in collegiate sports has become increasingly serious in modern times and merits significant attention. Accordingly, this chapter will briefly explore three areas worthy of concern: (1) Violence: The Causes and Effects; (2) Internal Controls: The NCAA; (3) External controls: The Courts. Most of the incidents referred to in this chapter involve professional sports. In fact, aside from a 1973 Ohio State—Minnesota basketball fight and a 1978 Gator Bowl football altercation which led to the firing of Ohio State coach Woody Hayes, most collegiate-level violence has received little public attention. The problem is a serious one on both levels. The similarity between collegiate and professional athletics involving the pressures creating violent behavior, the internal dispute resolution mechanisms, and the external legal standards, makes a study of professional sports violence indispensable to an understanding of the collegiate problem.

# VIOLENCE: THE CAUSES
# AND EFFECTS

As a result of an attempt in 1905 by the entire Pennsylvania football team to win a game by reducing the Swathmore star lineman to a bloody pulp, President Theodore Roosevelt threatened to abolish football by Executive Order unless the game could be made less violent (Marcus, 1972: 12). In my book, **Sports Violence, The Interaction Between Private Lawmaking and the Criminal Law** (1980), all aspects of this increasingly serious and significant problem are explored. The conclusions of the book are based on surveys sent to 1,490 amateur and professional athletes, coaches, owners, general managers, and prosecuting attorneys. One clear finding that emerges is that excessively violent conduct will continue to increase as long as the pressures and incentives to be violent remain. Although some pressures impact more on the professional level than upon college athletics, all must be briefly explored.

First, because violence and physical intimidation are accepted as legitimate parts of the professional game, the pressures to perpetuate violent collegiate conduct are that much more significant. In hockey, for example, violence and intimidation in excess of that permitted by the rules of the professional game are becoming integral parts of strategy. Players fight because it has become a condition of the job. Max McNab, General Manager and former coach of the Washington Capitols, explained, "Intimidation is a factor. Physical courage is our primary requirement" (Horrow, 1980: 13). Sports attorney Bob Woolf explains that "the premium the NHL puts on this aspect of the game was re-established every time I talked with the team on behalf of a draft choice. Invariably, the interview would get around to how well my client could fight. Sometimes, the hockey general manager sounds more like a boxing promoter trying to size up some kid coming out of the amateurs . . . to my endless amazement, the clubs, if they got the impressions the boy was not tough, frequently offered to enroll him in boxing classes" (Woolf, 1976: 146). William R. McMurtry, a Toronto attorney commissioned by the Canadian Minister of Community and Social Services to explore the causes and prevention of hockey violence, exclaimed that "what is recent and disturbing . . . is the emergence of a trend towards controlled and deliberate use of physical intimidation making full use of the present rules and the reluctance of the hockey establishment to eradicate fighting as part of the game" (McMurtry, 1974: 23).

Second, the perception that violence is tolerated and necessary is often coupled with the justification that an occasional fight or late hit is actually healthy. This catharsis argument is described in sociological terms: " . . . that the speed and body contact—the very nature of the game— causes an accumulation of aggressive impulses (frustration) which must be released, if not one way, then another, and that prohibiting fistfighting will result in more vicious and dangerous illegal use of the stick" (Smith, 1979: 1). Besides, several players responded that "no one ever gets hurt in a fight because the technique is awful and the footing horrendous" (Horrow, 1980: 24). Of course, the argument has little merit. However, the important point is that many of the professional and amateur players appear to believe this. One hockey player wrote: "I don't see any violence in two players dropping their gloves and letting a little steam escape. I think it's a lot better than spearing somebody. I think it's an escape valve because you know yourself pressure builds up and there is no way to release it and if fighting is not allowed, then another violent act will occur" (1980: 25).

Third, sports violence is taught and accepted by its participants as non-criminal at a very early age. This mentality revolves around the notion that each young "gifted athlete" is trained to believe that there is nothing "illegal" about fighting (or even more malicious conduct) if it is done during the course of the game. In hockey, Canadian boys typically enter organizational hockey around age seven. The ablest are quickly funneled into a highly competitive "select" league and begin intensive training which lasts until age sixteen. Those who have remained emerge "a tough fighting unit prepared for violence whose primary objective is to win a hockey games" (Vaz, 1976: 212). The junior leagues "have become a mini-business, cultivating 14-year-old professionals" (Horrow, 1980: 26). The "feeding grounds for the professionals" survive mainly on the $40,000 they receive from the National Hockey League for "each professional player" they produce. Some have argued that a youngster learns that violent acts are "legal" by watching, and thus emulating, professionals. In a sample survey of 604 Toronto junior players, 56 percent suggested that they had learned "how to hit a player illegally" from watching pro hockey, and 60 percent had actually used some of the tactics "at least once or twice" (Eastwood, 1974: 158). McMurtry concludes that "it is not surprising that virtually every boy playing hockey is profoundly influenced by examples portrayed in the NHL (1974: 20). Former National Hockey League star Henry Boucha, injured in a 1975 stick-swinging incident with Dave Forbes, indicated in testimony before the House Judiciary Subcommittee on Crime that "as part of my development of the young hockey player I was told repeatedly that in order to play professional hockey I would have to learn to be aggressive and to fight both offensively and defensively. This always bothered me because by nature I am not an aggressive person."[1] In football, much the same situation appears to exist, though the causes may be somewhat different. Intentional injuries will continue as long as high school players feel that they must demonstrate the ability to play a "hardnose game" in an effort to obtain a football scholarship to college; the same holds true for college players who, desiring to make a career in athletics, emulate the professionals in hopes of being drafted (Horrow, 1980: 28). Coach Vince Lombardi noted that "pro football, like the college game, is a violent, dangerous game. To play it other than violently would be imbecile" (1961: 122).

Fourth, once the "skills" of violence are learned, players are explicitly and implicitly pressured by teammates and coaches to continue their violent conduct. The hockey professional mentality is described by McMurtry, "It is extremely difficult for the player who is being provoked and being pushed to turn his back and appear to be running. The pressure from his own team-mates and from the many millions of fans make it an impossibility for him to do that" (1974: 23). The pressure to portray the "ambivalence to pain" image is prevalent at all levels. Further, the best that can be said for hockey and football coaches in this regard is that **most** of them will not overtly encourage violent conduct. However, studies have shown that if a coach asks his team to "play rough and aggressive," his players frequently translate this message into "take out the opposition any way you can" (Vaz and Thomas, 1974: 47).

Intense competition against teammates for roster positions—and against opponents—for victory lead to the mentality that the law of survival is the only law that governs. In testimony before the **Hackbart** court, former coaches John Ralston of the Denver Broncos and Paul Brown of the Cincinnati Bengals admitted that it was normal behavior for players to disregard the safety of opposing players. Ralston suggested that the pre-game psychological game should be designed to generate an emotion equivalent to that which would be experienced by a father whose family had been endangered by another driver who had attempted to force the family car off the edge of a mountain road. The precise pitch of motivation for the players at the beginning of the game should be the feeling of that father when, after overtaking and stopping the offending vehicle, he is about to open the door to take revenge upon the person of the other driver (Horrow, 1980).

Furthermore, most players accept the fact that some less-talented players must be more violent to compensate for inferior ability. Thus, the sports establishment appears to condone the actions of certain "enforcers," even though these actions go beyond those which would be tolerated from more skilled players. It seems clear, therefore, that excessive violence will continue to increase as long as pressures and incentives to be violent continue to emanate form the social context of all levels of sport, including inter-collegiate.

# INTERNAL CONTROLS: THE NCAA

In 1876 a group calling itself the Intercollegiate Football Association established 61 rules that were meant to govern football. Of those, only two were concerned with safety. After the Roosevelt threat to abolish football in 1905, a new independent rules committee was formed under the name of the Conference Rules Committee. Its members met with the original Intercollegiate Football Association Committee on January 12, 1906. The committees met under the title of the American Intercollegiate Football Rules Committee. This group led to the inspiration and creation of the National Collegiate Athletic Association (NCAA) in 1910. The NCAA governs the conduct of intercollegiate athletics by enacting and enforcing rules which purport to cover every aspect of collegiate sport. Regulation of "during-the-game" conduct occurs on three distinct levels. Control of the actions of student-athletes and representatives of the various NCAA member institutions is primarily the responsibility of each institution. Playing rules, which are developed by rules committees, also provide measures of control. In addition, policies such as the disqualification statement, which is applicable during NCAA championship competition, have been developed.[2] Three specific levels of governance must be discussed here: (1) Codes of Ethics; (2) Rules Committees and during-the-game penalties; (3) NCAA tournament disqualification and suspension.

# Codes of Ethics

The basis of ethical authority is derived from Article III, #6 of the NCAA Constitution:[3]

It should be a member institution's responsibility to apply and enforce the following principles: (a) individuals employed by, or associated with, a member institution to administer, conduct or coach intercollegiate athletics and all participating student-athletes shall deport themselves with honesty and sportsmanship at all times so that intercollegiate athletics as a whole, their institutions and they, as individuals, shall represent the honor and dignity of fair play and the generally-recognized high standards associated with wholesome competitive sports.

The rulebook for each sport contains a "coaches and players code of ethics." For example, the 1980 NCAA Baseball Code provides the following:

Coaching Ethics: (1) it is the duty of the coach to be in control of his players at all times in order to prevent any unsportsmanlike act toward opponents, officials or spectators; (2) coaches are expected to comply wholeheartedly with the intent and spirit of the rules. The deliberate teaching of players to violate the rules is indefensible; (3) coaches should teach their players to respect the dignity of the game, officials, opponents in the institutions which they represent; (7) coaches should refrain from any personal action that might arouse players or spectators to unsportsmanlike behavior.

The Hockey Code of Ethics contains the following language:

A coach should be thoroughly acquainted with the rules of hockey. He is responsible for having his players understand the rules and should make certain that both the spirit and the letter of the rules are adhered to . . . a coach's actions should at all times bring credit to himself, his institution and the game of hockey.

# Rules Committees and During-the-Game Penalties

The NCAA Constitution and Bylaws make it clear that the rules committee of each sport has sole rule-making responsibility. Bylaw 10, #5, names 12 "sports committees" with "responsibilities for formulating the official playing rules in their respective sports." Each sport, therefore, is subject to the appropriate, specific rules.

In hockey, the rule structure provides for penalties based upon the severity of the violent act. Ranging from a two-minute minor penalty [Rule 4, & 2 (a)], to a competitive disqualification [Rule 5, & 5(a)]. Section 5(a) provides the core distinction between regulation of professional and amateur hockey. While National Hockey League rule structure appears to accept and condone fighting, the NCAA rule structure seems to afford an adequate deterrent. Section 5(a) states:

> A disqualification player penalty, consisting of a suspension for the remainder of the game, plus a major penalty, shall be imposed upon any player who fights, attempts to injure an opponent, or commits other serious penalties as outlined in these rules... (b) the progressive game disqualification structure will be as follows: first disqualification penalty—that game plus 1. Second disqualification penalty—that game plus 2. Third disqualification penalty—that game plus 3. Fourth disqualification penalty—that game plus 4. The progression will continue after the fourth disqualification penalty.

In baseball and basketball, the rules provide the game official the power to award an unsportsmanlike conduct foul (Rule 2, & 6), and eject the player or coach from the game [Rule 3, & 7(c)], respectively.

In football, Rule 9, & 1 sets out very specific prohibitions for certain types of contact. Most specifically, it shall be a personal foul for a player to "strike an opponent with the knee, or strike an opponent's head, neck, or face with an extended forearm, elbow, locked hands, palm, fist, or the heel, back or side of the open hand during the game or between the periods" [Article 2(a)]. It is also a personal foul for a player to trip [Article 2(c)], spear [Article 2(m)], "charge into a passer when it is obvious the ball has been thrown" [Article 2(o)], or deliberately use his helmet to butt or ram an opponent [Article 2(1)].

The NCAA Football Rules Committee has provided noble direction in the area of player safety. The three divisions of the NCAA are represented on the committee by four members from Division 1 and three from Divisions 2 and 3. The secondary schools and junior colleges using NCAA rules are each represented by a member at large. A chairperson and secretary editor, elected at large, complete the committee. For example, during recent years, the American Football Coaches' Association attempted to eliminate the "chop block" through its Code of Ethics and appeals to the coaches, but results were unsatisfactory. In 1980 the Football Rules Committee placed a prohibition against the chop block in the rules. This block had formerly led to a number of serious injuries (particularly broken legs) when a defensive player, while in contact with an offensive player, was knocked at or below the knee (Nelson, 1980: 4). The Football Rules Committee admits that "football is no longer classified as a fatality sport, but it is a high-injury risk sport with an incidence of catastrophic cases higher than is acceptable." As such, the Football Rules Committee, since 1969, has made 51 injury prevention rules changes involving personal fouls, penalty enforcement, and unsportsmanlike conduct.

# NCAA Tournament Disqualification and Suspension

The NCAA tournament regulation and disqualification power is derived from Article II, & I (f) of the NCAA Constitution. It states that one of the purposes of the NCAA is "to supervise the conduct of, and to establish eligibility standards for, regional and national athletic events under the auspices of this association." Additionally, Executive Regulation 2-2-1, which governs conduct during NCAA championships, requires that:

A governing sports committee, or the games committee authorized to act for it, may (i) reprimand publicly or privately, and/or (ii) disqualify from further participation in the NCAA championship involved, and/or (iii) ban from participation in a subsequent championship of the sport involved a student-athlete or representative of an institution who is guilty of misconduct occurring at or at any time preceding or subseqent to the competition during the official dates of the meet or tournament.

"Misconduct," for these purposes, shall mean any conduct contrary "to the principles set forth in NCAA Constitution 3-6(a) and may be found upon informal hearings granted to the student-athlete or representative involved."

Identical disqualification language appears in tournament handbooks drafted by the NCAA Divisions I, II and III Football Committee, NCAA Division I Basketball Committee, NCAA Ice Hockey Committee, and the Baseball Subcommittee, or the (games committees authorized to act for them).

Disqualification of a player under these rules may affect the competitive standing of a team as well. Executive Regulation 2, Section 4, states as follows:

(F) When a student athlete representing his institution in a team championship is declared ineligible subsequent to the tournament . . . the record of the team's performance shall be deleted, the team's place in the final standing shall be vacated and the team's trophy and the ineligible student athlete's award shall be returned to the Association.

Some authorities have criticized the intricate network of NCAA rules and regulations. The House Subcommittee on Oversight and Investigations of the Committee on Interstate and Foreign Commerce wrote in 1968, "The rules contain many minor and so widely perceived as vague, confusing, unenforceable and containing traps for the unwary that they create more resentment than respect and thereby serve more to undermine the NCAA than to properly regulate intercollegiate sports." It may be important to note that the formal disqualification procedure has not been used for an incident involving during-the-game violence. As a practical matter, therefore, the game penalties created by the various rule committees provide the only real deterrent to excessively violent collegiate conduct. NCAA Assistant Executive Director Thomas C. Hansen argues that the threat of NCAA Tournament disqualification acts as a strong deterrent, since the college student "appreciates the once-in-a-lifetime opportunity represented by tournament participation." Hansen concludes by suggesting, "We have found this policy to be effective in minimizing incidents of questionable conduct on the part of participants in NCAA championships."⁴

The NCAA appears to be involved in other aspects of safety as well. The NCAA has joined with other amateur groups and their equipment manufacturers to form The National Operating Committee on Safety in Athletic Equipment to improve safety through improved equipment. Further, the Competitive Safeguards and Medical Aspects of Sports Committee has directed its attention to rules changes, improved conditioning programs and proper coaching techniques, which, combined with the equipment improvements, have helped to lower the number of deaths in football over the past 10 years from 24 in 1967 to four in 1969. There has been a much lower incidence in the rates of head and neck injuries as well.

# EXTERNAL CONTROLS: THE COURTS

Despite the enormous pressures working to keep sports violence cases out of litigation, an increasing number of cases are reaching the courts. The civil and criminal justice systems have power to deal with excess sport violence through laws prohibiting assault and battery and cases defining the scope of negligence. The argument used most often to justify court involvement in during-the-game violence is advanced by Gary Flakne, County Attorney for Hennipin County, Minnesota, and prosecutor in the leading American sports violence case, **State v. David Forbes,** "The mere act of putting on a uniform and entering the sports arena should not serve as a license to engage in behavior which would constitute a crime if committed elsewhere. If a participant in a sporting event were allowed to feel immune from criminal sanction merely by virtue of his being a participant, the spirit of maiming and serious bodily injury may well become the order of the day" (Horrow, 1980: 3). Most incidental contact is a normal and legitimate part of the game; other contact is harmful, malicious, repugnant, and no doubt illegal. The key question, therefore, is: Where do you draw the line between the two? In at least one case in each major sport, courts have grappled with this problem in decisions affecting both college and professional athletics.

In football, the leading case is **Hackbart v. Cincinnati Bengals,** a case arising from a 1973 game in which Charles "Booby" Clark, upset because the Bengals were losing the game, hit Denver Bronco safety Dale Hackbart on the back of his head with his right forearm while Hackbart was on one knee with his back to Clark after an interception. The blow resulted in three broken vertebrae, muscular atrophy in his arm, shoulder, and back, and a loss of strength and reflex in his arm. Hackbart filed suit in 1975, seeking $1,000,000 in damages. The lower Federal court judge ruled against Hackbart, reasoning that "the level of violence and frequency of emotional outbursts in NFL football is such that Dale Hackbart must have recognized and accepted the risk that he would be injured. There can be no recovery." On appeal, Judge William E. Doyle of the Tenth U.S. Circuit Court of Appeals decided that Hackbart, indeed, could sue for damages and that a football team could be held accountable. In so ruling, Judge Doyle emphasized that the act in question was an intentional one which was specifically prohibited by the NFL rules. As such, it could not be an inherent part of the game nor something the risk of which was assumed by Hackbart. On October 29, 1979, the United States Supreme Court refused to hear the case, which in effect, allowed the Appeals Court ruling ordering a new trial to stand. Thus, the Supreme Court has cleared the way for one player to sue another as a result of excessive, unwarranted contact. Further, the case demonstrated that it is possible for a team or a college athletic program to be held accountable for the actions of its players. Though the new trial is not scheduled to begin until early 1981, the Hackbart theory will have serious ramifications. Attorneys for the Bengals and Broncos agreed that the ruling will lead to many more such lawsuits. Further, the case would set a precedent that a player will be liable for any intentional violence that results in injury, even if no penalty has been called or punishment has been assessed by game or league officials.

In hockey, a September 21, 1969, incident gave rise to **Regina** v. **Green** (16 D.L.R. 3d 137, Prov. Ct. 1970) and **Regina** v. **Maki** (14 D.L.R. 3d 164 Prov. Ct. 1970). Boston Bruin Ted Green almost lost his life after being struck by a hockey stick wielded by Wayne Maki of the St. Louis Blues. Green "came off the boards and cuffed Maki with the back of his glove." Maki retaliated with his stick, coming straight overhead "like a logger splitting a stump."[5] Two charges were brought, one against each participant. The incident was condemned both in and out of hockey, but despite the severity of the injuries and the intentional violence involved, all the criminal charges were dismissed. Both defendants were acquitted on the basis of self-defense. Following the 1970 acquittals, Canadian Attorney General McMurtry wanted to avoid such prosecutions but could not because he thought the law was extremely clear. As a result of a get-tough policy on the **amateur** level, close to 100 convictions have been secured in Canada since 1969 (but none in the professional ranks).

In the United States, the major case is **State** v. **David Forbes** (No. 63280, Dist. Ct. Minn., July 19, 1975), a Minnesota case arising from a January 1975 game between the Boston Bruins and the host North Stars. The Bruins' Dave Forbes, returning to the ice from the penalty box during a stoppage in play (he was penalized for a previous fight with North Star's Henry Boucha), took a swing at Boucha. Although missing with his gloved hand,

Forbes struck Boucha with the butt end of his stick and, after Boucha fell to the ice covering his seriously injured face, Forbes jumped on Boucha, punching him until the two were separated by a third player. Surgery was needed to repair a small fracture in the floor of Boucha's right eye socket. Forbes was prosecuted under the Minnesota criminal assault statute. The jury could not agree on a verdict, however, and Prosecutor Flakne decided not to retry the case because of the likelihood of ending up with another deadlocked jury. By taking the **Forbes** case to trial at all, Flakne believed that he has "put the sports world on notice" that acts involving intention to cause serious bodily injury to another would not be tolerated in his jurisdiction. Though failing to set a definitive precedent, the **Forbes** case was significant if only because it focused legal attention on the issue of sports violence.

In basketball, the case of **Rudy and Sophie Tomjanovich and the Houston Rockets** v. **California Sports, Inc. (The Los Angeles Lakers),** (C.A.H. - 78-243, S.D. Texas, 1979) began on December 9, 1977, when Houston Rocket forward Tomjanovich was hit in the face by Laker Kermit Washington after an on-court scuffle between Washington and Houston player Kevin Kunnert. Soon after the incident, NBA Commissioner O'Brien fined Washington $10,000 while suspending him without pay for 60 days. Not satisfied with the League's action, the Tomjanovichs and the Rockets filed two separate suits on March 6, 1978. On August 7, 1979, after hearing two weeks of testimony from Rocket and Laker players, trainers, general managers, officials, and doctors about the incident and its aftermath, the five-man and one-woman jury deliberated for five hours and returned a verdict of $1.8 million in actual damages and $1.5 million in punitive damages for a total of $3.3 million—an award of some $600,000 **above** what attorneys for Tomjanovich had asked.

The jury found that Washington committed a battery, acted with "reckless disregard for the safety of other"; that Washington struck Tomjanovich "maliciously"; that the blow "was not accidental or unintentional, but was an intentional act"; that the Lakers were negligent because they "failed to adequately train and supervise" Kermit Washington; and also showed negligence because they retained Kermit Washington after they became "aware that he had a tendency for violence while playing basketball." Almost as important was what the jury **did not** find: that Kermit Washington was **not** acting in self-defense; that, since the "blow struck by Washington was far beyond any type of conduct permitted by the rules and customs of the game," Tomjanovich did **not** "consent to such conduct"; finally, Judge Singleton would **not** allow the jury to decide whether "violence, fighting, slugging or punching occurs in all sports," nor whether "it has been accepted" as a part of the game. Significantly, the jury apparently decided that individual acts of violence are not part of the game of basketball; the award will, therefore, help draw the line between violence and physical play on both the collegiate and professional level.

Despite the legal precedents, the courts cannot resolve the problem of "during-the-game" amateur or professional violence until the line separating legitimate, aggressive play from excessive, illegal contact is clearly defined. There are four separate reasons for this conclusion.

First, judges and juries must interpret laws which were not written to cover the case of sports violence. Typically, the legal battle pits the plaintiff (or the "state," if it is a criminal case) trying to prove that the athlete **intended** an assault and battery (or negligently disregarded the safety of his victim) against the defendant athlete, trying to prove that he acted in self-defense or out of an "involuntary reflex"; or that, by playing the game, the victim "consented to" the contact and "assumed the risk" of getting hurt. Sometimes, the team or athletic department can be sued under the theory that it is responsible for any of its employees' or agents' actions. It can also be sued under the theory that its "supervision" is negligent if it allows a violent player to play. All of these theories are used daily in the courtroom with relative ease; yet in a sport violence case, they are quite difficult to prove. The popular view is that people participate in athletics out of the love of the game, not of a malicious desire to harm an opponent. Therefore, it is much harder to make the case that one athlete **intended** to injure another one. If an athlete argues that he acted in self-defense, the general principle is that he could have used whatever force was necessary to protect himself. If he retaliated beyond what was necessary, however (as the courts found in **Hackbart** and **Tomjanovich**), he could not successfully argue self-defense. Some athletes have argued that their actions were not intended, but rather, were the product of an involuntary reflex to act. In the **Forbes** hockey case, the defense successfully argued that "since athletes are trained from age four that violence is part of the game, a player is conditioned from boyhood to react to violence without even thinking; thus, such violence is the product of an instinctive reflex and should not be penalized." Other athletes have argued that their victims have "consented to being hit" or "assumed the risk" of it. Most courts agreed that there is some merit to these arguments, but the familiar problem arises: drawing the line separating conduct that is consented to as part of the game and conduct that is beyond the scope of consent, and thus—illegal.

Second, many prosecutors simply do not want to file a criminal charge against a collegiate or professional athlete for something he does during a game. In the criminal system, filing charges is basically the decision of the prosecutor. In **Manning** v. **District Court of Rocksbury** (Mass. S.C. Adv. Sh. 1977, p.749), the court ruled that a Massachusetts prosecutor had every right to refuse to prosecute pitcher Ross Grimsley for hitting a Fenway Park spectator in the head with a pitch, even though the spectator pleaded that Grimsley be taken to court. Based on results from surveys which were sent to prosecutors who have jurisdiction over all professional sports teams, it seems that many of them do not view sports violence as a serious problem. According to one who would not bring charges: "The conduct is not prominent in most people's view of socially threatening behavior" (Horrow, 1980: 128).

Third, some argue that the courts should stay out of this area because criminal penalities have little deterrent value since most players do not think they are breaking the law. The fact that the four major hockey assault cases have all ended in an acquittal or hung jury reinforces this argument. Sports attorney Bob Woolf mentioned that within a year after the 1969 **Green** and **Maki** acquittals, the players were raising their sticks and "using" them again. Sociologists refer to this as the "community subgroup rational"; that the act becomes less criminal since everyone else in a subgroup performs similar acts. When there is trial, players wonder whether a defendant is being unfairly used as a "scapegoat" for the level of violence in the entire sport. This is similar to the argument of William Calley used in defending the atrocities his unit committed in Vietnam. In deciding not to prosecute Wilf Paiement for violently swinging his hockey stick in October of 1978, the Wayne County (Detroit) Prosecutors Office indicated that charges might not "have any deterrent effect at all, and might even encourage more violence in contact sports such as hockey." This argument is always made in connection with the need to "keep these cases within the family"; that NCAA administrators know better than anyone what conduct is unreasonable in the heat of the game; that these administraors will mete out punishments evenly, unlike the courts whose results will vary from jury to jury and state to state. That, as in an assault and battery case between husband and wife, court action will only increase hostility between athletes who must compete against each other frequently; and that court action will make the game less competitive if athletes must be concerned about going to jail for a clip in football or a slash in hockey.

Fourth, court cases have generally been unsuccessful in the past because of the problem of convincing jurors (some of them sports fans) that some violent conduct should be illegal even if it occurs during the game. Since there are no statutes dealing specifically with sports violence, juries "have no real sense of standards norms in these areas."[8] In the **Forbes** case, for example, both attorneys spent considerable time questioning many witnesses on "normal hockey play" (such as ways of carrying the stick and what is accepted body contact) yet the jury was too confused to make a decision. Even if the jury grasps the facts of a particular incident and understands the context of the sport, it is difficult for it to decide that the athlete they have seen many times on television or read about in the newspaper actually **broke the law.** In prosecuting the **Forbes** case, for example, Flakne attempted to select jurors who believed that it would make no difference "whether the assault took place during an athletic competition, in a bar, or on the street." Despite one of the most repugnant incidents of sports violence in hockey history, the jury was still not convinced. A mistrial was considered in the **Tomjanovich** case because the jury asked for a copy of the judge's instructions (with Rudy Tomjanovich's autograph) to keep as a souvenir. It is difficult to believe that a jury that knows even a little about amateur or professional sports would treat an athlete exactly as it would a "normal" defendant.

Despite the numerous problems involved in court intervention, there have been recent attempts to clarify the standards which govern court involvement. The Sports Violence Act, introduced into the United States House of

Representatives by Representative Ronald Mottl on July 31, 1980, and again on March 3, 1981, states that a player who "knowingly uses excessive physical force and thereby causes a risk of significant bodily injury to another person shall be fined no more than $5,000 or imprisoned not more than one year, or both." Excessive physical force as specifically defined by the bill is force that (a) has not reasonable relationship to the competitive goals of the sports, (b) is unreasonably violent, and (c) could not be reasonably foreseen or consented to by the person affected. The statute, H.R. 7903, attempts to define a clear line that separates normal and aggressive behavior from excessively violent and repugnant conduct. The original bill included language which would have covered both professional and amateur athletics (participants in all "otherwise lawful athletic events"). The subsequent proposal was amended to cover only professional athletes. It was thought that though the criminal sanctions would apply only to players in professional sport, the deterrent effect of a symbolic federal statement on the problem will "trickle down" to the youth and amateur levels of each sport.

The increasing trend of court intervention in during-the-game violence confirms the belief that organized sport, at any level, does not exist in a legal vacuum and that the operation of law does not stop at the ticket gate of a collegiate or professional sporting event. As this trend becomes even more significant, the responsibility for institutional and organizational control of violence in sports will be even greater.

## FOOTNOTES

[1]Testimony at congressional hearing on Sports Violence Act, Washington D.C. September 30, 1980.
[2]Letter from Assistant Director of NCAA Events, Dennis L. Poppe: May 19, 1980.
[3]All references to the NCAA constitution, bylaws and rules are from NCAA (1979).
[4]Personal Interview. May 16, 1980.
[5]From testimony of Boston Bruin hockey coach, Milt Schmidt, during a National Hockey League disciplinary hearing, 1969.
[6]Interview with Maricopa County attorney (Phoenix) Charles F. Hyder: 1978.

# REFERENCES

Eastwood, J.
1974    "The Effects of Viewing a Film of Professional Hockey on Aggression." *Medicine and Science in Sports.* 6: 158-163.

Horrow, Richard B.
1980    *Sports Violence: The Interaction Between Private Lawmaking and the Criminal Law.* Arlington, Virginia: Carrollton Press.
Lombardi, Vince and T. Cohane
1961    "Why Pros Play Better Football." *Look.* 25:122.
Marcus, Richard M.
1972    "Sport Safety: On the Offensive." *Trial Magazine* 8:12-13
McMurtry, William R.
1974    *Investigation and Inquiry Into Violence in Amateur Hockey.* Ottawa, Canada: Report for the Canadian Ministry of Community and Social Services.
National Collegiate Athletic Association (NCAA)
1979    *NCAA Manual 1978-79.* Shawnee, Kansas.
Nelson, David M.
1980    "Chop Block: Changes in NCAA Football Rules for 1980." *NCAA News* (February 15):4.
Smith, Michael
1978    "Social Determinants of Violence in Hockey: A Review." *Canadian Journal of Applied Sport Sciences.* 15 (December):

1979    "Towards an Explanation of Hockey Violence: A Reference-Other Approach." Unpublished paper.
Vaz, Edmund W.
1976    "The Culture of Young Hockey Players: Some Initial Observations," Pp. 209-213. In Andrew Yiannakis, T. McIntyre, M. Melnick, and Dale P. Hunt (eds.) *Sport Sociology: Contemporary Themes.* Dubuque, Ia: Kendall/Hunt.
Vaz, Edmund W. and Dianne Thomas
1974    "What Price Victory? An Analysis of Minorleague Players' Attitudes Toward Winning." *International Review of Sport Sociology.* 9: 33-35.
Woolf, Bob
1977    *Behind Closed Doors.* New York: New American Library.

# THE LAW AND COLLEGIATE ATHLETICS IN PUBLIC INSTITUTIONS*

By
Cym H. Lowell

Collegiate athletics is one of the most publicly prominent elements of the university community. The success or failure of an institution's athletic teams is carefully followed by its students, alumni, and friends, and may have significant effects on such disparate elements of the institution as campus morale, alumni giving, and the structure of financial budgets. The prominence of athletics programs is also reflected by social, financial, political, and legal problems that the programs pose in the university community—to which the articles in this journal bear ample testimony.

The legal issues that an active athletics program can generate constitute one of the most currently troublesome aspects. While a number of matters have been simmering, probably the most publicized has been the federal government's role in collegiate sports programs. This issue has been crystallized in connection with the obligation of colleges and universities to provide equal opportunities for sports participation to both male and female students (under the aegis of the Higher Education Amendments of 1972, as implemented by regulations promulgated by the U.S. Department of Health, Education, and Welfare, and the Fourteenth Amendment to the Constitution). Other issues have received less public attention but are equally important. These issues concern the nature of the relationship

*Reprinted from *Educational Record*, Vol. 60 (1979), pp. 482-98. c 1979 by American Council on Education. Used by permission. The article is adapted from *The Law of Sports* by John C. Weistart and Cym H. Lowell (Charlottesville, Va.: Michie/Bobbs-Merrill Law Publishing, 1979) and omits legal citations and other technical references that appear in chapter 1 of *The Law of Sports*. The author acknowledged in the *Educational Record* article his gratitude to Mary F. Kish for her contribution to the paper.

between a college or university and the other principal parties involved in athletic activities—athletes, athletic associations, and the federal government.

The legal issues posed by the relationships have not been resolved, but have been sufficiently defined to suggest that each relationship raises a number of considerations which should be carefully scrutinized by the collegiate athletics community. My purpose will be to review (in a nontechnical manner) the principal legal relationships that a public institution encounters in connection with its athletics programs; identify how the courts have characterized these relationships; and suggest some implications of the characterizations.

# RELATIONSHIP OF INSTITUTION TO STUDENT ATHLETES

The initial relationship to be considered is that of the institution to the student athletes to whom it provides financial assistance in the form of scholarships or grants-in-aid. The legal nature of this relationship has never been clear in the case of students in public institutions, and its ultimate characterization could cause some serious problems for both parties. (Slightly different principles may affect the relationship between a private institution and its students, but they are not addressed here.)

The relationship could be viewed first as traditionally academic. The argument in favor of this view would be that athletics is a part of the general concept of education. Colleges and universities are not monolithic, and their programs include a variety of activities that contribute to the overall educational process. The courts have in some contexts supported this view. In this sense, the student athlete would be viewed as a participant in the institution's athletic activities as part of its educational program who receives financial aid to defray the cost of education. That the aid given the athlete may be subject to the condition that he or she maintain athletic eligibility would not detract from the aid's educational nature, since staying eligible is a frequent condition of financial aid provided to students participating in other activities. For example, the student athlete would be perceived on the same basis as is a student who is required to maintain a given grade-point average to retain a financial award or a music or drama student who is given assistance with the expectation that he or she will perform publicly as part of the educational program. For relationships so characterized, few adverse consequences for either the institutions or the athletes would result, since this characterization is traditional.

The relationship could, alternatively, be viewed as a contractual arrangement in which the athlete agrees to participate in athletics in exchange for the promise by the educational institution to provide financial support. The argument in favor of this view would be that athletics is not a part of the educational process, but is, rather, a business activity conducted by the institution and the support is actually for services rendered. Under this view, a condition requiring that the athlete maintain eligibility would be distinguished from similar conditions placed on grants to other students. A requirement that a student maintain a given grade average or participate in musical or dramatic activities would be seen as not contributing to the financial advantage of the institution, as compared with an athletic program that in many schools may make a significant financial contribution. Although public performances improve the skills a music or art department seeks to "teach," the skills displayed in intercollegiate athletics reflect less clearly the educational functions of the institution. It may also be suggested that it should be of little importance that the student athlete-institution relationship occurs in an academic environment and is commonly believed to be noncontractual, inasmuch as the law should be applied to the factual situation as it arises.

# THE INSTITUTION AS EMPLOYER

Under the contractual view, the possible consequences to the parties are far different from those commonly understood. The institution could be deemed an employer of the athletes, so that it might have to comply with the various requirements of laws that apply to or regulate the terms of employment. These requirements would include state workmen's compensation laws, federal tax withholding rules, the Fair Labor Standards Act, the Occupational Safety and Health Act, and the National Labor Relations Act. A contractual characterization of the relationship could also have other consequences for the institution. For example, it might lead to an assertion that its principal revenue-generating sports constitute a business of institution, which could lead to other problems, such as an assertion that the income derived from these events, including broadcast revenues, would be subject to federal income tax as business income that is unrelated to the tax-exempt activities of the institution. Although this prospect may seem to be somewhat fanciful, the Internal Revenue Service has suggested this possibility in the past few years. A contractual characterization would also have unfortunate consequences for the athlete, who might have to pay income tax on the stipend. These are not the kinds of consequences that are generally thought to flow from the athlete-institution relationship.

Although the nature of the student-institution relationship has not been resolved, several recent court decisions suggest that in some circumstances it can be viewed as contractual. These cases have arisen in three basic areas.

The first involves the legal status of a scholarship or a grant-in-aid. If the stipend were viewed as academic, then it would constitute a gift from the institution, though it might be subject to conditions—for example, that the athlete maintain eligibility in accordance with specified rules and regulations—and it would raise few legal issues. If, on the other had, it were viewed as contractual, the consequences noted above would then become much more plausible.

# THE ATHLETE AS EMPLOYEE

In the few cases that have considered financial aid awards, the courts have clearly indicated that these could be considered contracts and have found not only that the motivation for their conferral is often to induce the recipient to attend the conferring institution and be of assistance to its athletic program, but also that there is inherent in the award a requirement that the athlete participate in the athletic program. The most important case dealing with financial aid awards is **Taylor v. Wake Forest University,** 16 N.C. App. 117, 191 S.E. 2d 379 (1972). The university had awarded a four-year football scholarship to a promising young athlete. The grant was conditioned only on his complying with the rules of the Atlantic Coast Conference, the National Collegiate Athletic Association, and Wake Forest University, all of which required the maintenance of eligibility. The university also had a policy, unwritten when the award was conferred, of terminating financial aid if an athlete failed to attend practice sessions. The athlete participated in the football program during his first year, but after achieving low grades decided not to participate further. The school then terminated the scholarship because he failed to participate in football. When the athlete's parents subsequently sued to recover his expenses in completing his education, the court found that the scholarship was a contract, since the athlete had agreed ''in consideration of the scholarship award,... to maintain his athletic eligibility, and this meant both physically and scholastically.'' The athlete's failure to maintain physical eligibility by not participating was seen to indicate that he ''was not complying with his contractual obligations'' and could not, therefore, prevail.

The result in **Taylor**—that the athlete was unable to recover the costs of his education—seems reasonable enough on its facts. But the court's opinion is troublesome because of the effect that its basic conclusion (that the athlete agreed to participate in consideration for the award) could have on other athletes and institutions, which were noted above. (The court in **Taylor** did not consider—and it was apparently not argued by counsel—the possibility that the award could have been construed as an educational grant with a condition that the student athlete maintain eligibility in accordance with established rules and regulations of the school, conference, and national association.)

The second group of cases in which the courts have had an opportunity to consider the nature of the student—institution relationship involves situations where workmen's compensation recovery, which is available only to ''employees,'' has been sought for injuries to athletes. These cases are important to the extent that they indicate under what circumstances a collegiate athlete will be considered to be an ''employee'' of his or her institution. Briefly, the courts have concluded that, as a general proposition, a college or university athlete will not be considered an employee merely because he or she is the recipient of financial aid, but where there is evidence of a contractual relationship between an athlete and an institution (so that the receipt of a scholarship or other benefits can be viewed as consideration for the performance of athletic services, as in **Taylor**), the athlete may be treated as an employee for workmen's compensation purposes. The cases do not stand for the proposition that a truly amateur athlete who participates in sports an as avocation and receives financial aid only to defray educational expenses will be found to be an employee.

# THE TAXIBILITY OF SCHOLARSHIPS

The final area in which the courts have made determinations about the status of athletes who participate in amateur athletics has been in federal income tax cases. The most important tax issue involving amateur athletes is the taxability of scholarships or grants-in-aid. The Internal Revenue Code provides that when a student receives a scholarship at an educational institution, it will generally not be includable within his or her gross income if it carries no requirement of any substantial quid pro quo from the recipient.

Although no cases deal directly with the question, it has been considered in a recent public ruling. The Internal Revenue Service, in Revenue Ruling 77-263 (1977-2 C.B. 47), was asked to rule on the taxability of awards given to students who expected to participate in athletics. The awards were governed by the rules of an intercollegiate conference, which required, among other things, that the recipient be accepted by the university under its normal standards. In addition, the award could not be cancelled for non-participation in the year of its grant. On these facts, the service concluded that the award was a nontaxable scholarship, reasoning that the recipient was not required to participate in order to receive the award and that the university requires no particular activity of any of its scholarship recipients. Although students who receive athletic scholarships do so because of their special abilities in a particular sport and are expected to participate in the sport, the scholarship is not cancelled in the event the student cannot participate, and the student is not required to engage in any other activities in lieu of participating in the sport. In light of the IRS's emphasis on the absence of a requirement that the recipient participate in athletics as a condition to the award (even if the non-participation is a result of a "student's unilateral decision not to participate"), the existence of such a requirement could make the award taxable.

In short, the courts have had several opportunities to consider the nature of the relationship between academic institutions and athletes who receive scholarships or grants-in-aid, and in some circumstances the relationship could be deemed to be contractual. Such a conclusion is at odds with the conventional understanding of the parties; its wide application would produce a range of consequences that would require a critical re-evaluation of the entire relationship.

A number of implications could be drawn from this possibility, but college or university administrators should make sure that the risk of such a contractual ruling is minimized to the greatest extent possible. Rules on the structure and terms of financial aid arrangements should not provide any basis for an assertion that the awards are conferred in exchange for a promise by the student to engage in athletic activity. The practices of a particular institution should be supervised to make sure that the handling of awards (within the rules of a particular athletic association) also does not provide support for a contractual characterization of the relationship.

Cases such as **Taylor** also suggest the necessity for delegating to someone within the organized collegiate athletics community responsibility for staying abreast of litigation nationally that touches on the nature of the student-institution relationship. Decisions having implications like those in **Taylor** could be avoided if the "academic" nature of the relationship were carefully presented to the court, and if the court were advised of the potential consequences of a contractual characterization. Situations such as **Taylor** might also be avoided if cases presenting particularly troublesome issues (and factual circumstances) could be settled without trial (or appeal) and the possible publication of a decision. These steps should reduce the likelihood that other courts would so clearly conclude that the relationship in particular cases was contractual.

# INSTITUTION AND ATHLETIC REGULATORY ASSOCIATIONS

A second relationship that may pose a wide range of legal concerns for a college or university relates to the athletics associations or conferences—regional and national—of which it may be a member. Their basic purpose is to facilitate competition and provide a forum in which each member institution may benefit from the judgement, experience, and expertise of other members in the analysis and solution of common problems. In this sense, an association will accomplish the practical business of administering the athletics activities of its membership.

This function will be performed through a formal structure, as reflected in a constitution, bylaws, and detailed rules and regulations setting forth policies and procedures for the association. Each member is obligated to comply with these various provisions (to the extent that they are lawful and enforceable). The association also investigates whether impermissible conduct has occurred at a member institution, and, if it has, decides whether sanctions should be imposed on the wrongdoing party.

In other words, athletics associations exercise a considerable degree of control over the athletics-related activities of their members and they act as legislative, judicial, and executive bodies for the activities within their ambit of authority. The existence and exercise of this control have caused much controversy in the athletics community during the past several years, and many of the disputes have found their way into the courts. It is unlikely that the frequency of such disputes will diminish soon. Thus, the leading sports periodicals regularly feature articles on investigations conducted by athletics associations and the impact they have on the institutions under scrutiny. In addition, the differing economic needs of large and small institutions have caused some associations to adopt rules that are not consistent with the perceived needs or interests of all members, instances that have led to efforts by those members to overturn such rules.

In light of this situation, a review is warranted of the basic principles the courts have articulated to define some aspects of the nature of the relationship between institutions and athletics associations. This review will indicate the extent to which courts tend to review cases as they arise, and suggest limits for association action.

When disputes have arisen between an institution and an athletics association, the court traditionally reviewed the actions of the association, assuming that the action did not pose constitutional problems, on a very limited basis by applying the so-called rules of voluntary associations. According to this body of law, the general rule has been that the actions of an association will be held to be conclusive, except when mistake, fraud, illegality, collusion, or arbitrariness can be shown. These principles suggest that if an institution were unhappy with some particular action, its only recourse might be to withdraw from the association, though this may not be practicable if it wants to maintain a viable intercollegiate athletics program.

# REVIEWING ASSOCIATION ACTIONS

Recently, however, the courts have shown a much greater willingness to review the actions of athletics associations on their merits, especially when the interests of the institution affected by association action are substantial. Specifically, the courts have in some cases attempted to ascertain whether the powers entrusted to associations have been exercised in a manner that is reasonable and consistent with the more general requirements of felt public policies. In several of the more recent disputes between institutions and athletic associations, there is a rather surprising lack of attention to the traditional principles of voluntary associations. In some cases, the issue of their application is not considered by the court, and in others they are applied in a manner that indicates an inclination to scrutinize actions of athletics associations differently from what was thought to be the case just a few years ago. (In addition, the courts have been asked to review cases in which it is asserted that association action has affected the constitutional rights of an institution, and these cases have been reviewed on a much different basis.)

The limit of judicial review of athletics association actions is still unestablished; but the courts are regularly reviewing cases against associations on their merits. This trend is important because athletics association actions may no longer be treated as conclusive. The institution—association relationship is placed on a different basis, inasmuch as dissatisfied institu-

188

tions will have alternatives other than accepting association action or resigning. Rather, an institution can now have the appropriateness of association action determined by an independent third party, i.e., judicial review. Though little empirical information is available, it is likely that this trend has affected how associations act.

Should disputes between an institution and an association reach the courts, they will generally relate to the validity of certain association rules and the propriety of association procedures in determining whether an institution has violated a rule. Determining rule validity raises many important issues (which are discussed in **The Law of Sports**), but determining procedural propriety has attracted much more public attention.

# PROCEDURAL VALIDITY

The procedures an association follows to enforce its rules consist of several levels of activity, which are of a distinctly investigatory, prosecutorial, and adjudicatory nature. When it is believed that improper acts have taken place, the association investigates the surrounding circumstances, and, if there are grounds for believing that such acts have occurred, it will then conduct such proceedings as are necessary to determine whether its rules have been violated.

The validity of these procedures in a particular case—whether they provide adequate procedural protection for the institution's interests—will generally be determined by the procedural due process requirements of the Fifth and Fourteenth Amendments to the Constitution. To trigger the due process requirements, two facts must be present in a given situation. The first is an act undertaken by a person or entity that is affected with "state action"; i.e., the constitutional requirements apply to only public, as opposed to purely private, action. Over the past few years, it has become clear that an athletic association having public institutions in its membership will be deemed to be within the state action concept. The second factor is the deprivation of a right or interest that is sufficiently important to require constitutional protection. The range of protected interests has not been defined precisely, but some courts have held that the interest of institutions (or athletes) in athletic participation will qualify for protection, though other courts have found to the contrary.

If it is determined that an institution's interests are entitled to constitutional protection, the next step will be to determine what process is due. Generally, the procedural safeguards required in a given situation will be governed by its particular facts and circumstances. A court will make a determination by balancing each party's interests including such factors as the importance of the jeopardized interests, the type of proceeding in which the interest is presented, the appropriateness of the procedure requested to prevent the arbitrary deprivation of a protected interest, and the costs of requiring such a procedure. The seriousness of the sanction imposed may also be considered.

The balancing process may demonstrate the necessity of specific procedures in particular circumstances, but the basic requirement of procedural due process is that before any action may be taken, the affected person must be given a "fair hearing," which will include notice and a hearing. The formality of the notice will depend on the seriousness of the interest. When significant interests are at stake, the notice should recite the time and place of hearing, as well as a statement of the specific charges and the grounds, which, if proven, would justify the imposition of a sanction, and should be given long enough before the hearing date to allow time for preparation of a proper defense. Although the nature of a hearing depends on the particular case, the hearing must enable the decision maker to hear both sides of the situation and should entail the rudiments of an adversary proceeding.

Thus, in cases involving significant potential penalties, it may be necessary that the affected person be accorded the right to counsel, given a list of the charges that are to be presented, provided with a list of the names and facts to be elicited from adverse witnesses, and be allowed to undertake reasonable discovery activities. Once the hearing has been held, the findings and conclusions may have to be published and made available for inspection. In short, an institution subjected to the enforcement activities of an athletic association should have the opportunity to appear, be heard, and make an intelligent and informed defense to the preferred charges.

# PROCEDURAL PRINCIPLES AND ENFORCEMENT

The application of these procedural principles has been considered in a number of cases. Some of the problems regarding procedural propriety are still basically unresolved; these arise relatively frequently in the context of enforcement activities of athletics associations.

One such problem results from the overlap in the institution-athlete and the institution-association relationship: the procedures an athletic association follows to determine whether its rules and regulations have been violated may involve only the member institution and not the athlete whose conduct may have precipitated the investigation. If a violation is found, the association may then impose a sanction upon the institution; and if the college or university does not take appropriate action with respect to the athlete, additional sanctions may be imposed against it. The question then becomes, is the athlete entitled to procedural rights in the intitial proceeding, even though he or she may not be a direct participant in it? The argument against granting the athlete such rights would emphasize that the institution need not take action against the athlete, though if it does not, it may itself be sanctioned by the association. Also, the athlete may have no interest that can be constitutionally protected, so that there is no need for his or her participation. The athlete, however, might argue that he or she may have an interest that can be protected; if a violation is found, he or she is the one who will feel the eventual punishment. Recent cases seem to confirm that an institution may have to comply with the association's decision, since failure to comply may jeopardize its entire athletics program.

# A DIFFERENT DILEMMA

A "compulsion" to comply could put an institution in the vise of a difficult dilemma. A contractual obligation to an association to act as specified by the association may conflict with its constitutional duty to protect the athlete before complying. If, in protecting the athlete, additional facts not presented in the association-institution proceeding show that the athlete should not be punished, then the institutional decision makers would be in a precarious position. In light of this potential dilemma, athletes could be given procedural rights in the initial proceeding.

A further question results if the association and institution hold separate proceedings: can the association, consistent with constitutional requirements, compel the institution to declare an athlete ineligible if the institution's proceedings show that the athlete should not (or may not) be punished? Though resolution of this issue is also not clear, the institution's public constitutional duty would seem to take precedence over its private contractural obligation if reasonable evidence were generated by its proceedings that there had been no violation that would cause an athlete to be made ineligible.

An additional aspect of enforcement activities that may raise interesting procedural questions relates to the availability to institutions of prehearing judicial relief to compel an association to follow appropriate procedures. Improper preliminary procedures may cause an institution to suffer damage that could not be easily remedied, even though an ultimate suspension or other penalty may eventually be overturned for lack of requisite procedural formality. Accordingly, in many cases it will be important to determine the extent to which an institution could compel an association to conform its procedures to applicable due process requirements, or, if it has already adopted procedures that conform to those requirements, compel adherence to them.

This discussion of the various legal principles that define some aspects of the relationship between academic institutions and athletics associations is important for a number of reasons. The basic reason is that the terms of this relationship can be critically important to an institution. Athletics associations control to a large extent the structure and conduct of an institution's athletics program, and it may be essential to determine the limits of that control or the extent to which it can be challenged successfully. In addition, the many cases that have enunciated the principles indicate that a significant number of disputes about regulation of athletics programs have arisen. The number of disputes suggests that many institutions perceive that they have substantial interests in their athletics programs and that these interests have not been satisfactorily advanced or protected by the pertinent athletics associations. This dissatisfaction with association protection is illustrated by the controversies that have churned for several years over the conduct of investigations by national associations into the athlete recruiting practices of colleges and universities, scrutinized in congressional hearings, as well as in the popular press. Such disputes have resulted in the filing of several suits against the investigating associations by institutions that have felt that they were not treated fairly under an association's internal procedures.

These cases may also indicate that the relationship between academic institutions and athletics associations is changing, though the change may also be the result of a number of other factors; for example, the increased economic importance of athletics programs (both in the positive sense of producing revenue and in the negative sense of consuming funds, in some cases, from general sources) and the litigious nature of our society being reflected in the relationships in the collegiate athletics community.

The institution-athletic association relationship is important in the administration of an institution's athletics program, and it is apparent that it carries the potential for generating significant legal problems.

# INSTITUTIONS AND THE FEDERAL GOVERNMENT

An additional relationship that should be considered is that between academic institutions and the federal government. This relationship has developed along many lines over the past two or three decades, as educational programs have increasingly benefited from public funding. Although the flow of funds is economically beneficial, the attendant governmental regulation may be much less welcome. College or university administrators often complain that the federal government has become increasingly involved (or has increasingly interfered) in the conduct of academic programs traditionally free of such outside scrutiny. Although federal support of athletics programs is quite small, it has attracted the scrutiny of governmental regulators.

As noted above, a recent important development in collegiate athletics has been the evolution from a system of private administrative regulation of athletics to one that increasingly involves public supervision of the acts of the private adminstrators. This charge has resulted partially from the courts' willingness to review the merits of the grievances of those who are affected by association action. There has not been a perceptible effort by federal agencies to supervise directly the administration of collegiate athletics, probably not so much from lack of concern as lack of incentive. Many of the conflicts in collegiate athletics have either been negotiated or resolved judicially. A federal involvement (through the enactment of legislation and implementing regulations) would then be anticipated only where specific problems are either not resolved privately or by the courts or are resolved in a manner that is not satisfactory to the Congress.

Two separate situations are possible that might bring federal involvement. One would be passage of legislation intended to remedy problems prevalent in our society generally and in collegiate athletics. In this situation, the scheme could severly affect relationships in the athletics community. The primary example of such legislation is Title IX of the Higher Education Amemdments of 1972, which prohibits discrimination on the basis of sex in federally funded educational programs. The regulations that have been adopted to implement the Title IX requirements have generated significant controversy in the collegiate community, partly because legislators failed to take account of the nature of athletics matters in educational institutions. Some collegiate athletics administrators have suggested that the regulations could precipitate the demise of major college athletics as they are now known. Although the ultimate effect of the regulations is not yet clear, it is apparent that when Title IX was passed, its effects on athletics received little analysis. It is also clear that it will have, and has had, a significant impact on the participation of females in competitive collegiate athletics. Similar developments could occur in other areas if statutory schemes of general application are imposed upon collegiate athletics.

The second type of situation in which federal involvement could affect collegiate athletics would be the passage of legislation specifically designed to resolve problems in the athletics community generally that have enough public impact to require specific legislative resolution. Though no such comprehensive legislation has been enacted, Congress passed the Amateur Sports Act of 1978 to rectify problems in administering American participation in international competition (for example, in the Olympic and Pan American games). A brief review of this legislation and its history suggests that the spectre of federal involvement in collegiate athletics is not as fanciful as may have been thought just a few years ago. This existence of this legislation indicates Congress is not committed to perpetuating vested interests in the athletics community if legislators feel that the public interest is not being served. Moreover, the history of the Amateur Sports Act suggest the remote possibility that other legislation might bring direct federal control of some aspects of athletics. Once such control is established, it could be too easily broadened to include all areas of athletic activity (even collegiate sports) within its purview.

# AN EXAMPLE OF FEDERAL INTERVENTION

Congress felt a need to intervene in international competition administration to correct several separate, but related problems. The first problem was inadequate performance by the United States Olympic Committee (USOC), which has under various names governed American participation in the Olympic games since 1950. After hearing testimony on the problems relating to the USOC, the Senate Committee on Commerce in 1974 concluded that the USOC had failed to meet its obligations to its members, athletes, and the American public for a variety of reasons. A second, but closely related, problem was the long-term feud between the Amateur Athletic Union and the National Collegiate Athletic Association. These bodies are responsible for American participation in international amateur athletics. Both had been said to have "an inordinate capacity to engage in petty disputes [and] . . . a fierce determination to perpetuate their own rule over amateur sports."

From lengthy hearings, the Senate Committee on Commerce concluded that "it is no longer advisable to permit elements of the present amateur sports structure of the United States to continue without substantial reform ...[and] that needed change will not come about voluntarily, . . . " The legislative proposals which accompanied these comments in 1974 called for an independent federal agency to oversee international competition. This proposal met with substantial resistance and was ultimately defeated in favor of a restructuring of the USOC, which involves a much less sweeping change.

This instance of legislative intervention in international amateur athletics suggest the type of legislative response that may be expected when unresolved (or unresolvable) problems develop in the sports community. The findings and conclusions that underlay this legislation portend potentially far-reaching consequences for other aspects of sports activity in this country. The clear message of the sponsors of the legislation was that Congress will not allow the rights of those involved in athletics or the public to be reduced by the people or institutions (or both) responsible for the administration of sports activities. Thus, collegiate athletics must not be administered in a manner that will result in federal regulation. Though individual institutions cannot direct sports "governance" nationwide, collectively they can.

The relationship between the federal government and colleges and universities regarding athletics programs is not at all well developed at this point. There has been no groundswell of feeling that there is any need for comprehensive federal regulation of collegiate sports activities, but important public policies may require that such a relationship be explicit. These policies are embodied in Title IX and the applicaton of its requirements to collegiate sports; the congressional hearings on enforcement activities of some athletic associations; and the enactment of the Amateur Sports Act of 1978. Perhaps the lesson from these developments is that collegiate athletics administrators should conduct their programs so that the public is reassured that federal intervention is not needed.

The conduct of an athletics program by a college or university will require that it maintain important relationships with a number of different groups. The technical, legal terms of many of these relationships have not been fully developed at this point, and definitive guidance will probably be forthcoming only if disputes between the parties to the relationships require judicial resolution or congressional action. The nature of these relationships must be carefully examined by the athletics community, since each poses the potential for generating legal complications. It is not possible for administrators to avoid all of these possible difficulties, but many can be circumvented if the relationships (and their implications) are kept in mind in structuring and administering programs (at the individual institution and athletics association level). The emerging issues regarding collegiate athletics will continue to evolve. It will be of interest to see whether the "shoal waters" suggested by these issues can be avoided. Such avoidance will require careful navigation by those who are responsible for administering athletics programs.

# COMMUNITY INTERESTS AND INTERCOLLEGIATE ATHLETICS

By
Erik K. M. Kjeldsen

The problems of intercollegiate athletics need little, if any, elaboration since they are examined extensively in both this set of readings and elsewhere (e.g., Michener, 1976; Underwood, 1980). These problems, however, provide the foundation of concern for this analysis. How is it that a subsystem of an institution devoted to pristine intellectual and problem-solving goals can be so susceptible to corruption and that the institution finds it so hard to rid itself of what Tom Meschary (1972) described as the "disease in sport"? Many have attempted to analyze these questions and have made extensive sets of recommendations for the change in intercollegiate sport. The Carnegie Commission (Savage, 1929) and the American Council on Education (Hanford, 1974) are just two examples. The impact of these and similar reports has been negligible. Very often the reason for lack of change rests with the inability of university administrations and intercollegiate athletic regulatory bodies to understand and control the influence of external constituencies on athletic programs.

The present essay will analyze the sources of pressure on athletic departments which emanate from community groups which have an apparent vested interest, either political or economic, in intercollegiate athletics. It is suggested that many of the problems of intercollegiate athletics are not the result of the activities of villainous individuals, but are the outcome of certain systemic conditions (e.g., norms of winning at all costs, financial rewards) which will captivate any member of the system no matter what is his/her value position.[1] Because we have directed suggestions for change at individuals and not the system, it is no wonder the tide of corruption has not been curtailed.

# INSTITUTIONAL CONTROL AND COMMUNITY INTEREST

The National Collegiate Athletic Association (NCAA), in its continuing struggle to deal with athletic excesses, specifies that athletic councils (or other governing bodies) be comprised of more than 50 percent faculty and/or administrators (NCAA Constitution, 1979: 3-2-[a] and [b]). Needless to say, this regulation is designed with the objective that institutional control will keep athletics in its "proper place" relative to academic functions in the institution. It is also evident that this objective has not been realized in many colleges and universities. Part of the reason for this failure lies in two problems with the nature of the rules. One of these problems is in the lumping together of faculty and athletic administrators. If the purpose of the rule is to maintain the priority of the academic function of the university by placing "academics" in a numerical majority, the rule-makers overlook the fact that athletic administrators develop a vested interest in the growth and development of the athletic department itself. Therefore, their words, as members of such councils, must be examined with a degree of skepticism when they make statements relative to academic priority. It would not be surprising if their words in support of academic priority were somewhat inconsistent with their actions in support of athletic program growth. To the degree that athletics is seen as a source of organizational benefit in the form of financial return (television, bowl and play-off returns) and positive public relations, athletic administrators will be tempted to look the other way when academic considerations are circumvented. This logic would dictate that athletic councils should be dominated by academics (faculty only or faculty and university academic administrators) who have no vested interest in the athletic program. Athletic administrators would serve only in a non-voting advisory capacity under this plan. Domination of the council by academics with no connection to the athletic departments does not guarantee decision-making with academic concerns as the highest priority. The influence of alumni, athletic administrators and others with vested interests in athletics often reaches the level of appointing committees, assuring that only "friends" of intercollegiate sport are appointed to athletic councils. These "friends" are often so motivated by the symbolic and status rewards of association with the glamour of athletics that they frequently promote growth and athletic "hoopla" with nearly the same enthusiasm as athletic directors themselves. While no organization wishes to invite a "fox into the chicken house," if only supporters of athletic giantism are appointed to athletic councils, the stage becomes set for abuse.

The second problem relative to the rules themselves lies in paragraph 3-2-(b), which is devoted to external contituencies of the athletic social system. This paragraph refers to the responsibility of the institution "for the acts of an independent agency, organization or individual when the institution's executive or athletic administration has knowledge that such agency, organization or individual is promoting the institution's athletic program . . . " This statement is completely inadequate to deal with the substantial number of community interest groups which, for a variety of reasons, wish to play some role in the athletic functions of the university. Those interested in the Athletic Department include, but are not limited to, such groups as local business persons; commercial suppliers of food, equipment, and other materials for the Athletic Department and others in and around the university; and, finally, fans and other hangers-on of the athletic teams who have come to be emotionally involved with the success of the athletic teams.

These interested parties may be organized into formal groups such as "booster clubs" (under one or another name) or may act as separate interest groups or may communicate their concern as individuals. In all cases, they back up their interest with extensive verbal and financial support, thereby providing considerable influence on the Athletic Department both directly and indirectly through their network of associations within and without the university. In conjunction with alumni spokespersons, they form an organized and vocal coalition which exercises strong influence over the key administrators charged with the conduct of the athletic program and, through them, exercise control over the program while disorganized faculty and administrators powerlessly express their concern over the "evils of intercollegiate athletics."

From the standpoint of reference group theory, the athletic director is surrounded by a number of "significant others" and responds to those most able to support their expressions of concern with sanctions (either gratifying or punishing) which are relevant to his values and priorities. Most athletic directors are former players and coaches in the "major" (i.e., spectator) sports (Ceglarski, 1979: 9) and, understandable, have a strong emotional commitment to the growth and well-being of those sports. Also, as any bureaucrat, the athletic director has a vested interest in the growth and security of his organizational unit and, therefore, responds enthusiastically to expressions of interest in the growth and expansion of the athletic department (as long as such growth does not adversely affect "his" sport, of course). Hence, the picture emerges of an athletic director receiving influence attempts from a variety of personal and organizational sources and selecting from among those inputs according to his/her own personal concerns for program development, ego gratification and career advancement through organizational growth. It is not difficult to see from this analysis how the athletic department personnel, the alumni and these "community interests" naturally reinforce one another's concerns for a "bigger and better" athletic program. Together they form a coalition which, through its affiliations and control over resources, is able to resist the attempts of faculty and others to intrude disturbing questions based on educational concerns into the conduct of the athletic program.

To this point the analysis has focused on the organizational goals of financial return, positive public relations and/or the personal returns of ego-enhancement and career advancement. Such goals of both organizations and individuals are inherent in human life, and much that is enhancing to human culture has been achieved in pursuit of such ends. Where, then, is the problem? The problem, of course, lies in the methods utilized to achieve the goals and the consequent effects of these methods on both the organizations and individuals which comprise the system. When individual athletes are exploited in the interest of achieving organizational objectives and/or the personal goals of others, the system is no longer a "symbiotic" relationship; that is, it is not working to the good of all concerned. As long as individual athletes leave the intercollegiate sport system without being educated (or at least trained) for a meaningful role in society it may be claimed that the sport subsystem is exploitative (Sack, 1977). It may also be argued that methods utilized within sport which are antithetical to the principles of the educational system of which they profess to be a part are destructive both to the individuals who have to cope with the inconsistency as well as to the public image of the educational system.

And what of "winning"? Many have alluded to the idea that the evils of sport are the result of the pursuit of victory being shifted from a means to educational ends to an end in itself (thereby permitting the violation of educational principles in the pursuit of the higher goal—victory). The present analysis, on the other hand, is based on the idea that winning is still a means to an end. However, it is the ends that have been shifted. Instead of the growth and development of the individual being the goal in many institutions today, the ends being pursued are the growth and development of the athletic department or university as an organization and the career advancement of the sport bureaucrats, with the individual participant being exploited in the pursuit of each of the aforementioned goals. In short, as organizational theory informs us, the client (the student-athlete) has become the servant of the institution (the university) and is manipulated for the good of the institution itself.

Soon after the emergence of intercollegiate athletics, the great public interest in these activities was perceived by college administrators and the outcomes of this enthusiasm on the university as a whole were not lost on them. Since then, intercollegiate athletics have been seen by many administrators as an arm of the university, and student-athletes have been consciously or unconsciously used as agents of the university in the pursuit of the good of the institution. A brief examination of these perceived outcomes in the light of present-day research should be instructive in understanding the motivations for the takeover of intercollegiate athletics by university administrators.

Much promotion of intercollegiate athletics has been carried out in the name of the good of the university achieved through alumni contributions and the fear of the loss of these contributions. Many justify big-time sport (even after it is shown to be a losing business for most) through the belief that alumni donations rise and fall with the "success" of the "focal" athletic team(s), particularly football. Recent research has not supported this belief (Sigelman & Carter, 1979; Sack & Watkins, 1980). It appears that intercollegiate sport ranks quite low on the priority list of alumni (Frey, 1981; Rossi, 1981). The belief in strong alumni interest seems to result from the efforts of a few in power positions among alumni groups as a result of occupancy of formal positions in alumni organizations or of being large financial contributors (Frey, 1981; Sack & Watkins, 1980). The reality seems to be that for the large majority of institutions the high interest in athletics expressed by the vocal few does not seem to be shared by large segments of alumni populations and that financial contributions do not appear to rise and fall in direct relationship with the success of the athletic program.

What of the belief in direct financial return from the conduct of an athletic program? It has long ago been shown that there are only a few institutions which actually realize a profit from athletics (Jackson, 1962). For the rest, large sums poured into big-time sport would appear not only to be a drain on monies which might be used to support recreational sport, but are also a diversion of capital outlay money which might otherwise go into the construction of academic buildings. "Middle-time" institutions hoping to "cash-in" on the financial returns of intercollegiate athletics should look very carefully before leaping into the "big-time" pond.

Non-financial returns such as increased visibility resulting in higher public awareness and better recruiting of both faculty and students also seems limited to the small percentage of universities which are able to appear repeatedly on television. The costs of achieving such interests by the television networks through the development of championship teams should cause administrators to consider hiring a good public relations firm to promote their cause rather than depending on the supposedly "free" publicity received through athletic success. While other intangible rewards such as organizational pride and cohesiveness have been used to justify intercollegiate sport, the evidence to support the causal role of sport is lacking and, if effective at all, it may actually be misdirecting the loyalties and values of the university community. Perhaps investment in activities which are more consistent with the educational objectives of the university may serve equally well in the development of organizational pride and cohesiveness. The example provided by schools which have dropped football in recent years does not indicate serious deleterious effects on academic institutions from the elimination of big-time sport.

Michener (1976) argues that public universities are seen as having a responsibility to provide public entertainment through spectacle sport. While he bases much of his subsequent analysis on an examination of the outcomes of that premise, he does not provide any justification for that position. Under the best of circumstances, the logical connection would be weak; but where programs have been shown to be exploitative of participants and conducted in such a manner that the practices of the subsystem violate the principles of the larger system, the responsibility for the provision of public spectacle is difficult to justify on any grounds other than mere precedent.

Stripped of the rhetoric of justification of athletics by the doctrine of "Good Works," it appears as if the primary beneficiaries of intercollegiate athletics are: (1) the few outstanding athletes who go on to a career in professional sport (and this should only be accepted with reservations concerning their long-range benefit), (2) the few athletes who receive a meaningful college education which they would not ordinarily receive, (3) athletic and other university administrators who achieve career advancement through the development of "successful" athletic programs, (4) a small number of alumni (and "subway-alumni") who realize a measure of ego-gratification through psychological identification and/or social affiliation with a prestigious institution, (5) community business people who either directly provide services and/or supplies to the athletic department or who benefit from the infusion of money into the local economy, and (6) the seeker of entertainment services who realizes a period of diversion from the normal routines of life.

Even if these are the only beneficiaries of intercollegiate athletics, one might ask the question, "Why not?" The answer would seem to be that the benefits appear to be realized at great cost. Not only do big-time athletic programs costs a great deal of time, energy and money, but they also exact a toll in human costs. Many individuals are sacrificed (physically, psychologically and/or vocationally) for the benefit of the few. It is not for this writer to make a value judgement for the reader, but it does appear that "big-time" intercollegiate athletics is sufficiently inefficient in both human and financial terms to question its continued existence.

The reality of big-time intercollegiate athletics today is that it serves only a small minority of the student body. The primary benefactors of the program are individuals within and without the university who are supposedly hired to run the programs for students or who profit by offering services for these programs. Even "organizational benefits" are hard to support with tangible evidence. Athletics has been taken over by an "administrative class"[2] which runs athletics primarily for its own benefit behind the rhetoric of the doctrine of "Good Works." These good works supposedly provide recreational and educational services for students and positive public relations for the university as an organization. In fact, however, the promised services fail to appear, and the primary beneficiaries are the administrators themselves and the external groups with personal and/or financial vested interest in athletic success. This takeover appears to parallel similar changes experienced by industry in the early twentieth century and seems to be inherent in bureaucratic growth whether in the military, the church, education or sport.

# RECAPTURING CONTROL: SUGGESTIONS

Analysis and understanding are but initial steps in a change process. The remaining step is to recommend an action procedure which will institute change if it appears necessary. Each assessment of intercollegiate sport has brought its own set of recommendations for change. From "institutional control" of 1905, to a stronger role for university presidents in 1929 (Savage, 1929), to student take-over in 1971 (Scott, 1971), there have been periodic calls for the restructuring of athletics in order to preserve what is perceived as good about sport while eliminating the evils which seem to grow like barnacles on the less visible portions of the ship of sport. Given the repeated appearance of problems, one might legitimately ask if it has not come time to scuttle the ship in order to save the passengers and crew. However, like James Coleman, after his analysis of high school athletics led to the conclusion that sport was a diversion from the main purpose of the high school (1961), I will also refrain from joining those who call for its elimination. As was previously stated, intercollegiate sport does provide benefits to some, The problem lies in the costs it enacts on others. Intercollegiate sport must find ways to reduce those costs or face the threat of being eliminated by forces in the society acting through the legal system on behalf of those upon whom the costs are enacted. Already congress has conducted an investigation of the NCAA, and several athletes have turned to the courts for recompense when, at the conclusion of their collegiate careers, they found that they were not sufficiently competent to enter the professional realm of sport and realized that they had not received an academic education nor alternative vocational training in return for their four years of play for the university.[3]

Restructuring the NCAA and its rules is not the answer. Already the rule book with its interpretations is too thick to assimilate. Strict enforcement of the regulations is a practical impossibility. An enforcement staff, no matter how large, could not eliminate the offenses. It would then become a game whereby the violation of rule is not the offense, but getting caught is the offense.

Ideally, the answer should lie in a reorganization of our values to the "sportsmanship" ideology whereby a philosophy of humanism and consideration of the good of the individual guides our actions, but in a real world sense that goal is unrealistic to expect, given the great potential for personal reward which exists in the sport subsystem.

This analysis leads to the conclusion that there is no permanent solution to the problems facing intercollegiate athletics. There will always be the potential for gain through sport, whether it is organized or informal. Human nature being what it is, there will always be individuals and interest groups who will attempt to maximize their gain at the expense of others. In short, sport, by its very nature, is competitive and political, both on the field and off. If there is no resolution to the problems facing intercollegiate sport, what then? Must the ship be scuttled? While the resolution of the problems facing sport may be impossible, perhaps it is not too much to hope that they may be managed and that the cost/benefits ratio may be tilted in the direction of benefits through effective management techniques.

Specifically, it is through the application of modern management science techniques that intercollegiate athletics has its best chance for survival. This application must not be utilized simply by athletic directors to insure greater effectiveness in the pursuit of more victories at less cost. It must permeate all levels of the university and, as called for earlier (Savage, 1929), the executive officers of the colleges and universities must actively participate in athletic governance by holding athletic directors accountable for contributing to the educational goals and principles of the university itself. Without such a commitment to principle by university executive officers, the events of the past century will repeat themselves until there is no doubt that the ship must be scuttled to prevent the chaos on board from corrupting more and more.

The fundamental objective of management efforts must be to regulate and coordinate the various interest groups enthused about sport. Both the strength and the weakness of sport programs is the wide spectrum of people and groups that are interested in them and who wish to be associated with them. These enthusiasms must be channeled and oriented toward the educational good of both participating and non-participating students. Creative management techniques must be sought to bring these interest groups **into** the system and to be certain that their energies are treated as a valuable resource to be utilized in the pursuit of the educational goals of the university. Exclusion will not work. Even if attempts at exclusion were to be successful (which is a doubtful probability), the resources of the interest groups would be lost to the system and, as a result, it would be less effective than its potential. Existing regulations may preclude their membership on councils as voting members, but their input can be brought into the system by the formation of an advisory board which can provide a voice for their concerns (and the concerns of other constituencies as well). A latent outcome of such an action may be to provide a forum in which such individuals can be informed and persuaded of the appropriateness of moderation and academic priority.

The foregoing argument may be summarized in the terminology of systems theory (Parsons, 1951) by stating that, first, successful managers of intercollegiate athletic programs must be certain that their subsystems be **adapted** to surrounding subsystems and to the larger systems of which they are a part. Second, the subgroups of such programs must be **integrated** within themselves so that the components of the system (students, faculty, alumni, boosters) know the goals of the subsystem and the supra-system and understand their roles and the roles of others in the pursuit of those goals. As part of this adaptation and integration, "outside" groups with legitimate interests in the athletic department may have to be assimilated, but this must be done in such a way as to insure that the goals of the program are not corrupted. Such assimilation is likely to be more effective in control measures than any attempts at exclusion. Third, managers of such programs must assure some measure of **goal attainment** by all elements of the system. These goals must be prioritized into primary and secondary goals and intermediate and long range goals. Managers must understand, however, that lack of some minimally satisfying degree of goal achievement by an organizational component will almost undoubtedly result in efforts to increase net benefits from participation which may be harmful to the system as a whole or in the withdrawal and consequent removal of the time, energy and/or financial contribution of that component of the subsystem. Finally, the manager must be skilled in maintaining the stability of the organization over time. Specific responsibilities include: (1) forethought in the recruitment of new members, (2) the training of those new members and (3) the management of tensions which arise in the normal course of organizational life. Whether such tension management takes the form of "stroking" the ruffled feathers of some losing coach or disgruntled fan, explaining apparent lack of justice in the distribution of rewards, acting as social director for some organizational get-together or taking the blame for some subordinate's "goof," the director, as the symbolic leader, bears this responsibility. If any of the foregoing "needs" of organizations are not met, either the effectiveness or efficiency of the organization, or both, will suffer.

Systems theory tends to be somewhat abstract in its terminology and not sufficiently down-to-earth in its prescriptions for action. A more tangible approach is taken by management science as it specifies the various functions to which an effective manager must contribute. These managerial functions may be summarized by the four cue words: planning, organizing, directing and controlling. Let us look at each in turn to see how they apply to a department of intercollegiate athletics when it is viewed from a social systems perspective.

# Planning

A major responsibility of an administrator is the development of plans. This has normally been future-directed, with an emphasis on goals for growth toward expanded programs supposedly serving more students or for increased "quality," that is, more wins (or profits) by a specified date. Planning, however, must also be goal-directed in the sense of the purposes of the larger institution. Statements of mission must be developed which specify how the athletic program contributes to the educational goals of the university. If such contributions are taken for granted or are assumed to take place automatically, one can be almost certain that they will not be made after a period of evolution in both personnel and methods of operation. Priorities change, "squeaky wheels get greased," and soon practices evolve which are inconsistent with the goals of the institution. Plans must be the product of input from each of the constituencies and must be consistent with the goals of the university. They must be periodically examined and updated both in terms of larger aims and specific objectives. Such plans must be distributed to all constituencies, and supervisory procedures must be instituted to insure that the various subunits know their role and contribute their appropriate function.

# Organizing

Once plans have been made relative to both goals and methods, the implementation phase begins. The administrator must organize a working system including advisory councils comprised representatives of the various interest groups. The organization must be staffed with people who are competent at their jobs and who understand how their position contributes to the goals of the department and the university. A major responsibility in this area is for the administrator to act as an educator. The councils and staff will undoubtedly consist of people with varying backgrounds and resultant divergent priorities, values and attitudes. The athletic administrator must be able to lead by provision of information, persuasion and example (as well as by reward and punishment) in order to develop a well-integrated, efficient system of operation.

## Directing

After the system has been organized and staffed, the athletic administrator must provide for on-going direction of the program. Appropriate organization of the supervision process will undoubtedly facilitate this, but continuing efforts must be made to be certain that supervision is effective in implementing the program as planned. Skillful use of symbolic and material rewards as motivators can result from an understanding of the unique qualities of the personnel making up the organization and is very important to effective direction. "Management by Objectives" or some other such approach should facilitate the effectiveness of these efforts.

## Control

Direction and control are often not clearly distinguished in the minds of administrators. Direction may be thought of as a one-way process, while control is inherently a two-way process. The administrator must insure that the information flow into the department is not only "downward." Effort must be invested in determining the reactions of the first-line personnel and the clientele to the program itself. "Upward" communication must be planned for and fostered, given the tendency for people to be reluctant to express frustration to persons of higher status until the people are extremely dissatisfied. Control in this sense must be thought of as in cybernetics, that is, knowing what is happening in every part of the system so that one can adjust procedures and processes before the dissatisfaction creates frictions which are dysfunctional to either effectiveness in goal attainment or inefficient in the sense of human costs. This feedback is also important in assuring accountability on the part of each of the subunits in the system. Administrators must not unquestioningly accept the reports of their units supervisors. Receipt of information through other channels (such as the previously mentioned athletic advisory board consisting of student, community and faculty interests) is essential in testing the reality of official reports. Unit supervisors understandably present the best image possible, and the reality of their perception must be tested with information received through independent channels.

The foregoing suggestions for the effective management of sports programs are no different from suggestions which might be made for any organization. The sport organization is not essentially different from any other bureaucracy. Sport itself, however, is so captivating, so emotionally engrossing, that too often those involved become lost in the excitement and detail of the program itself. The sport administrator must remain "above the fray" and keep his/her focus on the relationship of the department's programs with the university and the interests of the constituent groups. Too many athletic directors have failed to do this (perhaps due to their lack of management training), and this "internal" perspective has contributed to the problems we presently face. This is also a strong argument against the combined position of coach/athletic director.

The foregoing adminstrative suggestions were oriented to the athletic director him/herself. Earlier, the observation was made that effective management included the supervision of the athletic director by some executive officer. Athletic departments fit into organizational schemes of universities in a variety of ways. Therefore, in one case the athletic director may be supervised by a dean (of a school or physical education, for example), or a vice president (for student affairs, for example), or the president. There is probably no one best way; however, effective supervision requires real supervision on the part of the higher administrator. Let us examine how such supervision can help keep programs under control.

Supervision by the higher-level administrator undoubtedly begins with the hiring of the athletic director. Hiring the right person (i.e., one with a compatible philosophy as well as the competencies), clarifying expectations relative to goals, and defining parameters regarding methods set the tone for subsequent supervisory efforts. After the hiring and "settling in" period the supervisor should request periodic reports, and through these, demonstrate a continuing concern for the expectations and standards specified during the hiring process. Additionally, the supervisor should do what is within his/her power to provide resources to do the job that is expected. One of the most predictable ways of creating a problem is to communicate expectations without provision of resources to enable the person to get the job done. Supervisors should also do what is possible to minimize the pressure toward producing winning teams by publicly declaring that winning is only one of many standards on which athletic personnel will be judged. The supervisor must often reinforce the athletic director's efforts to educate and persuade a victory-hungry community that there is more to educational sport than victories. However, supervisors must tread carefully on this thin ice or be prepared to go under with both the coach and athletic director. The supervisor must resist the temptation to bend the athletic program in such a way that it serves as an organizational "tool." Moreover, he/she must make certain that the athletic director does not perceive it as his/her job to do this. Student-athletes are not agents of the administration; it is not their job to recruit, manipulate public opinion and/or influence the legislature and/or alumni to provide more funds. If these are unintended outcomes of a program organized for student benefit, the program is mutually beneficial; but the first step toward manipulating the program is also the first step toward corrupting the program and exploiting student-athletes. Finally, the supervisor must be sensitive to the potential negative influence of external constituencies and must assist the athletic director in his/her efforts to keep them in a manageable position in the system. It would be tempting for a supervisor to improve "town-gown" relationships by recommending a particular course of action beneficial to a community group, but this, too, is the first of a series of steps toward a corruption of the program.

# SUMMARY

It has been argued that the best hope for the survival of intercollegiate athletics is improved management designed to regulate the influence of interest groups as each attempts to manipulate athletics to its benefit. Specific suggestions have been forwarded as to how these management principles can be applied by the athletic director and his/her supervisor in order to achieve this regulation. Unfortunately, implementation of the above suggestions cannot be legislated or otherwise imposed. It is to be hoped that university executives will see the need for strong action from within the system itself. History tells us that attempts at regulation from outside the university are futile. The NCAA cannot act as an enforcement body. Already it is under fire for its action in trying to obtain evidence in order to sanction a particular basketball coach. Also, regulations from outside educational circles (i.e., legislation and/or the courts) are likely to be so restrictive that schools will in all probability drop athletics rather than submit to such perceived interference with their programs. The last and perhaps only hope is improved internal management on a school-by-school basis. This improvement will depend largely on university executive officers taking vigorous action to manage their own programs through the control and regulation of the constituent groups which comprise its own sport system.

Elimination of these problems and controversies is highly unlikely given the imperfection of human social systems in general. Hence the dilemma of "educational sport" will be with us for a long time. Creative, innovative, principled and well-skilled sport managers and university administrators are needed to keep athletics educational as well as attractive sporting activities. This can be achieved only by continually coping with the everchanging problems induced by enthusiastic, energetic groups which are often mistakenly seen as external to the system of intercollegiate athletics.

## FOOTNOTES

[1]Recent studies applying a systems perspective and organizational analysis to understanding athletics include Santomier, et al., (1981) and Frey (1978).

[2]In an address to the University of Massachusetts community, Joseph Litterer of the School of Business faculty referred to a "third culture" to be added to C.P. Snow's "World of Two Cultures." This third culture consisted of a class of administrators trained neither in the humanities nor the sciences but in the arts of social

organization. According to Litterer, members of this third culture are as isolated from communication with the other two cultures as they are from one another. Applied to the present analysis, it may be that sport administrators are isolated from the concerns of both the university as an educational community and the student body seeking recreation through sport. As such, they tend to serve the system rather than serving the clients of the system.

[3]Cited in a CBS broadcast of "60 Minutes," 1980.

# REFERENCES

Ceglarski, Mark A.
1979    "A Survey of the Qualifications of Directors of Intercollegiate Athletics," Unpublished master's thesis. University of Massachusetts/Amherst.
Coleman, James S.
1961    *The Adolescent Society.* New York: The Free Press.
Frey, James H.
1978    "The Organization of American Amateur Sport." *American Behavioral Scientist.* 21 (January/February):361-378.
1981    "The Place of Athletics in the Educational Priorities of University Alumni." *Review of Sport and Leisure.*
Hanford, George H.
1974    *An Inquiry into the Need for and Feasibility of a National Study of Intercollegiate Athletics.* Washington D.C.: American Council on Education.
Jackson, Myles
1962    "College Football Has Become a Losing Business." *Fortune,* 66 (December):119-121.
Meschary, Tom
1972    "There is a Disease in Sports Now." *Sports Illustrated.* 37 (October 2):56-58, 63.
Michener, James A.
1976    *Sports in America.* New York: Random House.
National Collegiate Athletic Association (NCAA)
1979    *NCAA Manual, 1978-79.* Shawnee Mission, Kansas: NCAA.
Parsons, Talcott
1951    *The Social System.* New York: The Free Press.
Rossi, Peter H.
1981    "Survey of University of Massachusetts Alumni." University of Massachusetts. 12 (December):6.
Sack, Allen L. and Charles Watkins
1980    "Winning and Giving: Another Look." Paper presented at the first annual meeting of the North American Society for the Sociology of Sport, Denver, Colorado, October, 16-19.
Santomier, J.P., W.G. Howard, W.L. Piltz and T.J. Romance
1980    "White Sock Crime: Organizational Deviance in Intercollegiate Athletics." *Journal of Sport and Social Issues,* 4 (Fall/Winter): 26-32.

Savage, Howard
1929        *American College Athletics.* New York: The Carnegie Foundation.
Scott, Jack
1971        *The Athletic Revolution.* New York: The Free Press.
Sigelman, Lee and Robert Carter
1979        "Win One for the Giver? Alumni Giving and Big Time Sports."
            *Social Science Quarterly,* 60 (September):284-94.
Underwood, John
1980        "The Writing is on the Wall." *Sports Illustrated,* 52 (May 19): 36-72.

# WIN ONE FOR THE GIVER? ALUMNI GIVING AND BIG-TIME COLLEGE SPORTS*

By

## Lee Sigelman and Robert Carter

For many Americans, rousing half-time speeches in which frenzied coaches attempt to rally their downtrodden charges epitomize intercollegiate athletics, thanks in large part to a 1940 movie that depicted Notre Dame's Knute Rockne beseeching the Fighting Irish to "win one for the Gipper" (former Notre Dame player George Gipp). In the years that have passed, a premium on winning has come to pervade college sports for more self-serving reasons, such as the athletes' need to establish national reputations so they can graduate into professional ranks and the coaches' need to build winning records so they can entrench themselves in their positions or move on to even better things. Clearly, big-time college sports (football and, to a lesser extent, basketball) are no longer considered merely pleasant diversions from the important business of life—if they were ever seen in that light. Americans may smirk at the unrefined athletic fanaticism that ignited a "soccer war" between Honduras and El Salvador, but how different are the passions that rage each autumn when the game of the season is played between Army and Navy, Texas and Oklahoma, Ohio State and Michigan, USC and UCLA, or Harvard and Yale?

Although "the Gipper" is no longer with us, college football and basketball teams are still trying to win for the sake of the alumni. Many old grads are staunch supporters of the athletic department, its personnel and its policies; are faithful followers of the school's teams; and are prolific donors to the school's annual fund. But if the football or basketball team falls on hard times, athletic directors, coaches and even college presidents become a target for disgruntled alumni groups. Because alumni are thought to be so attuned to their school's athletic fortunes, it is widely believed that alumni donations soar after a successful season and plummet in the wake of athletic failure. In the words of the old saw, "Alumni are for giving but not forgiving."

*Reprinted with permission from *Social Science Quarterly*, 60(September, 1979): 284-294.

# THE EXISTING EVIDENCE

How valid is the idea that alumni giving varies according to a school's success or failure on the playing fields? Clark Kerr, former president of the University of California, has characterized sports as a major factor in spurring alumni giving, vitally important to the success of many schools (Klein, 1967: 1). A wide variety of others, including sports writers, athletic directors, college fund raisers and sociologists, concur with Kerr's assessment. "Winning in some visible sport," Richard Moll, the director of admissions at Bowdoin College says, "charms alumni to give money" (Herman, 1974; see also Sievert, 1971; Sack, 1977; Amdur, 1971).

What evidence is there that athletic success stimulates alumni giving? Probably because so many people have taken this relationship so much for granted that it has not seemed necessary to research it, we have only a smattering of evidence which can be summarized as follows.

• A favorite example for demonstrating the economic clout of college athletics involves Ohio State University, a perennial football power. In 1965, the Buckeyes won seven games and lost two, and alumni contributions to the school totalled $1,247,698. The next year, when the team's record fell to 4-5, alumni giving fell, too, by almost $500,000 (Amdur, 1971: 125).

• T. Marshall Hahn, President of Virginia Tech, said that after his school's basketball team won the National Invitation Tournament in 1973, thousands of dollars were pledged to the college treasury. Hahn added that in the future alumni, corporations and the state legislature would look more favorably upon the school because the victory conveyed the image of Tech as a successful university (**Sports Illustrated**, 1973: 2).

• According to Joseph M. Ray, President of the University of Texas at El Paso, the fact that his school (then named Texas Western) won the NCAA basketball championship in 1966 "helped focus attention on us. The acceptance of our supporting community came easier after that" (quoted by Klein, 1967: 1).

• Amdur (1971: 125-29) has catalogued several similar cases, although he is extremely critical of the college sports establishment. For example, after the University of Georgia's football record fell from 6-4 in 1960 to 3-7 in 1961, alumni contributions dipped by some $37,000. At the University of Missouri, alumni contributions almost doubled, from $227,000 to $442,000, when the football team improved its record from 6-5 in 1959 to 10-1 in 1960. At Amherst, hardly a "football factory," alumni contributions increased each year during the 1960's save two, 1961 and 1966—the very years in which Amherst did not win the Little Three football championship. Amdur also notes a dramatic jump in alumni giving at tiny Wilkes College in Pennsylvania between 1964 and 1966, a period when the fortunes of the football team were improving sharply (Amdur, 1971: 125-29).

On the other hand, there are some indications that big-time athletic programs are not the spur to alumni giving that both their staunchest supporters and their most strident critics seem to believe.

• Marts (1934) tried to determine whether the efforts of many schools to use football success to gain national visibility had paid off in dollars and cents. He studied 16 schools that had attempted to build strong football programs, as well as a control group of 16 similar schools that had made no such effort. According to Marts, the aggregate endowment of the 16 schools that had decided to emphasize football increased by 105 percent between 1921 and 1930. By comparison, the endowment at the 16 non-football schools increased at an even faster rate, 126 percent. Moreover, the financial condition of some of the football schools was pitiful because they had incurred such large debts in building their athletic programs (Marts, 1934: 14-15).

• In most recent years, dozens of schools have simply given up varsity football. In an analysis of some of the 151 colleges that dropped football between 1939 and 1974, Springer (1974) finds that officials at all the schools he studied were initially concerned about the potential impact on alumni giving. But, Springer states, "The experience of almost all the schools was that it had no significant negative effect and in some instances had considerable positive results." Many schools launched successful fund-raising drives at the very time they were dropping football, and alumni identification with the alma mater seemed unaffected. Obviously, this does not mean that any school should feel free to drop football; as the President of one university (a member of the Southwest Conference) observed, "I'd like to get rid of sports recruiting and big time football, but I couldn't stay in this state for two days" (Cady, 1974). But Springer's conclusions do provide an interesting counterpoint to some of the more extreme claims that have been made about the impact of varsity sports on alumni giving.

• Finally, Budig (1976) has attempted a statistical test of the relationship between alumni support and athletic performance. Budig used data on alumni giving at 79 colleges and universities for four years during the 1960s and 1970s to determine whether total alumni giving was higher at schools that had greater football or basketball success than it was at schools with poorer records. Budig's analysis did not support the hypothesis that football records were significantly related to total alumni support. Basketball success, on the other hand, was somewhat more closely tied to total alumni giving, but the relationship was, of anything, inverse; the better the basketball record, the lower the alumni giving. More generally, significant relationships between athletic success and a alumni giving seemed so random and infrequent that they could be attributed to sheer chance rather than to any systematic linkage.

Where does all this evidence and counter-evidence leave us? Not very far, it would seem, from where we began, for none of the existing evidence is particularly persuasive.

Dramatic cases like Ohio State, Virginia Tech and Texas Western are convincing only until one examines them more closely. For example, although alumni dollars flowed into Virginia Tech just after the NIT tournament win in 1973, a check of financial records maintained by the Council for Financial Aid to Education (CFAE) reveals that alumni giving at Virginia Tech was not unusually high that year in comparison to immediately preceding and succeeding years (CFAE, 1970-76). The University of Texas at El Paso may have gotten a great deal of publicity the school was widely portrayed as a "jock factory" because its starting team was composed of five blacks from outside the region, none of whom ever graduated from the school. And anyone who bothers to consult CFAE's figures on alumni giving over the years at Ohio State will find very little relationship between the generosity of that school's graduates and the Buckeyes' gridiron record. Similar problems continually crop up whenever one closely examines the instances in which football or basketball success or failure is supposed to have influenced alumni giving.

The same must also be said about the existing counter-evidence. The Marts study is now little more than a historical footnote. Springer's analysis of what happens when a school gives up football, interesting as it is, is not definitive because, as Springer himself recognizes, schools that drop football are hardly representative of schools that play football. That being the case, giving up football should hardly be expected to have had a major impact on alumni giving at those schools. Nor does the Budig study provide a fair test of the hypothesis that alumni giving is tied to athletic success. What Budig tested was the proposition that the total volume of alumni giving varies from school to school as a function of relative athletic success—that schools with better football or basketball teams tend to receive more alumni dollars than do schools with poorer athletic records. But not even the most rabid supporter of big-time college athletics is likely to make such a claim, for differences among schools in overall levels of alumni giving are products of many factors that have nothing to do with athletics. Two of the most obvious of these are the sheer number of alumni a school has and the social class composition of the alumni. Football and basketball notwithstanding, Harvard will always attract greater overall alumni support than Appalachian State, because Harvard has more, as well as more affluent, alumni. Budig's attempt to explain overall levels of alumni giving, then, fails because it attempts to explain the wrong thing: total alumni giving. The speculation that one continually hears—that alumni giving rises and falls with the fortunes of the football and basketball teams—should have been tested. The hypothesis that alumni giving tends to increase when a school enjoys athletic success and to decline when a school suffers athletic failure has remained untested. What we have is a wealth of speculation and a lack of conclusive evidence concerning the impact of athletic success on alumni giving.

# TESTING THE LINKAGE BETWEEN ATHLETICS AND ALUMNI GIVING

## Data and Methods

The subjects of this analysis were the 138 colleges and universities that maintained Division I (or big-time) intercollegiate football programs as of the 1975-76 academic year, the most recent one for which the relationship between athletic success and alumni giving could be analyzed. [1] This marks a considerable increase in the number of schools that play big-time football; in 1960-61, the initial year in our analysis, only 96 schools competed in Division I. Thus our analysis was based on a somewhat larger number of schools for more recent years than for earlier years.

School-by-school data on alumni giving were obtained from the annual surveys conducted by CFAE. Since the 1954-55 academic year, CFAE has surveyed American educational institutions in order to obtain detailed information about their sources of voluntary financial support. In the early years, CFAE often experimented with question wording, and its coverage of institutions was spotty. As a result, CFAE figures prior to 1960-61 are not very reliable, and we therefore took the 1960-61 academic year as the starting point for our analysis. The initial CFAE surveys were biennial, but since 1965-66 they have been conducted on an annual basis. The most recent survey at the time our research was undertaken was for the 1975-76 academic year. Accordingly, we had alumni giving data for 14 different academic years during the 1960s and 1970s.

CFAE conducts its surveys by mail, and rates of response, although high, are not perfect. In the 1975-76 academic year, for example, only 108 of the 135 schools responded to the CFAE survey, which means that we had to drop 20 percent of the schools that would otherwise have been available for the analysis for that year. Moreover, not all schools that did respond provided all the information we needed to measure the aspects of alumni giving in which we were interested. As a result, our analysis had to be based on something less than the total set of Division I CFAE respondents for any year; for 1975-76, our analyses were based on between 90 and 100 schools, depending on the specific dimension of alumni giving that was being examined.

Three separate dimensions of giving seemed particularly important to us. First, and perhaps most crucial, is the increase or decrease in the total volume of alumni giving. Fortunately, CFAE has asked about total alumni donations in each of its surveys since the 1960-61 academic year. Accordingly, as an initial measure of the increase or decrease in alumni giving, we simply calculated the percentage change from one year to the next in total alumni giving for each school. For the 1975-76 academic year, for example, this figure was calculated as follows:

$$\frac{\%\ \text{Change in Total}}{\text{Alumni Giving}} = \frac{\text{Total Giving 1975-76} - \text{Total Giving 1974-75}}{\text{Total Giving 1974-75}}$$

Because the CFAE data were available for 14 academic years, we were able to calculate 13 different yearly rates of change in total giving for each school that had responded to the surveys.

A second dimension of giving involves the average dollar value of the gifts that a school receives in a given year. The CFAE surveys do not indicate the total number of donors to any school, an omission that makes it impossible to calculate the value of the average gift. CFAE does, however, provide yearly figures on total alumni giving to each school's annual fund, and matches these figures with the number of alumni contributing to the annual fund. These figures on alumni giving to the annual fund were used to calculate a measure of the dimension of giving:

$$\text{\% Change in the } \$ \text{ Value of the Average Gift} = \frac{\$ \text{ Value of Average Gift to Annual Fund 1975-76} - \$ \text{ Value of Average Gift to Annual Fund 1974-75}}{\$ \text{Value of Average Gift to Annual Fund 1974-75}}$$

Due to the vagaries of the CFAE data, these figures could be computed for only the 10 most recent academic years of our study, 1966-67 though 1975-76.

Finally, because it is possible that total or average alumni giving could be swollen by a few large contributions, it is also important to consider how many of a school's alumni contributed in any year. Again, this had to be computed from figures on alumni giving to the annual fund:

$$\text{\% Change in Proportion of Alumni Who Gave 1975-76} = \frac{\text{\% Giving to the Annual Fund 1975-76} - \text{\% Giving to the Annual Fund 1974-75}}{\text{\% Giving to the Annual Fund 1974-75}}$$

Again, these figures could be calculated for only the 10 most recent academic years, 1966-67 through 1975-76.

School-by-school athletic records were taken from yearly NCAA football and basketball guides (NCAA, 1961-77). For each year, the percentage of games won by each team was used as the measure of success in both basketball and football (with a tie counting as half a win in football). In addition, we also noted whether each football team had participated in a post-season bowl game in a given year, and used the resulting dummy variables in the analysis.

Thus, allowing for missing data, we had six separate variables per year for each of the 135 Division I schools. The purpose of the statistical analysis was to determine whether the three alumni-giving variables were related to any or all of the three athletic variables (winning percentage in basketball, winning percentage in football and bowl appearances). The fact that we had data for so many different years meant that we could conduct several independent tests of these relationships—13 yearly tests for the total alumni-giving measure, and 10 apiece for the average gift and proportion-giving variables.

# Findings

How closely are increases or decreases in alumni support tied to success or failure in basketball and football? In order to find out, we used correlation and regression analysis to relate each school's alumni-giving change figures for a given year to its three athletic success measures for the same year. That is, we used football performance during the fall of a given academic year and basketball records for the spring semester to try to predict changes in alumni giving over the entire academic year. Let us use the statistical results for the most recent academic year in our study, 1975-76, to take a close look at these relationships, and let us then turn to the results for the other years.

The results for 1975-76 are summarized in Table 1. The first, third and fifth rows of Table 1 provide the simple correlations between each athletic success measure, on the one hand, and percent change in total and average alumni giving and in the proportion of alumni making contributions, on the other. None of the nine correlation coefficients is of even moderate magnitude, the highest being a meager .141 between percent change in the value of the average gift and football records. Three of the correlations were not only low, but were actually negative; that is, there was some tendency (albeit an extremely modest one for alumni giving to fall off at schools that had better athletic records. More generally, not a single one of the six correlation coefficients is significant at the .05 level of probability.

Other major findings for the 1975-76 academic year relate to the standardized regression coefficients (betas) in the second, fourth and sixth rows of Table 1. These regression coefficients summarize the independent statistical impact that each of the three athletic success factors had on each of the alumni-giving measures, correcting for the the influence of the other two athletic success factors. What these betas reveal is similar to what we have already seen: none of the athletic success measures is closely related to changes in alumni giving. Even the highest of the betas, .203, does not approach statistical significance; that is, we cannot be confident that even the strongest relationship we observed reflects anything more than a purely random association.

Although each of the three measures of athletic success, taken separately, is essentially unrelated to any of the three dimensions of change in alumni giving, it was still possible that all of the three athletic success measures, considered jointly, could account for changes in alumni giving. But the tiny coefficients of determination ($R^2$) for each of the alumni-giving dimensions rule out this possibility. For 1975-76, at least, these coefficients mean that knowing a school's degree of success in football and basketball would tell us nothing at all about whether the alumni were becoming more or less supportive than they had been in the previous years in terms of their financial contributions to the school.

Of course, these results pertain only to a single academic year. How representative are the 1975-76 results of those obtained for the other years in our analysis? Recall that, for the first alumni-giving measure, we were able to conduct separate analyses of the impact of athletic performance for 13 different years (including 1975-76). This means that we had a total of 39

TABLE 1
Statistical Results for 1975-76 Academic Year

| Alumni Giving | Basketball Record | Football Record | Bowl Appearance | Number of Colleges | Adjusted $R^2$ |
|---|---|---|---|---|---|
| % change in total | .001 | .131 | .098 | 100 | .000 |
| alumni giving | .000 | .111 | .036 | | |
| % change in $ value | -.053 | .141 | .005 | 92 | .000 |
| of average alumni gift | -.035 | .200 | -.106 | | |
| % change in proportion | -.054 | .112 | -.048 | 92 | .000 |
| of alumni giving | -.035 | .203 | -.160 | | |

NOTE: In each cell, the first entry is the simple correlation coefficient, $r$; the second is the standardized regression coefficient, beta. None of the individual terms or the overall equations approaches statistical significance at any conventional level.

different beta coefficients summarizing the independent impacts of the three athletic success measures on total alumni giving—one beta per measure per year. Similarly, because we were able to conduct separate analyses of percent change in the size of the average gift and in the proportion of alumni making contributions for 10 different years, we had 60 additional betas to consider.

Of this total of 99 beta coefficients, only two proved to be statistically significant. This means that in fully 97 of the 99 instances we had to conclude that the relationship between athletic performance and changes in alumni giving was random. Moreover, the only two significant relationships (between football records in 1974 and percent gain in the proportion of alumni making contributions in 1974-75, and between going to a bowl in 1970 and change in the value of the average donation in 1970-71), actually ran in the wrong direction; schools with winning football records in 1974 tended to attract proportionately fewer new alumni givers than did schools with losing records, and schools whose football teams attended postseason bowls in 1970 were significantly less likely than other schools to receive larger average alumni donations.

In view of these negligible results, it would be pointless to present these results in any greater detail. Instead, we can summarize our findings by stating that according to a number of different statistical criteria we have found no support for the thesis that alumni giving is connected to athletic performance.

One further possibility still had to be investigated. Could our consistent failure to uncover any relationships between athletic performance and alumni giving be traced to the methodological choices we had made? If we had measured our variables differently or used different means of relating them, would our findings have been different?

In order to address these questions, we undertook several additional statistical analyses. First, it occurred to us that even if athletic success does have an impact on alumni giving, that impact might not be immediate. Accordingly, we completed a new set of correlations and regressions with a one-year time lag between the three athletic success measures and the three alumni-giving variables. Second, we wondered whether improvement in athletic records from one year to the next, as opposed simply to athletic success in a given year, might be the key to greater alumni giving. We therefore redefined the athletic success variables so that they would reflect change from year to year, and ran still more correlations and regressions (both with and without the one-year lag). Third, we tried measuring the three alumni-giving variables simply in terms of yearly change rather than percent yearly change; that is, we eliminated the denominators from these variables as they were defined above. Having done so, we could examine several more sets of correlations and regressions (with both the original and the newly defined athletic success measures, and with and without the one-year time lag). Finally, we also undertook separate correlation and regression analyses—with both the original and the redefined measures—for the public and private schools in our sample.

Presenting the results of all these reanalyses in any detail would be superfluous, for they did nothing to alter our original conclusions. For example, the same-year relationships between the original alumni-giving variables and the newly defined athletic success measures were significantly different from zero in only four of 99 instances, and three of these relationships were inverse. None of the other reanalyses provided results that were substantially different, and as a result we had to conclude that we could find no support in our data for the notion that alumni giving rises and falls with the fortunes of big-time intercollegiate athletic programs.

# CONCLUSION

In recent years, as the costs of running a big-time athletic program have skyrocketed, approximately 70 percent of the NCAA's member athletic departments have been operating in the red (Raiborn, 1970; Hanford, 1974). In this situation, much attention has been called to the indirect economic benefits purportedly associated with big-time college sports. The most frequently cited is the greater alumni giving that successful athletic programs are said to spark.

Two basic points need to be made about this contention. In the first place, even if there were a strong relationship between athletic success and alumni giving, this would probably be of little practical consequence, because most schools obtain only a small portion of their support from alumni (Froomkin, 1974). CFAE figures reveal that in the 1975-76 academic year alumni giving in the United States totaled $588 million, or roughly $52.50 per student. Although this may sound like an impressive amount, it was a mere drop in the bucket—about 1.3 percent of the total institutional expenditures of $44.8 billion in 1975-76, or $4,000 per student (CFAE, 1975-76, 4-6). Of course, some schools, particularly academically prestigious private schools, do lean heavily upon their alumni for financial support; but these also tend to be the very schools that have the hardest time competing in big-time intercollegiate athletics. In any event, our statistical analysis has revealed that there is simply no relationship between success or failure in football and basketball and increases and decreases in alumni giving.

In the final analysis, however, the lack of any relationship between success in intercollegiate athletics and increased alumni giving probably matters a good deal less than the fact that so many people believe that such a relationship exists. Debates concerning the role of college sports tend rapidly to turn into ideological confrontations. For radical sports critics, the idea that athletic success causes alumni giving symbolizes the twisted values and perverted priorities underlying big-time college athletics. For hard-core athletic supporters, it exemplifies the tangible benefits that varsity sports can confer upon a school. Because the idea can be debated so nicely from a variety of ideological outlooks, it will doubtless continue to be widely held despite the contrary evidence presented here.

## FOOTNOTES

[1]From the list of Division I teams, we omitted the three service academies because of their unusual financial situations.

# REFERENCES

Amdur, Neil.
1971    *The Fifth Down: Democracy and the Football Revolution.* New York: Coward, McCann and Geoghagen.
Budig, Jeanne E.
1976    "The Relationships among Intercollegiate Athletics, Enrollment, and Voluntary Support for Public Higher Education," Ph.D. dissertation, Illinois State University.
Cady, Steve.
1974    "Educators on Sports Recruiting: 'Roman Circus' Must Go." *New York Times* (March 19).
Council for Financial Aid to Education.
1960-    *Voluntary Support of Education.* New York: CFAE.
1976
Froomkin, Joseph.
1974    "Sports and the Post-Secondary Sector," in George H. Hanford, *An Inquiry into the Need for and Feasibility of a National Study of Intercollegiate Athletics.* Washington, D.C.: American Council on Education: Appendix F.

Herman, Robin.
1974    "How the College Crowd Feels about IT: Jeers Outscore Cheers,"
        *New York Times* (March 19).
Klein, Frederick.
1967    "Bring in the Brawn: Recruiting of Athletes Intensifies as Colleges
        Seek Prestige, Money," *Wall Street Journal* (April 11).
Marts, Arnaud C.
1934    "College Football and college Endowment," *School and Society,* 40
        (July 7): 14-15.
National Collegiate Athletics Association.
1960-   *NCAA Official Basketball Guide* (Shawnee Mission, Kansas:
1977    NCAA).

––––––.
1960-   *NCAA Official Football Guide* (Shawnee Mission, Kansas: NCAA).
Raiborn, Mitchell H.
1970    *Financial Analysis of Intercollegiate Athletics* (Shawnee Mission,
        Kansas: NCAA).
Sack, Allen L.
1977    "Big-Time College Football: Whose Free Ride?" *Quest,* 27
        (Winter): 87-96.
Sievert, William A.
1971    "Financial Pinch, Waning Interest Hurting Some Sports
        Programs,"*Chronicle of Higher Education* (January 25).

––––––.
1973    "More Basketball Business," *Sports Illustrated.* (April 16): 21.
Springer, Felix
1974    "The Experience of Senior Colleges That Have Discontinued Foot-
        ball," in George H. Hanford. *An Inquiry Into the Need for and
        Feasibility of a National Study of Intercollegiate Athletics.*
        Washington, D.C.: American Council on Education: Appendix I.

# PART IV:
# THE FUTURE

# INTRODUCTION

There are many forces exerting influence on athletic governance. The battle lines appear to be drawn between those groups representing the campus community (e.g., administration, faculty) and those representing external interests (e.g., boosters, regulatory bodies, courts). What the future holds for intercollegiate athletics will be determined by the outcome of this struggle.

The final selection paints a rather pessimistic picture for institutional control by representatives of the academic community, particularly for "big-time" programs. These programs will be controlled by a coalition of alumni, boosters, athletic directors and, sometimes, coaches. The coalition will be so formidable that any efforts by college administration, faculty or student body to reduce the coalition's effect or break up its control will be fruitless. Academic representatives will have considerably more influence over smaller and less intense programs, although their role in governance will still be circumscribed by legal entities and regulatory bodies.

# INTERCOLLEGIATE ATHLETICS IN THE FUTURE: BOOSTER COALITION, INSTITUTIONAL CONTROL AND THE PURSUIT OF SCARCE RESOURCES

By
James H. Frey

American intercollegiate athletics have reached a point in their evolution where they face a dilemma of a magnitude unlike any confronted at any time in their glamourous, yet controversial, history. The quandary rests on the ability of athletic programs, particularly those designated as "big time," to acquire enough resources to maintain current levels and, for some, to expand. Despite a trail of crises, mostly of an ethical nature, growth and expansion seemed to be the norm, especially in the 1960s and early 1970s. More sports, including those for women participants, were added to already lengthy lists on most campuses; television was feeding money to national regulatory bodies for dispersion to members; fans were attending at stadium-bursting rates; intercollegiate events had captured the hearts and minds of students, faculties, and administrators; and these same events were even promoted as major folkloristic celebrations or public art forms crucial to the survival of American society (Cady, 1978; Novack, 1976). The picture, indeed, was rosy until recently.

During the last five to seven years, many college athletic programs have fallen on hard times. Very few are profitable, and the financial question remains a major hurdle for most, given the trends of tax-cutting legislation, mandated growth in women's sports, and large inflationary bites out of the American leisure time and charitable dollar. In addition, revelations of scandal and impropriety, of discrimination and inequality, of education irresponsibility and illegal financial wizardry have presented additional obstacles to justifying the growth and expansion of athletic programs. There is also evidence that fewer quality athletes are available to fill the labor pool required to maintain high-level programs. Thus, faced with financial and labor supply problems unlike any previously encountered, college and university athletic decision-makers will have to make some hard choices in the 1980s.

It is not clear what the future of intercollegiate sports will bring in the face of this dilemma. Will these programs continue to grow and prosper; or, will they suffer drastic change, or possibly even a structural and ideological "demise"? It is my prediction that American intercollegiate athletics will evolve into a formalized two-class system with a small, elite group of institutions maintaining very prosperous and visible programs; and, a larger, but less fortunate, group will operate programs of limited scope, if they have any program at all. The major source of survival for the elite corps of programs rests in their ability to draw maximum resources from an organizational coalition of athletic administrators and alumni/boosters who represent the political and economic power in the community or region contiguous to the institution. The role of this coalition in the maintenance—and even survival—of athletic programs will be more prominent than that of the faculty, students or even college presidents. Thus, while the 1980s will be "the last hurrah" for the bulk of college athletics programs, for both men and women, this time period will see even greater glory for the surviving elite group.

# POLITICAL REALITY: CONTROL OF ATHLETICS BY ALUMNI/BOOSTER COALITION

Boosterism has a long history in America, particularly in association with colleges (Boorstin, 1965). As the country grew and expanded, a group of individuals, usually the economic elite of an area, took on the task of promoting their community. They were optimistic, growth-oriented, and willing to take risks even if it meant going outside the law (1965: 3). An easy way to mark a community as "up and coming" or destined for greatness was to establish hallmarks of permanence and legitimacy. According to Boorstin these were a newspaper, a hotel, and a college. Not to boost a community showed total lack of community spirit and a lack of business sense

(1965: 117). A college in town not only enhanced the image, but it also increased land values; that is, it was profitable for the booster. It was only natural that college be promoted and controlled by boosters, since this was the way American institutions were established—by community, not royal or ecclesiastical, decree. If a social unit did not have the support of the booster element, it usually could not survive politically or economically.

When any social unit has political priority, it means it has the power to guide the outcome of decisions in its favor. It is able to procure resources necessary for its survival and growth—even if it means the opposite for other units within the same system (Thompson, 1967). The power usually emanates from strong valuational or ideological support since that unit is producing a valued product. Being in this position means a social unit is autonomous; that is, it can act on its environment and even be impervious to the demands of other environmental components.

For generations intercollegiate athletic programs have been able to operate from a position of political autonomy and priority because a coalition of alumni/boosters, coaches, and athletic administrators represented a formidable structure of allies. The booster—alumnus provided the interconnection with the business and the political world; the coach provided the winning product; and the administrator guided the athletic program through the academic maze. The promotion of athletics was enhanced by support from academic administrators, even in the face of faculty distress over the emphasis on athletics. Presidents supported athletics because they believed that a winning program attracted students, financial contributions, and favorable legislative appropriations. Athletics was apparently the only element of higher education which could unite all of its diverse constituencies.

It was good business to promote athletics, particularly a winning athletic program. Businessmen saw athletics as a stimulus to their profits, and since most athletic programs ran deficits, even in their early history, it was only natural that they "boost" the activity with a financial subsidy.[1] These boosters/alumni were viewed as necessary to the development and maintenance of a "big time" athletic program because legislative appropriations, university budgets, or gate receipts did not provide sufficient funds for a high-level program (Atwell, **et.al.**, 1980). Faculties were either disinterested or had given up all hope of rekindling educational goals with athletes; or, professors became the athletic department's greatest fans. Students, who once controlled and operated intercollegiate athletics, willingly gave up decision-making authority when inter-school contests became too complex for their administration, too expensive to operate, and too important to alumni (Lucas & Smith, 1978). However, the truth of the matter is that presidents, faculty, and students will always lose the control battle because they do not have the resources to compete with those available to the booster coalition. Academics could not fund and supervise an athletic program with extrinsic, commercial goals; a booster coalition could, and still does today. If the latter can provide the money, then it can also command some power in athletic decision-making. Therein lies the focal point of the current controversy over "institutional control," that is, the academic institution's ability to run the athletic program consistent with its own policy and goals, not necessarily with those of community interests.

The coalition is often represented by three types of organizational forms affiliated with university athletic departments. The first usually takes on a name like "Cougar Club" or "Tiger Club" that clearly demonstrates this affiliation. These are what have come to be known as "booster clubs." These groups raise money for the athletic department through various promotions and by soliciting direct gifts, either in-kind or cash. These groups will also subsidize coaches' salaries, entertain prospective athletes, provide cars for coaches and administrators, and provide influence for political, economic and media favors on behalf of athletes and athletic programs. Booster Club members have also been known to influence event scheduling, subsidize team travel, and provide incentives in the form of monetary reward to coaches, administrators, and players. It is these groups which have attracted the most attention from the National Collegiate Athletic Association (NCAA) enforcement division (Evans, 1974; Denlinger & Shapiro, 1975; Looney, 1978).

The non-profit foundation, incorporated independently of the university, has the major purpose of securing funds for land procurement and capital expansion. Its ability to raise money is amazing. One school in the southeast was able to raise over four million dollars in less than a month for a stadium renovation (Marcin, 1979: 26). The Sun Angel foundation at Arizona State raised $4.5 million to expand a stadium and also provided funds for the construction of a baseball field and golf course (1979: 26).

A third type of athletic organization which includes booster/alumnus association is that of the independently incorporated athletic department. Many "big-time" schools where athletic departments do not receive legislatively apropriated monies (e.g., University of Michigan, University of Kansas) have corporate status with the state apart from the university. This poses questions of accountability to the larger institution, and the extent to which credit lines can be negotiated for capital funds with or without university approval. The booster coalition may be able to establish a "hidden interest" in this corporation by virtue of the fact that the independent corporation apparently exists under rules and procedures that may or may not be consistent with the sponsoring organization. Thus, it is easier to influence an athletic program without the encumbrances of institutional rules.

Rarely are athletic fund-raising efforts tied into the larger developmental operation of the university. Athletic administrators see a great deal of difficulty in bringing these groups under internal control. Efforts to control these groups have been largely superficial since the need for their existence is so great. As a result of the financial dependence of the athletic department on booster groups, the latter are able to exercise a great deal of influence, direct or indirect, on athletic policy. Program and personnel decisions often cannot be made without consulting these groups. In fact, these groups will even withhold donations if the current athletic situation is not to their liking (Atwell, **et al.**, 1980).

While it is profitable for the athletic department to have affiliated booster organizations, these groups also become the source of tax and other economic benefits for their members.² For example, the booster groups can become a major vehicle by which one can attain access to the political and economic elite. Booster membership can be the source of reciprocal business arrangements (e.g., "If you purchase your trucks from me, I'll give you a discount and give you my plumbing business"). Booster members also receive "perks" or special treatment from athletic departments in the form of complimentary tickets, free rides on charter flights, etc.

The affiliation of booster clubs with colleges and universities is not new. What is apparent, however, is that these groups have dropped their general interest in the functioning of the university and concentrated their attention on athletics.³ This is because academic governance has been largely financed by government dollars and private philanthropy is not as significant as it once was. However, more importantly, athletics can do more for booster political and economic interest than can philosophy or sociology. The booster coalition represents a network of individuals who reap economic and political benefit from their common association with athletics. Historically, their power was measured by the ability to attract immigrants to a growing community (Boorstin, 1965); today, that power is measured by the ability to attract high-caliber athletes and coaches to a growing and successful athletic program. The college or university athletic program with a well organized booster club of political and economic elite will survive in the 1980s; those without will not survive. The cost of surviving is great—the loss of academic control of athletics.

# INSTITUTIONAL CONTROL

Institutional control of athletics by the academic side of an institution is virtually impossible in the face of the influence exercised by the booster coalition. This is particularly true for the colleges and universities which belong to Division I in the NCAA organization. These schools operate the most expansive programs demanding the greatest resources. They would not survive financially without booster support. The power of the coalition is actually beyond the comprehension of most faculty and academic administrators. The coalition is run by individuals who are used to getting what they want; they make decisions daily that involve millions of dollars and thousands of people; and these are the individuals who have the most political influence. No one faculty member or administrator can stand up to their power. Athletic directors, who are modern-day "managers," not old coaches, tend to hold ideological and behavioral similarities to boosters; that is, they are cut of the same mold. Therefore, athletic directors rarely provide a source of resistance to booster enthusiasm and involvement. Colleges and universities cannot deny these groups the opportunity to forge their allegiance to the campus, unless the institution has alternative bases of political and fiscal support.

Nothing raises the cynical anger of a professor more than abuses of the educational goals of higher education by the athletic department (e.g., circumventing entrance requirements or pushing athletes into "easy," irrelevant courses). Rarely, however, does the faculty member follow his verbal assault with concerting collective action. University senates pass resolutions that are ignored; faculty leaders discuss the problem in ineffectual, informal settings; committees are created and dissolved with no result; or the control of abuse is left to a faculty athletic committee which is often a mouthpiece of the athletic program and easily circumvented by external booster interests. Faculties will never be effective in controlling large-scale athletic programs because they do not operate at the same political and economic levels as boosters/alumni. The faculty voice might be more readily acknowledged if it came from an organized group (e.g., a labor union), but the prospects for this are not good (Blackburn and Nyikos, 1974). Faculties have simply lacked the courage and organizational apparatus to tackle the athletic program. They have, in their intellectual arrogance, absolved themselves of responsibility for the academic credibility of athletics or any other extramural activity. Organizing the faculty will stimulate activism and subsequent demands for greater input and control of the athletic operations on campus, but unless faculties can move in the circles of the elite, these efforts will be in vain.

Faculties can lend an air of respectability to athletic programs by asserting themselves in such areas as admission standards, academic counseling and eligibility reviews. This has been suggested as a mechanism by which faculties can control athletic operations (Blackburn & Nyikos, 1974; Hanford, 1974; Plant, 1961; Marco, 1960). But when it comes to decisions about the level of program, key personnel and general policy, the booster coalition has the greatest influence.

There is evidence that college presidents and faculties are asserting their authority in NCAA governance and rule-setting practices in order to win back the long-lost control. However, the NCAA devotes only one section of three brief paragraphs to the topic of institutional control (**NCAA Manual,** 1980-81: 15-16). Their position is to hold the weakest component, the faculty, responsible for control. The regulatory power of the NCAA, and any other athletic regulatory body, is compromised by the fact that the interests of these bodies are the same as those of the booster coalition—athletic growth for economic and political benefit. The NCAA is a cartel-like organization designed to promote the athletic enterprise. It does so by monopolizing athletes' labor value and mobility as well as controlling the commercial aspect, for example, TV monies (Koch, 1971; Sage 1979). Regulatory bodies need the booster coalition to maintain attractive and financially profitable (to these bodies at least) athletic programs. NCAA rules hold the institution responsible for acts of boosters. The result is that although the regulatory body sanctions individuals—that is, asks them to disassociate themselves from the athletic program—it would never request dismantling of the group representing the booster coalition.

Academic control of athletics will exist only at a moderate or even superficial level at schools with high-level ambitions. Those with lesser goals will find academic control more feasible. Big-time programs require more resources than an institution can provide by its own efforts. The booster coalition is needed for financial and political solvency for the most expansive programs. Even the NCAA will not be able to combat the forces of boosterism. In fact, it may be replaced as a regulatory body by an association of elite schools which will develop regulations that permit more flexible procedures and a more advantageous division of the athletic financial pie. Such an association has already been proposed in the form of the College Football Association (CFA). The sixty or so members of this group desire an autonomous organization in order to circumvent current NCAA television restrictions that prevent these schools from getting maximum television coverage and, therefore, more dollars for their programs. Miller (1980) proposes a biennial audit of athletic programs, which is similar to accreditation procedures for professional schools. This audit, which would be directed primarily at football and basketball programs, would review the extent of compliance with rules governing sports. If there were problems, schools would have a one-year immunity or grace period without penalty to clear up these violations. Audit teams would be a neutral group of coaches and administrators from an independent audit firm.

# FINANCIAL CONTINGENCIES AND BOOSTER ACTIVITY

The growth dilemma presents itself at this time because the traditional financial resources of athletes are stabilizing and even decreasing. Consequently, athletic programs are placing more emphasis on maintenance rather than growth. The result is what has been called the "stationary state" (Nisbet, 1979) or state of negative entropy (Frey, 1978a). Athletic programs are consuming more energy than they are able to generate. Several factors have produced this condition.

## Attendance and Gate Receipts

Even though it may not appear to be true, stadiums have reached their saturation point, both in terms of the number being constructed and in the rate of attendance. Between 1960 and 1965 attendance at college events rose 21 percent; between 1965-1970 it was up 19 percent; it rose only 7.5 percent between 1970 and 1975; and since 1975 attendance is up only 2.1 percent. Since 1975 there is evidence that attendance is on the decline (Broyles **et al.**, 1976). The rate of attendance is declining while the costs of athletic programs, which are predominantly dependent on gate receipts, are up 61 percent since 1972 (NCAA, 1978). Thus, revenue from gate receipts, as a portion of the total athletic budget for income, is on the decline (Atwell, 1980).

In addition, the exclusive right of season ticket holders (including corporate entities, who now take up a large portion of the seats in any stadium and arena) make it physically impossible to expand the market by attracting or creating "new" fans.' For example, one school in the West has not added a new booster-season ticket holder for over two years because of the unavailability of seats in a basketball arena. These restrictions reinforce the elitist connotation of the college game plus limit the supportive "sense of community" that every institution seeks to create surrounding its athletic program. This means that college programs will have to get more money from the same number of persons. Only those schools with well-organized booster groups will be able to turn this trend.

A second factor, which will contribute to the decline of community interest in local or regional athletic programs as well as gate receipts, is the development of cable television. Beginning January 1, 1978, all cable systems could carry non-network programs from distant television stations (Hochberg, 1979). Microwave or satellite distribution makes it possible for a viewer in Denver, Colorado, to watch a sporting event originating in New York, Chicago or another distant city. While cable television triples the potential audience for an event, it can also be harmful to local gate receipts. Fans may stay home to watch an event originating from elsewhere, rather than attending the local event. In effect, college competition will be placed in rivalry with professional athletics even though a pay-for-play franchise is not located in or near a college or university. Many of the successful collegiate programs such as Ohio State, Oklahoma and Nebraska attribute some of their notoriety to the fact that they are the "only game in town." Schools can gain revenue because they will hold the copyright to the broadcast and can sell permission to broadcast at a fee. However, problems arise because a game may not be purchased by the cable TV outlet unless it has national appeal. This means intersectional scheduling, which is becoming prohibitively expensive for most institutions. Financial restrictions on national scheduling can be overcome by programs which have a large contingent of booster dollars available to subsidize travel.

# Legislative Appropriations

The reduction of available tax dollars will prevent the expansion or creation of new athletic facilities and programs on campuses. More frequently, legislators will give higher priority to capital improvements that are more consistent with the educational goals of the university. Presidents and alumni will also lobby less actively for athletic appropriations because they will be fighting for favorable appropriations for other university functions, thus leaving the door open for the capital expansion of athletic facilities to be financed by booster interests. This has already occurred on many campuses (Marcin, 1979). Athletic programs cannot expect to improve upon their appropriation, because of the larger problem of fewer dollars available for any social or educational program. Combine this fact with the decline in gate receipts, and the result can only be either to change the level of program—no growth or declining growth—or to increase the booster coalition contribution.

## Insurance

More practical economic factors will make it difficult for athletic programs to maintain their current practices. Rising liability and medical insurance rates, particularly for football, are forcing schools into a severe cost crunch with some programs. For example, in 1975 the University of California paid a liability insurance premium of $437,602; in 1977, it was $1,144,000. The "sue syndrome" plus the tendencies for injuries to favor the plaintiff have contributed to escalation of product liability suits which cost considerable money regardless of outcome (Appenzeller, 1979).[5]

## Inflation

In addition, inflation and rising energy prices can have serious effects on travel, equipment purchase and facility utilization. If a team cannot travel, it cannot maintain the kind of schedule that gives its program the notoriety, exposure and financial guarantee it needs. Add these problems to the exigencies of Title IX regulations, even with the football exemption, and changes in traditional operations will have to take place.[6] Economic problems are even more significant when it is noted that 81 percent of the NCAA football programs lost money in 1977, and only 30 athletic programs operated in the black. The athletic revenue growth rate for institutions has been just over eight percent, but inflation has been rushing away at 11-12 percent (Raiborn, 1977).

## Constituency Support

These economic problems are exacerbated by the fact that even the potential pool of contributors is dwindling. First, college enrollments have leveled off and in many areas are on the decline. This will make fewer alumni available for political and financial support in the future. Additionally, the alumni who do exist will have fewer real dollars for peripheral contributions and expenses. Also, these alumni will be less likely to contribute because they can draw on few intimate and positive experiences with the athletic programs of their schools. One study of alumni found that less than one percent of alumni felt athletics represented their most remembered experience in school (Frey, 1978b). This same group listed athletics as number 11 on a list of 12 priorities for university spending, and they also resented the preferential treatment received by athletes and other special groups of students. Few were involved in direct participation, since only a select number had the talent and skill it took to participate in a college athletic program. As a result, athletics may not carry the extensive alumni support that is so often suggested by athletic protagonists.

This same study demonstrated that the board of directors of the surveyed alumni group were strong supporters of athletics. Thus, athletics remain a priority, despite the apparent lack of support from the total alumni body, because the strong association of alumni with athletics is an artifact of of the membership of the elite alumni in booster groups which strongly endorse the athletic program.[7] Presidents and athletic directors tend to listen to the influential, not average, alumnus.

In addition, recent studies of college students demonstrate that a large percent feel that college sports are operated on behalf of outside interests, not students. Fifty-eight percent of the students in one study felt the boosters controlled athletics, not the institution (Frey, 1980). Just under half felt that athletics were more important to the community than the school and were run on behalf of alumni rather than students. Seventy-six percent agreed with the notion that students have no voice in athletic governance. In another study (Jensen, et al., 1980), 42 percent of the students felt that the "big business" aspect of college athletics is a perversion of educational goals. Yet these students, and those in the Frey study, generally supported athletics on campuses. They believed athletics were valuable from the traditional standpoints of character development and campus social life. What is important here is to note that the percentage favoring athletics is not as high as the promoters of these programs would have us believe. I predict that future studies will reveal a lowering of the student support quotient for athletics.

## Labor Supply

Successful athletic programs obviously cannot operate without a substantial pool of athletic labor from which to draw the most talented performers. Until recently, this supply seemed endless. Virtually any school could recruit athletes at any level of sophistication and intellect. If they were not admissible under normal circumstances, entrance requirements could be circumvented by the use of junior college enrollments, manipulated transcripts, bogus courses or minority admissions variances. Recent NCAA rulings have made it illegal to use certain courses or schools in attaining eligibility. Championship rules make it more difficult and problematic to allow a transfer student to play. These factors, combined with the exclusivity of college athletics, means that fewer athletes—particularly male—qualify, from the standpoints of brains or brawn, for college athletics.

There has, in fact, been a first-ever decline in the number of males who participate in college sports. While women's participation doubled from 32,000 in 1972 to 64,000 in 1978, men's participation declined from 172,000 to 170,384 during this same period (U.S. Commission on Civil Rights,

1980). Still, schools spend twice the money per capita on male athletes as compared to female athletes. As the supply of available labor declines, the competition for the remaining qualified few will be intense. The edge may be provided by the resources of booster coalition.

Affirmative Action and Civil Rights legislation has opened the doors of opportunity, to some extent, for one of the major subgroups of athletic labor—the Black. At one time, the only avenues out of the ghetto and an existence of despair were athletics and entertainment. College coaches flocked to the play-grounds and athletic fields of American urban centers to find the "diamond in the rough" who would lead their team to glory (Telander, 1978). The black and white communities supported this association of success and athletics. However, it was not long before the injustice of this effort and attention became known.

For every athlete from these circumstances who made it either to the collegiate or professional big-time, a thousand did not. For those who made it, the career was short-lived, with few long-term benefits of money or fame. Many a "star" was forced back to his origination with only stories of his experience, some reputation, but few tangible assets (Jordan, 1979). It was not long before stories and reputation lost their luster. It is possible that many Blacks who could have been athletes will pursue vehicles of success other than athletics because they have become aware of these injustices. In fact, leaders of the Black community such as Jesse Jackson and Harry Edwards are openly challenging Black youth to look at alternatives to athletics and to funnel their energies to pursue careers which have a more reliable pay-off, in addition to making some contribution to society.[8] If such admonitions are taken to heart, the labor pool available for college athletics will suffer a considerable deficit. The Black portion of that labor pool will be even more decimated if faculty assert themselves on admission and degree requirements and expect higher standards of academic performance. Then, only a few academically and athletically qualified Blacks will be available.

Athletes, in turn, are becoming more sophisticated about the recruiting dynamics; that is, they recognize that they have a product that is in demand. It is only natural to sell one's services to the highest bidder. The bids are ordinarily channeled through "representatives of athletic departments," e.g., athletic boosters. Money payments, use of cars, travel for relatives, and other incentives are offered, and often requested by, the athlete. As a result, few schools will be able to stay in the bidding market for the elite athlete without the external sources of support, both legal and illegal.

The labor pool of athletics is also decimated by the high rate of disabling injuries which can keep a player from performing for a season or even a lifetime. It is estimated that nearly one million high school players, 70,000 college players and all of the players on the National Football League suffer injuries in one year (Underwood, 1978). Thus, additional player resources are required. The decline of available scholarships, smaller number who are eligible or desire to play, and lowered skill of those available to replace the "star" potentially reduce the quality of the available athletic resources of a winning season which, in turn, leads to lowered alumni and booster support. In addition, if a team has no star to attract media attention, program visibility as well as revenues will also be reduced. It truly is a vicious circle.

The problem of maintaining the labor pool for college athletics is further complicated by the fact that an increasing number of high school districts are dropping some sports, particularly football. Between 1969 and 1979, there was a 2.3 percent and a 10.0 percent decline in the number of schools offering football and basketball, respectively (National Federation of State High School Associations, 1975). During this same time, the number of participants dropped 6.7 percent for football, 9.5 percent for basketball.

Many high schools no longer carry coaches as faculty and, therefore, must recruit as part-time, interested persons. In all but seven states, coaches are no longer required to have a teaching credential in order to be employed by a school system (Sefeldt & Gould, 1980). Both of these facts point to the prospect of fewer well-trained athletes being available for college programs.

Finally, just as we have a "Poverty Establishment," there now exists a "Sport Establishment"—a network of organizations and occupations that depend on athletics as currently construed for their maintenance and survival (Frey, 1978A).

As college programs become more rationalized and organized under this athletic-industrial complex, the athlete, realizing that athletics is a business, will be less loyal to his team, or nation. He/she will be less willing to sacrifice himself/herself for the sake of the team. The reason for his/her participation is extrinsic and based on self-interest, which means higher turnover of personnel. A player will not remain at "Good Ole U." for the sake of teammates and tradition. He will transfer to a school that will give him the most toward meeting his goals (e.g., professional career). As any foreman or manager will tell you, high turnover of key personnel is disruptive of productivity.

# CONCLUSION

All of these factors are intertwined. The environment of intercollegiate athetics is deteriorating. The supports are no longer there; they are missing not because of Title IX or another singular element, but because of systematic conditions which are subtle yet pervasive. It is only a matter of time before drastic changes in the intercollegiate athletics world will come.

The most significant change will be that only a few schools will be able to grow or expand their athletic program. These schools will become an elite corps which will dominate any national attention that athletics receives. Schools like Alabama, University of Southern California and Nebraska University, with programs augmented by a strong booster/alumni coalition, will form national conferences, dominate television coverage, secure the services of the best available athletes and will essentially operate regulation-free. These programs will represent the last stage in the nationalization of college athletics and the professionalization of the college athlete. The affiliation with a college or university campus will remain only one of convenience and tradition. The elite sports clubs of America will exist in connection with a university; the booster groups will be sponsors of these sports clubs, and provide them with the resources necessary to compete in the national marketplace for the elite athlete in a declining labor pool.

The less endowed or committed schools will see the 1980s as their "last hurrah." These institutions will bear the brunt of all financial, and thus program, cutbacks. Title IX is only a temporary roadblock for the elite athletic programs, but Affirmative Action plus other financial exigencies represent the death knell for many smaller, less-endowed programs. The rich get richer and the poor fall by the wayside. The final result will be a two-class athletic system which will be only a facsimile of current organization.

## FOOTNOTES

[1]As early as 1852, businessmen "boosted" an intercollegiate event to enhance their economic interests. The owners of the Boston, Concord and Montreal Railroads paid all of the expenses for Harvard and Yale crews to compete in the very first intercollegiate event—a regetta on Lake Winnipesaukee. The aim of the railroads was to get people to use rail transportation to the event. It worked, the businessmen and the athletes made money (Smith, 1976).

[2]The involvement of business and political elite in booster groups has an analogy with professional team ownership. Few professional teams make money, yet potential owners line up in order to purchase an available team. It has been suggested that through player depreciation allowances and the ability to demonstrate an "on-paper" loss, team owners are able to accrue considerable tax advantages (Noll, 1974). In fact, major conglomerates find it desirable to own a losing team in order to be able to demonstrate that the profit in one company was drained to service another. Thus, overall earnings are shown to be minimal and less available to taxes. Contribution to booster clubs and booster foundations provide a similar tax advantage to the contributor. It may also give him the vicarious thrill of ownership, since along with his contribution comes decision-making influence as well as all of the excitement of being an "athletic groupie."

[3]Booster groups can continue to influence college and university administration because of their ties to state legislatures and the governing boards of the institution. Regent and trustees are often also booster club members or they represent groups which have dealings with other booster members.

[4]An analysis of the list of booster club members of one institution revealed that 26 percent held corporate memberships. This figure is most likely conservative because many who were listed by name, such as medical doctors or lawyers, probably purchased memberships (i.e., made donations) through a business account.

[5]At this time, there are over 100 football helmet-related injury cases pending in court with claims totaling over $300 million.

[6]It is interesting to note that many athletic directors are viewing women's sports as a possible salvation from the financial requirements of maintaining a winning athletic program. From one standpoint, transferring money to women's programs can be justification for de-emphasizing some men's sports, including the major pro-

grams. On the other hand, accelerated women's sports can mean additional revenue-producing avenues including gate receipts and women boosters-alumnae. Schools were to come into compliance with Title IX by September 1979; few have fully met the requirement.

[7]Sigelman and Carter (1979) have demonstrated statistically that no relation exists between win-loss records and donation patterns by alumni. Sach (1980) reanalyzed the Sigelman and Carter data and reached the same conclusion.

[8]The major problem with the arguements of individuals like Jackson is that they suggest the pursuit of professional careers (e.g., doctor, lawyer) as an alternative. Success in these careers is unlikely. Greater emphasis should be placed on the acquisition of more generalized skills such as writing or mathmatical proficiency, which can be utilized in a number of job arenas.

# REFERENCES

Appenzeller, Herb
    1979    "Product Liability Litigation Continues to Escalate." *Athletic Purchasing,* 3 (June):17-20.
Atwell, Robert H., Bruce Grimes and Donna Lopiano
    1980    *The Money Game: Financing Collegiate Athletics.* Washington, D.C.: American Council on Education.
Blackburn, Robert T. and Michael S. Nyikos
    1974    "College Football and Mr. Chips: All in the Family." *Phi Delta Kappan*, 56 (October):110-113.
Boorstin, Daniel J.
    1965    *The Americans: The National Experience.* New York: Random House.
Broyles, Frank, Robert D. Hay and Harry A. French
    1976    "Some Facts about College Football Attendance." *Athletic Administration.* 10(Summer):13-15
Cady, Edwin H.
    1978    *The Big Game: College Sports in American Life.* Knoxville: The University of Tennessee Press.
Denlinger, Kenneth and Leonard Shapiro
    1975    *Athletes for Sale.* New York: Thomas Y. Crowell.
Evans, J. Robert
    1974    *Blowing the Whistle on Intercollegiate Sports.* Chicago: Nelson-Hall.
Frey, James H.
    1978A    "The Organization of American Amateur Sport: Efficiency to Entrophy." *American Behavioral Scientist.* 21(February):361-78.
    1978B    "The Priority of Athletics to Alumni: Myth or Fact?" *Phi Delta Kappan.* 60(September):63.
    1980    "Survey of College Students' Participation in Athletics and Intramurals." University of Nevada, Las Vegas. Unpublished report.
Hanford, George H.
    1974    *An Inquiry into the Need for and Feasibility of a National Study of Intercollegiate Athletics.* Washington, D.C.: American Council on Education.

Hochberg, Phillip R.
1979        "Cable Television's Impact on College Athletics." *Athletic Administration.* 14(Fall):6-7.
Jensen, Ted M., Wilbert M. Leonard and Robert D. Liverman
1980        "College Students' Attitudes toward Intercollegiate Athletics: An Exploratory Model." Paper presented at the meetings of the North American Society for the Sociology of Sport. Denver, Colorado. October.
Jordan, Pat
1979        *Chase the Game.* New York: Dodd, Mead.
Koch, James V.
1971        "A Troubled Cartel: The NCAA." *Law and Contemporary Problems.* 38: 129-150.
Looney, Douglas S.
1978        "Deep in Hot Water in Stillwater." *Sports Illustrated.* 49(July 3): 18-23.
Lucas, John A. and Ronald A. Smith
            *Saga of American Sport.* Philadelphia: Lea and Febiger.
Marca, S.M.
1960        "The Place of Intercollegiate Athletics in Higher Education: The Responsibility of the Faculty. *Journal of Higher Education.* 21: 422-27.
Marcin, Joe
1979        "Booster Clubs: Boon . . . or Bane?" *Sporting News.* (November 17): 26-27.
Miller, Fred L.
1980        "The Ongoing Crisis—a Solution: Part II, Mechanics." *Athletic Administration.* (Winter): 23-24.
National Collegiate Athletic Association (NCAA)
1978        "The Sports and Recreational Programs of the Nation's Universities and Colleges." *NCAA Manual, 1980-81.* Shawnee Mission, Kansas.
National Federation of State High School Associations
1979        *Sports Participation Survey.*
Nisbet, Robert
1979        "The Rape of Progress." *Public Opinion.* 2 (June/July): 2/6.
Noll, Roger G.
1974        *"The U.S. Team Sports Industry: An Introduction."* Pp. 1-33. in Roger G. Noll. *Government and the Sports Business.* Washington D.C.: The Brookings Institution.
Novack, Michael
1976        *The Joy of Sports.* New York: Basic Books, Inc.
Plant, Marcus L.
1961        "The Place of Intercollegiate Athletics in Higher Education." *Journal of Higher Education.* 22 (January): 1-8.
Raiborn, Mitchell H.
1978        *Revenues and Expenses of Intercollegiate Athletic Programs.* Report to the National Collegiate Athletic Association.
Sack, Allen H.
1980        "Another Look at Winning and Giving." Paper presented at the meetings of the North American Society for the Sociology of Sport.

Sage, George H.
1974        "Socialization of Coaches: Antecedents to Coaches' Beliefs and Behaviors." *Proceedings: National College Physical Education Association for Men.*

Seefeldt, Vern and Daniel Gould
1980        "Physical and Psychological Effects of Athletic Competition on Children and Youth." Washington, D.C.: ERIC Clearinghouse on Teacher Education.

Sigelmen, Lee and Robert Carter
1979        "Win One for the Giver? Alumni Giving and Big Time College Sport." *Social Science Quarterly,* 60(September): 284-294.

Smith, Ronald A.
1976        "Reaction to 'Historical Roots of the Collegiate Dilemma'." *Proceedings. Natural College Physical Education Association for Men.* (January): 154-161.

Telander, Rick
1978        *Heaven is a Playground.* New York: Grosset and Dunlap.

Thompson, J.D.
1967        *Organizations in Action.* New York: McGraw-Hill.

Underwood, John
1979        *The Death of an American Game.* Boston: Little, Brown.

United States Commission on Civil Rights.
1980        *More Hurdles to Clear: Women and Girls in Competitive Athletics.* Clearinghouse Publication. Number 63. (July).

68470061